P9-CJH-208

The Best American Food Writing 2020

WITHDRAWN

GUEST EDITORS OF
THE BEST AMERICAN FOOD WRITING

2018   RUTH REICHL
2019   SAMIN NOSRAT
2020   J. KENJI LÓPEZ-ALT

The Best American Food Writing™ 2020

Edited and with an Introduction
by J. KENJI LÓPEZ-ALT

Silvia Killingsworth, Series Editor

MARINER BOOKS

HOUGHTON MIFFLIN HARCOURT

BOSTON • NEW YORK   2020

Copyright © 2020 by Houghton Mifflin Harcourt Publishing Company
Introduction copyright © 2020 by J. Kenji López-Alt

ALL RIGHTS RESERVED

The Best American Series® is a registered trademark of Houghton Mifflin Harcourt Publishing Company. *The Best American Food Writing*™ is a trademark of Houghton Mifflin Harcourt Publishing Company.

No part of this work may be reproduced or transmitted in any form or by any means, electronic or mechanical, including photocopying and recording, or by any information storage or retrieval system without the proper written permission of the copyright owner unless such copying is expressly permitted by federal copyright law. With the exception of nonprofit transcription in Braille, Houghton Mifflin Harcourt is not authorized to grant permission for further uses of copyrighted selections reprinted in this book without the permission of their owners. Permission must be obtained from the individual copyright owners as identified herein. Address requests for permission to make copies of Houghton Mifflin Harcourt material to Permissions, Houghton Mifflin Harcourt Publishing Company, 3 Park Avenue, 19th Floor, New York 10016.

hmhbooks.com

ISSN 2578-7667 (print)   ISSN 2578-7675 (ebook)
ISBN 978-0-358-34458-2 (print)   ISBN 978-0-358-34649-4 (ebook)

Printed in the United States of America
DOC 10 9 8 7 6 5 4 3 2 1

"Open Wide" by Burkhard Bilger. First published in *The New Yorker*, November 18, 2019. Copyright © 2019 by Burkhard Bilger. Reprinted by permission of Burkhard Bilger and The New Yorker.

"We All Scream" by Charlotte Druckman. First published in *Eater*, April 9, 2019. Copyright © 2019 by Vox Media, Inc. Reprinted by permission of Vox Media, Inc.

"The Man Who's Going to Save Your Neighborhood Grocery Store" by Joe Fassler. First published in *Longreads/The Counter*, April 2019. Copyright © 2019 by The Counter. Reprinted by permission of The Counter.

"Kitchen Shift" (originally published as "Kitchen Shift: The Chefs Behind North America's Most Hedonistic Restaurant Quit Drinking") by Hannah Goldfield. First published in *The New Yorker*, May 20, 2019. Copyright © 2019 by Condé Nast. Reprinted by permission of Condé Nast.

"A Real Hot Mess: How Grits Got Weaponized Against Cheating Men" by Cynthia R. Greenlee. First published in *Munchies*, February 14, 2019. Copyright © 2019 by Cynthia R. Greenlee. Reprinted by permission of Cynthia R. Greenlee and Vice Media.

"Here's What the Government's Dietary Guidelines Should Really Say" by Tamar Haspel. First published in *Washington Post*, March 26, 2019. Copyright © 2019 by Tamar Haspel. Reprinted by permission of Tamar Haspel.

"Fare Access: DC Restaurants Could Do More to Welcome Diners with Disabilities" by Laura Hayes. First published in *Washington City Paper*, April 4, 2019. Copyright © 2019 by Washington City Paper. Reprinted by permission of Washington City Paper.

"Yelp Reviewers' Authenticity Fetish Is White Supremacy in Action" by Sara Kay. First published in *Eater*, January 18, 2019. Copyright © 2019 by Vox Media, Inc. Reprinted by permission of Vox Media, Inc.

"Wet 'n Wild" by Katy Kelleher. First published in *Topic*, April 2019. Copyright © 2019 by Katy Kelleher. Reprinted by permission of Katy Kelleher.

"Where'd You Go, Rocco DiSpirito?" by Kat Kinsman. First published in *Food & Wine*, October 25, 2019. Copyright © 2019 by Kat Kinsman. Reprinted by permission of Kat Kinsman.

"The Provocations of Chef Tunde Wey" by Brett Martin. First published in *GQ*, March 6, 2019. Copyright © 2019 by Brett Martin. Reprinted by permission of Brett Martin.

"Whatever Happened to Portland?" by Meghan McCarron. First published in *Eater*, June 5, 2019. Copyright © 2019 by Vox Media, Inc. Reprinted by permission of Vox Media, Inc.

"New Coke Didn't Fail. It Was Murdered" by Tim Murphy. First published in *Mother Jones*, July 9, 2019. Copyright © 2019 by the Foundation for National Progress. Reprinted by permission of the Foundation for National Progress.

"Hard Times for a Hot Commodity, the Prized New Mexico Chile" by Amelia Nierenberg. First published in the *New York Times*, December 16, 2019. Copyright © 2019 The New York Times. Reprinted by permission.

"What the Heck Is Crab Rangoon Anyway?" by Dan Nosowitz. First published in *Atlas Obscura*, August 14, 2019. Copyright © 2019 by Dan Nosowitz. Reprinted by permission of Dan Nosowitz.

"The Kitchen at Per Se Was a Clean Place but Hard and Heartless Too," adapted from "Blood on the Eggshells," as published on eater.com, March 26, 2019. Copyright © 2019 by Kwame Onwuachi; from *Notes from a Young Black Chef: A Memoir* by Kwame Onwuachi with Joshua David Stein. Used by permission of Alfred A. Knopf, an imprint of the Knopf Doubleday Publishing Group, a division of Penguin Random House LLC. All rights reserved.

"The Demand for 'Authenticity' Is Threatening Kansas City's Homegrown Tacos" by José R. Ralat. First published in *Eater*, April 23, 2019. Copyright © 2019 by Vox Media, Inc. Reprinted by permission of Vox Media, Inc.

"It's Not Always Easy to Be Jamie Oliver" (originally titled "It's Not Always Excellent to Be Jamie Oliver") by Kim Severson. First published in the *New York Times*, August 20, 2019. Copyright © 2019 The New York Times. Reprinted by permission.

"Easy, Peasy, Japanese-y: Benihana and the Question of Cultural Appropriation" by Sho Spaeth. First published in *Serious Eats*, February 13, 2019. Copyright © 2019 by Serious Eats Inc. Reprinted by permission of Serious Eats Inc.

"When Jacques Pépin Made All the World an Omelet" by Joshua David Stein. First published in *Taste*, April 23, 2019. Copyright © 2019 by Taste. Reprinted by permission of Taste.

"Lean Cuisine Doesn't Want to Be Part of Diet Culture Anymore. Does It Have a Choice?" by Kaitlyn Tiffany. First published in *Vox*, July 24, 2019. Copyright © 2019 by Vox Media, Inc. Reprinted by permission of Vox Media, Inc.

"I Just Want to Eat Her Up!" by Alex Van Buren. First published in the *New York Times,* May 27, 2019. Copyright © 2019 The New York Times. Reprinted by permission.

"Peter Luger Used to Sizzle. Now It Sputters" by Pete Wells. First published in the *New York Times,* October 29, 2019. Copyright © 2019 The New York Times. Reprinted by permission.

"The Spice Trade" by Paige Williams. First published in *The New Yorker,* January 28, 2019. Copyright © 2019 by Paige Williams. Reprinted by permission of Paige Williams.

"A Critic for All Seasons" by Korsha Wilson. First published in *Eater,* February 20, 2019. Copyright © 2019 by Vox Media, Inc. Reprinted by permission of Vox Media, Inc.

Contents

Foreword

THE WORLD HAS changed so much so fast since the pieces in this volume were written and published that I'm convinced the book will read like a time capsule. Of course, in some ways that's very much the purpose of an anthology—a highlight reel from the past year—but this time it feels different. The year in which these 25 stories were told, 2019, feels radically distant; but in 2020 our project remains the same, if not all the more relevant.

We are here to champion voices and stories by highlighting the best writing about one of the biggest topics. As Ruth Reichl wrote in this series' inaugural edition, food writing used to be considered trivial, relegated to lifestyle publications and cookbook sections. But Americans have finally recognized that food is everywhere and touches everyone and everything. That will only become clearer, and our job will become more urgent, as the consequences of this global event unfold.

As I write this, we are in the thick of a pandemic, and we don't yet know the full extent of its destruction. All around the world, we've lost lives and livelihoods. The new coronavirus has had an especially grave effect on our food systems. For now, our lives have been stripped down to the basics: Do we have what we need to survive? And if we do not, how do we get it? A word continuously heard during these times is "essential"—who is an essential worker, what is essential travel? In Daniel Defoe's *A Journal of the Plague Year*, nearly half the instances of the word "food" are in the compound phrase "food and physic," which is to say, food and medicine—the ur-essentials.

Everyone has had to adjust to a new reality. Those used to consuming prepared foods, whether at restaurants or drive-throughs, now have to fend mostly for themselves. Others rely on the kindness of organized and generous strangers. Those of us who cook at home now have to account for three meals a day, which, if we have other mouths to feed, can feel like twelve. Between the limitations of our pantries and the repetitive nature of endless days without leaving the house, it begins to feel a bit like *Iron Chef: Groundhog Day* edition. We take inventory of our provisions and calculate how long we can stretch them, the better to minimize going outside. It feels like preparing for a long winter.

Going to the grocery store or local market has become a risky proposition, where it's even possible. And once you do get there, many of the shelves are bare. Gallons of milk are being dumped and tons of vegetables mulched and buried while thousands of workers in processing plants risk their lives and lungs to keep up with our insatiable appetite for meat. Our industrialized agricultural system is set up largely to supply institutions, companies, and warehouses, not individuals. There is food, but it can't get where it needs to go.

This harsh economic reality is also a reminder that in our modernized world, where supermarkets and delivery apps are the norm, we depend on each other in order to eat. Feeding the world is a civic project, even if most of the time it's an invisible one that relies on a complex and global supply chain. The pandemic has highlighted how much the industrialization of food has distanced us from the people who grow, raise, and make our food. If there is any silver lining to this crisis, it's that it will force us to reckon with unsustainable practices much sooner than we otherwise would have.

Restaurants—one of the last parts of the food ecosystem where the service of other people is not only visible but largely a feature (there's a reason it's known as the "hospitality" industry)—have been especially hard-hit. So many establishments across the country that fueled great food writing over the years have been shuttered, and the landscape as a whole has been decimated. It feels like I read another eulogy for a beloved local spot nearly every day. But for every one of those, I'm also reading stories of chefs using their otherwise dormant kitchens to feed frontline workers and provide takeout for their neighbors.

Over the past half century, restaurants became one of the main vehicles for cultural exchange. But they used to be much more functional—according to one favored etymological explanation, one of the earliest modern restaurants, in 18th-century Paris, was so called because it served *bouillon restaurants,* or "restorative broths." But of course, people have been feeding customers as a business model for much longer; they just called it something else. The *Oxford English Dictionary*'s earliest entries for such establishments date back to the 15th century.

One of the reasons I love that story about the first Parisian restaurant is that the proprietor's surname was none other than Boulanger, which is also the French word for "baker." Though he served mostly broths, one supposes Mr. Boulanger also offered bread to soak them up with. One also imagines that somewhere in his lineage, he was descended from an actual baker, and that he was carrying on in the great tradition of his name: providing others with their daily bread. After all, bread is the canonical foodstuff of France, and of human civilization more generally. It is "the most everyday and familiar of foods, the sturdy staff of life on which hundreds of generations have leaned for sustenance," writes Harold McGee in *On Food and Cooking.* "Bread introduced a new dimension of pleasure and wonder to the mainstays of human life."

In recent years, spurred by social media, bread became a renewed source of fascination for home cooks across the world. I was pleased by this development, having believed for years that Americans' relationship with bread was horribly damaged by low-carb diet fads. But I'm also aware that the trend of upper-middle-class millennials embarking on three-day-long odysseys for the perfect crumb shot is incredibly clichéd. "A sourdough starter is a tamagotchi for people in their 30s," tweeted Louise O'Connor. Touché, Louise.

That this latest bread boomlet coincided with a time when we were all forced to stay indoors struck me as not entirely coincidental. In Defoe's *A Journal of the Plague Year,* the narrator writes of his decision to "lock myself up and my family" upon the recommendation of his friend, Dr. Heath. The bubonic plague was raging through London, and he hadn't "laid in a store of provision for such a retreat." He bought two sacks of meal, "and for several weeks, having an oven, we baked all our own bread." Though it may not be out of the same level of necessity as Defoe's narrator, the tendency to turn to bread in a time of crisis strikes me as almost romantic. Bread is a foundational food that signifies bounty and ingenuity as much as it does depression and despair. With apologies to the gluten-allergic, bread has gotten us through tough times. If you can make bread—and you can—you can not only feed your family, you can also feel alive. At the very least, like all cooking, it's a good, meditative exercise in patience.

Even though this may be one of our toughest years on record, both economically and emotionally, I am cautiously optimistic that it will usher in even more great food writing. "What would happen if we were to start thinking about food as less of a thing and more of a relationship?" asks Michael Pollan in *In Defense of Food*. He was arguing for "a broader, more ecological—and more cultural" view of food. Food is functional, yes, but it is inextricable from what makes us human.

In a time of food insecurity, journalism will only become more important. Wherever there is food, there are people behind it, and wherever there are people, there are stories to be told. I believe that a good deal of our best work is still ahead of us. Please send me your submissions for next year's volume by December 31, 2020, at silvia.killingsworth@gmail.com.

SILVIA KILLINGSWORTH

Introduction

I HAD FINALIZED the list of articles to include in this compendium by early February of 2020.

Before I had a chance to write my introduction, the coronavirus pandemic hit, and everything else suddenly seemed trivial. What relevance does food writing have in a world where restaurants don't exist? What role could chefs play during a global pandemic? Why should I care about the death of the Kansas City taco or the local supermarket, when I have the potential actual deaths of hundreds of millions of people to think about?

In other words: What value did these stories, which seemed so relevant at the time, have in a world where restaurants and food writing as we know them have ceased to exist?

I, like many chefs and writers, work best under intense, immediate pressure, and by early March we were hurtling over the mountains with no landing strip in sight, building the plane as it was flying, and all I could see was that sheer rock face looming up in front of us.

At first, the work was figuring out how to keep our customers and staff safe. Do we need to stop selling salads? How many people can we seat at a time? How about the table condiments? Is it better to have servers wear masks for safety, or will that make customers assume that they are sick? I spent over a week on the phone with virologists, infectious-disease specialists, and food-safety experts vetting every aspect of our operations to ensure that our food posed as little risk to customers as possible. By March 8 we were using throwaway single-use menus, the condiment bottles had been removed from the tables, parties were staggered so that we filled only half the restaurant at a time, and servers were instructed to lean as far back from the table as they could during necessary up-close interactions.

A few days later, as the virus spread in the United States and the first deaths were being reported, we decided to shut down full-time operations, transitioning to a takeout-only menu. By the next day, it became official when San Mateo County mandated that nonessential services would be shut down entirely.

As a restaurant owner and chef, my business was placed under the "essential" blanket, allowing us to stay open for takeout and delivery service even as the businesses around us locked their doors for the indefinite future and fellow business owners hunkered down to shelter in place.

At first, the "essential" title was a relief. *We can keep at least some of our people employed. We can pay our rent. We can limp along until we're finally allowed to reopen.* I worked quickly with my partners and teams to brainstorm strategies for how we could best serve our community while bringing in at least some revenue for the business—ideas that changed daily as new information about the virus was received and new rules of operation were disseminated by the county. We talked about doing retail business, about take-home meal kits, about gift cards and drinks coupons, about Web-based classes and personal deliveries.

I started spending my nights at the restaurant, repurposing the inventory in our walk-in freezer and pantry to put together meal boxes that I delivered to hospital workers and community centers. I also left packed meals at the restaurant for our laid-off staff to pick up in case they were struggling with no job, children out of school, and in some cases, immigration statuses that left them ineligible for unemployment benefits. Meanwhile, my business partner Adam tended to his newborn baby while simultaneously navigating the bureaucratic and accounting nightmares involved with securing the loans and government bailouts we'd need to survive.

As I cooked alone at night, soaking 25 pounds of chickpeas for vegan meals, or sliding 80 pounds of marinated pork shoulder into the combi-oven to slow-roast overnight, I couldn't help but note the bittersweet luxury of having a kitchen empty of line cooks and a dining room empty of customers. The long communal tables that once seated 24 guests were big enough to be laid end-to-end with a full 120 compostable takeout boxes.

It was then that I realized why these stories—the stories written when restaurants still had more than a glimmer of hope—matter.

The value of good writers seems harder and harder to place in a media landscape that demands all writing be free and fast, and where smaller magazines, newspapers, television and radio stations, and bookshops are being swallowed wholesale by giants like Amazon. Joe Fassler's piece on the disappearance of grocery stores and regional supermarkets shows how the same problems media faced in the past decade will play out in the retail food industry in the next (spoiler: Amazon is at the center of the story in both cases). I can't help but think of the flotilla of mom-and-pop restaurants and food businesses that will founder in the wake of the coronavirus, and the possibility that neighborhoods once defined by their unique food culture may lose their individuality.

If you want to see the value of good writing in action, you need look no further than Meghan McCarron's piece celebrating the new diversity of Portland's food scene in a landscape that fell victim to its own hipsterism (and the veneer of diversity that was painted over Oregon's troublingly racist past).

Stories about people, places, authenticity, and the rich diversity of America's food scene seemed particularly relevant as the question of what it means to be American has been at the core of recent politics. I loved José Ralat's account of the rich history of the Parmesan-dusted Kansas City taco as a metaphor for Mexican immigrant life in Middle America at the turn of the 20th century, now being erased by the internet's demand for "authenticity" (and I'm glad I got to taste them last time I drove cross-country —make sure you do, too). Like Sho Spaeth, I'm a Japanese American *hapa* who is not quite sure how to feel about the caricature of pseudo-Japanese culture that is Benihana. (Side note: my first ever restaurant job was wielding spatulas behind a hibachi-style grill.)

If anything, these stories are even more powerful now during the coronavirus pandemic, as minorities and lower-income individuals face the highest odds of contracting the disease. The kitchen workers (often undocumented immigrants ineligible for unemployment benefits), truck drivers, farm laborers, and factory

workers that form the backbone of our food industry are being
forced into choosing their livelihood over their health and the
health of their communities.

My weekly free meal deliveries also include another group who
have been disproportionately hit by the coronavirus: the elderly
and mobility-impaired. Laura Hayes's matter-of-fact look at the
difficulties of dining out while impaired could not be more relevant now.

We're used to writers asking us: Is cheap food worth the hidden
costs? Is a factory worker's health worth $1.99-a-pound ground
beef? Should I care about that uninsured Amazon or McDonald's
worker when a value meal is such a value? But Kwame Onwuachi's
memoirs shows us that even in the exalted kitchens of Thomas
Keller himself, abuse and exploitation are the norm. Thankfully,
the industry has been changing steadily for the better in the two
decades since I started cooking professionally.

If Anthony Bourdain's *Kitchen Confidential* solidified the image
of the professional kitchen as the last bastion of sex, drugs, and
rock and roll, the #MeToo movement and Bourdain's own ante-
mortem regrets showed us why, perhaps, that macho culture and
the abuses it encouraged ought not to be tolerated anymore. The
restaurant industry is, ironically, trying to shed the very image that
made household names out of chefs in the first place, and that
irony is not lost on writers like Hannah Goldfield. Her piece on
the newfound sobriety of Joe Beef chef David McMillan encour-
ages the positive changes he's made in his kitchens while vividly
showing how things got so bad, and making us question whether it
should have ever been celebrated in the first place.

Cynthia Greenlee shows us the flip side of that coin in her piece
on the gendered weaponization of food in the most literal sense
(grits thrown at cheating spouses). So does Brett Martin, in his
piece on NOLA chef Tunde Way's political performance-art dinner parties.

Good food writing, just like good cooking, need not be too serious, and not all rockstar chefs made their names through bad
behavior. It's good to be reminded that the wholesomeness that
first made Jacques Pépin into the king of television cooking has
carried him through to the internet age. Joshua David Stein dives
into the history of how Pépin's five-minute, 52-second segment on

making a French omelet, first recorded for San Francisco's KQED in 1995, is now one of the most beloved and well-watched cooking segments on YouTube.

A pair of stories by Kim Severson and Kat Kinsman document the respective rise, fall, and potential rise again of Jamie Oliver and Rocco DiSpirito. They, like *The Sopranos* did for gangsters, show us the human side of seemingly once swagger-filled, infallible TV chefs (and unlike that show, are inspirational and hopeful in their advocacy of self-reflection and improvement).

While restaurant reviews seem almost like a cruel joke in the current situation (what restaurant needs to be criticized right now?), good writing is good writing, and nobody has perfected the art of the classy takedown like Pete Wells. When restaurants do finally, hopefully, reopen, we'd all do well to pay attention to writers like Korsha Wilson, who question who, exactly, are professional reviewers writing for, and how it would look different if Pete Wells (despite his eagerness to take down stalwarts like Peter Luger) weren't the one defining what good dining was in modern New York.

Even big businesses fail from time to time, and I always find it fascinating to peek behind the scenes. Kaitlyn Tiffany's look at how Lean Cuisine pigeonholed itself into a false-diet corner, Tim Murphy's retelling of the story we all thought we knew about how and why New Coke failed (it didn't die, it was killed by a southern rebellion), and Katy Kelleher's look at the dubious science and marketing behind the modern phenomenon of "raw water" make poignant connections between the very human individuals behind corporate-sounding messaging.

Finally, a pair of stories by Burkhard Bilger and Alex Van Buren about babies and food particularly struck me, as I simultaneously want to feed my daughter everything and eat her up at the same time.

More than anything, being in lockdown with a toddler who is unable to socialize and learn through the channels we have gotten so used to has shown me the value of socialization, the value of internal and external reflection, the value of having a good laugh, the value of neighborhoods and people, the value of diversity and culture, the value of history and technology, the value of education, and, more than anything, the value of being asked to participate in a world that extends beyond the boundaries of our four walls, of being challenged and provoked by thoughts outside of our own.

This is why food is important. These stories are not just stories about cooking and eating. These are stories about culture. About how food shapes people, neighborhoods, and history. Now, more than ever, as we face the very real prospect that the bars and cafés that have played pivotal roles in our social lives, the restaurants that have come to represent a neighborhood, might be lost forever, we must remember what it is that we risk losing and turn our minds outward, even as we are forced to isolate.

By mid-April I was able to hire back enough management and production staff to box up over 500 free meals per week. And when I finally was able to take my nose off the grindstone, I lifted my head to find a world in which organizers and everyday people had already begun figuring out ways to help people fill those very real needs for human connection. I was awestruck by the selfless frontline health-care staff working overtime to care for those in need, by the researchers who spent endless days and nights toiling in labs, by concerned out-of-work individuals reaching out to the elderly and homebound to make sure their needs were met. The pandemic has revealed the true heroes among us. Chefs and writers may not be heroes, but even heroes need to eat, socialize, and be provoked, and wherever there are empty bellies to be filled and too-comfortable minds that need poking and prodding, chefs and writers will be there.

J. Kenji López-Alt

The Best American
Food Writing 2020

KWAME ONWUACHI AND
JOSHUA DAVID STEIN

The Kitchen at Per Se Was a Clean Place but Hard and Heartless Too

FROM *Eater*

ONE OF PER Se's signature dishes is a white-truffle-oil-infused custard served with a ragout of black winter truffles. It's presented about midway through the chef's tasting menu, arriving on a silver platter, a small amount of silken custard in a hollowed-out hen's egg. The custard is made from egg, Thomas Keller's thinking goes, so why not serve it in an eggshell? At Per Se, the egg is held in a silver coil, with its top neatly cut off. A translucent tuile—a play on a potato chip—juts up from the opening like a jaunty geometric feather. It's no wonder that Keller never takes it off the menu: it's his masterpiece. But someone has to hollow out and clean the eggs, and for a month that job fell to me.

Unless you've ever needed to clean the inside of an egg—and there's no reason in the world you would, because it's an insane thing to do—you might not know that it isn't only eggshell, white, and yolk. Between the shell and the liquid inside, there are two thin membranes. In order to prepare the eggs, both membranes need to be removed. It's a tricky operation. The first step is to score a circle with a tourné knife (the smallest in a knife roll) a third of the way down the eggshell. Then score it again, to cut the top off cleanly. Then you carefully empty out the yolk and the white, separating them into bowls to be used later. To loosen the membrane, you use a mixture of vinegar and hot water that must be poured carefully into the now empty egg. It takes one minute and nine seconds. Any less and the membrane will stick.

Any longer and the shell becomes fatally fragile. After pouring out the water, you have to use your finger to scrape the membrane from the shell until it peels off like a snake's skin. This is where my troubles began.

Even in the best-case scenario, you lose about 30 percent of your eggs. Sometimes they crack funny, chipping at the point of incision. Some eggs are just not pretty enough to make the cut. Often, digging in to remove the membrane, you'd catch the edge of the shell and the thing would chip. And, since this was Per Se, one chip was one chip too many. Into the trash it went. The vinegar, meanwhile, is great at softening the bonds that bind the membrane to the inside of the shell but also at softening skin. The repetitive action of scraping the membrane off with the softening effects of the vinegar meant that halfway through the stack, my fingertips were pinkish and cracking. Three-quarters done, droplets of blood had begun to form. This I noticed with some alarm and, admittedly, some pride. Looking down at my perfectly clean eggshells, I saw each one speckled with blood.

Because I was on egg duty for a month, my fingerprints vanished. Basic training was working. Who I was before I walked into the kitchen at Per Se was gone. Even the knowledge I thought I knew, I didn't. There was the way everyone else does a task and the way it was done at Per Se.

The rhetoric of a restaurant is vastly different than what actually happens in the kitchen. When I first arrived, I took at face value the stated philosophy of only accepting the best. The anger I had witnessed from Per Se's chefs, I thought, wasn't justified but could be understood in part as a sort of intensely discriminating standard of excellence. Passion for the best, perhaps, overflows into uncontrollable passion. But one morning while I was in the prep kitchen, I became painfully cognizant of how what happens in a kitchen differs from what is said about what happens in a kitchen. We had just received a shipment of mandarin oranges. We used them to make demi-sec rounds that we served as an accoutrement to a fish main. It was my job not only to take off the membranes but to peel the segments, scrape off all of the pith, and dehydrate them. Even though they'd eventually be dried, it was important to use only the ripest, most flavorful mandarins since the dehydration doesn't take away flavor, it intensifies it.

The batch I was working with that day was clearly off. The oranges were already desiccated, their flavor paler than what I was used to. Part of my responsibility wasn't just to prepare the oranges but to taste them too. I knew that if a diner sent back a dish, or if it made it to the pass and chef de cuisine Eli Kaimeh kicked it back, it was my ass that was on the line. So when I saw these oranges and tasted them, I knew I had to say something. When the sous chef supervising the commis kitchen at the time passed by, I told him I didn't think we should use the oranges.

He grabbed a mandarin and looked at it. "We can still appreciate its beauty," he said, which was a very Per Se way to say STFU.

"I just don't think it tastes good, Chef," I replied.

"What the fuck did you say?" the sous growled, his cheeks flushing with anger. "Nobody asks your fucking opinion."

"Are you going to question my taste buds?" he went on bellowing. "Nobody wants you to be here!"

By this point I had recovered enough to realize I'd just driven into crazytown.

"Why the fuck would you tell me that? I'm not your fucking friend. We don't have fucking conversations," he continued.

There were other moments too, when I felt like I was being called the N-word with no one actually saying it. No one had to and maybe they were too smart to. So it was left to me to decide whether it was because I was Black or because I was just me that I was the only one greeted with a growling "Get the fuck back in the prep kitchen!" when I ran food out to chefs on the line. From that point on, I took those words to heart. I didn't have conversations. I came in and did my job, getting better and better each service, but I didn't look for friends or colleagues. I had my mask on and shield up. It was that old familiar feeling of being confused, scared, unsafe. And as I did as a boy, I did now as a man, cutting off the wires of my emotions. When the other chefs yelled at me I was no longer there.

When service began in earnest, around five o'clock, the afternoon apprentices either continued prep in the commis kitchen or, if you had proven yourself, you were allowed to assist the garde-manger in the main kitchen. There are seven to nine official courses at Per Se, but Chef Keller padded these out with amuse-bouches.

Since he opened the French Laundry, Keller has been making these salmon cornets. They're often the first bite of food a guest has, and so set the tone for the rest of the evening. The cornets are small sesame tuiles wrapped, while still warm and pliant, into tiny cones. These cones are then filled with similarly dainty scoops of salmon tartare with tiny bits of chive, to resemble ice cream cones with sprinkles. Thomas Keller, Dad Joke king of the kitchen. Having proved myself, my job during service was to man the cornet station, which was tucked right by the door to the kitchen, next to the garde-manger.

For an apprentice to be on the line during service at Per Se was an honor. And to have even a small role in the flow of dinner service was a big deal. Though the hierarchy of the kitchen can be cruel, there's still a sense of togetherness on the line during service. As soon as a waiter puts in an order and a ticket is generated, we became one body. We'd brace for whoever was expediting that night to call out a number, and as soon as he did the assembly line would spring into action. Me with my cornets, while at other stations other chefs began the beautiful and intricate dance of world-class cooking.

From my station on the line, I grew to understand what Keller meant by "sense of urgency" and understood why the overbearing chefs bore down so hard on all of us. If the intricate rhythms of the kitchen are interrupted by even one beat, the whole thing topples dangerously into cacophony. The sloppy *mise* of a morning commis, uneven knife cuts for instance, translates into vegetables of varying doneness at dinner. Even a moment of laziness in a line cook during service exposes the entire kitchen to disaster. Food dies under the heat lamps. Foams collapse. Meat grows cold. Yet none of this justifies the abuse.

By the time four months were up and I was approaching the end of my apprenticeship, I was ready to leave. My skin was bulletproof by this point but I hated that it had to be that way. At the end of service one evening, we were all sitting around the pass discussing the menu—well, I was standing, because as an apprentice I wasn't allowed to sit. Every single night we had to create a menu for the next day. It didn't matter what time it was or how long it took. We'd gotten to the main course and everyone was dog-tired. It was 2:00 a.m. and we had started work at 11 that morning.

Eli looked at our exhausted eyes and asked, "What are we going to do for tomorrow? No one knows? What is the fucking main course?" I took a chance: "Why don't we do wagyu, Chef?"

Everyone looked around to see who had spoken up. I stood there with a blank face, no emotion, but at the same time not backing down. I had my Per Se game face on, a face I now donned automatically every day when leaving the locker room to approach the kitchen. And as the rest of the kitchen turned toward me, I noticed maybe for the first time that they were all hiding behind similar masks.

"What did you say?" Eli demanded, his voice cutting into me.

Keeping my tone as steady as I could, I responded, "Why don't we do wagyu, roasted. With hakurei turnips, hen of the woods, and a marsala veal jus. Maybe we can put a quail egg on it and make it like a riff on steak and eggs."

The chefs de partie looked at each other, shook their heads, and rolled their eyes. Everyone, including me, braced themselves for an epic verbal assault. Which approach will he take this time? I wondered. Maybe it would be Eli's usual riff when he got mad: "You fucking scum, you don't even get to sit down and you think you can put a dish on this menu!" Perhaps he would go with, "Do you know how hard and long I've worked to be in my position? To put my blood, sweat, and tears onto this menu? Do you really think you can spew some off-the-cuff 'dish' and think you can make it onto the menu of the best restaurant in North America?"

To my surprise, Eli stared down at his notes, scribbled something, and looked back up at me. "Sounds fucking good. We will run it tomorrow." My dish, on the menu at Per Se. I should have been overjoyed. I suppose that somewhere inside of me, I was. But by this time nothing could get through the game face. I was too afraid to smile, too exhausted to rejoice, and too beat to celebrate. I left Per Se a few days later. There was no teary goodbye, nor was I expecting one. The kitchen at Per Se was a clean place but hard and heartless too. The hierarchy was a necessary one but the weight of it was crushing to those on the bottom. The brigade system ensures that food gets to the plate looking pretty; it also gives free range to rage-inclined pricks to indulge their worst impulses. The anger was like black mold in the air ducts, infecting everything. As I've opened my own kitchens, at times I've certainly been guilty of regurgitating the habits I learned at Per Se. But when I grow enraged, I also try to remember how it made me feel to be yelled at on the line. From Per Se, I try to extract the sense of urgency without the poison of anger.

"I Just Want to Eat Her Up!"

FROM *The New York Times*

IN *BAO*, A short animated film that won a 2019 Academy Award, a woman makes dumplings and is astonished when one suddenly sprouts limbs and begins to cry like a baby. She raises the dumpling, or *bao*, like a son. He grows a beard and acquires a blonde human fiancée. Spoiler alert: when he goes to leave the house for good, his mother—in a fit of despair—picks him up and eats him.

Screening just before *Incredibles 2*, this cannibalistic feat earned gasps from the parents in the theater but not, I noticed, from my two nieces, aged 9 and 10, who continued to throw elbows in their greasy race to the bottom of the popcorn box. Mom's decision to eat the kid seemed a fairly run-of-the-mill maternal punishment.

Why so blasé? Conflating food and babies is no longer so uncommon in our culture. A relative might gaze upon your chubby-legged newborn and say, "She's so cute, I just want to eat her up!" or "How delicious!"

Fetuses and embryos are subjected to this unorthodox language too. The pregnancy apps Ovia, the Bump, and What to Expect all compare them to comestibles. At week six, Ovia informed me, my future daughter was the size of a blueberry, evolving quickly to a butternut squash and at last a watermelon. If I preferred to think of her as a French pastry, she was a madeleine, a croissant, and a plump boule. Best-selling prenatal bible *What to Expect When You're Expecting* proclaims that the 26-week fetus is the size of a chuck roast.

Why do we talk about the species we're supposed to keep alive as something we would—in a pinch—fry up for supper?

It's not a new phenomenon. A representative for BabyCenter, the pregnancy and parenting website, claimed that they launched the current trend of comparing fetuses to produce in 1997. By 2008, the What to Expect books had followed suit.

Gina Nebesar, cofounder of Ovia Health, decided to incorporate produce comparisons in their pregnancy app when it launched in 2013 after seeing how common they were among midwives, gynecologists, books, and websites. Though the app's million-plus users can choose other themes to indicate fetus size, such as toys or cute animals, the fruit and vegetable comparisons trounce the others in popularity.

"A lot of women like to go out and buy the fruit, put it on the kitchen counter and make something with it," Nebesar said. "It's easy to understand and nonthreatening. Imagining an orange inside of you isn't daunting."

Dr. Jessica Zucker, PhD, a Los Angeles–based clinical psychologist specializing in reproductive and maternal mental health, agreed that comparing a fetus to a natural element could "ease anxiety potentially and concretize information that is so abstract and life-changing." Upon hearing that one Ovia user baked the French pastry representing her future child every week, Zucker pondered whether it was "an unconscious attempt at connecting with this developing fetus."

Dr. Amy Bentley, PhD, a professor of food studies at New York University, noted that "we compare a lot of things to food"—lovers, pets, things we treasure—and that "the connection between food and love is huge. There's no question that to serve and prepare food for someone is an expression of love."

"Outside of the womb," Bentley added, "babies are incredibly edible." She recalls her husband saying of their infants, "'I just want to eat that kid. It's so delicious, I love it so much. I just want to take that chubby arm and just bite it.'" For them, she said, it was "a way to express the visceral emotion that was wrapped up in our obsession with the baby."

"Cute aggression," a term coined by researchers at Yale University and studied at the University of California, Riverside, could be at play here. The Yale study concluded that adults who felt "overwhelmed with very strong positive feelings" when viewing infant photos often had aggressive responses, wanting to pinch cheeks and "eat them up." Data suggested that the positive emotion surge had provoked the aggressiveness, and that the latter restored emotional equilibrium.

These studies were small, however. As Kara Becker, associate professor of linguistics at Reed College, cautioned, this is hardly universal behavior. "You can find communities where people don't talk to children this way." She pointed to a study of Samoan caregivers suggesting that they don't use what academics call a "simplified register"—or baby talk—when speaking to infants. Though child-centered Westerners might babble to babies who can't talk back, in Samoa, she said, adults are more of the "I'm not gonna talk to you until you can talk back" mindset. "Eating up" cute babies is likewise a social construct, she suggested, and learned behavior.

Heather Paxson, professor of anthropology at MIT and author of *Making Modern Mothers: Ethics and Family Planning in Urban Greece,* agreed that babies are not regarded as cuddly or edible around the globe. In Bali, for example, "It's very formal. Babies are seen as divine and not fully human."

In some cultures, Paxson said, a stranger talking about eating a cute baby would be perceived as a threat. She's seen the "I'm going to eat this baby!" line employed by Greek and American mothers. But in parts of the Mediterranean, Middle East, and Latin America, to talk about eating someone *else*'s baby could be "suggesting envy, which is to invite a malicious sort of threat." One would even be cautious about praising the cuteness of the baby, lest one invite the "evil eye."

Although Paxson generally thinks that moms talking about nibbling on babies suggests a physical, asexual intimacy, she noted that in pre–World War II Greece, according to author Eugenia Georges, women actually salted squalling newborns. Georges writes, "The birth concluded with the ritual known as 'the salting of the baby.' After the mammi wiped the infant clean, she rubbed salt over its body."

The idea, posited Georges, was to "cure" and harden the baby's skin, like a ham, and to prevent rashes and disorders. Salt retains its positive associations in Greek culture. A foolish person might be described as "without salt," and "Has the midwife not salted you?" is an insult.

Paxson suggested that salt was a purifying agent, not a culinary one, in that scenario, but added that in many cultures, "salt wards

off evil spirits." As for whether it's made the jump from "purifying
agent" to "taste agent," she laughed, "My husband has stories of
his mother literally pouring salt on his arm and pretending to eat
him like a cob of corn."

Are we ignoring the nearly universal taboo on cannibalism with
this sort of "baby talk"? Paxson, author of the book on Greek fer-
tility and motherhood, parries that in many cultures, newborns
are not yet considered fully human. "Customarily, in Greece . . .
baptism is the point at which a baby becomes a human, a person.
Before then, a colloquial expression in Greek would be 'a little
dragon.' It's of the human world but not quite human." When
placed in the historical context of high infant mortality rates, she
said, it makes a sad sort of sense. "I don't think it's ever easy to lose
a baby, but it does make it a little bit of a different thing if it never
had a full name."

Learned behavior or not, conflating the language of food and
babies is seductive. Most of the academics I spoke to had pet food
names for their children. My newborn daughter has the name of
a French pastry I love.

Not to brag, but she looks absolutely delicious.

A Critic for All Seasons

FROM *Eater*

"IF ONE WERE offered dinner for two at any price, to be eaten in any restaurant anywhere in the world, what would the choice be? And in these days of ever-higher prices, what would the cost be?" the critic Craig Claiborne once asked in a restaurant review for the *New York Times*. His answer was a five-hour meal at Chez Denis in Paris, which Claiborne and his collaborator, chef and cookbook author Pierre Franey, won in a fundraising auction sponsored by American Express. In a spectacularly blasé tone, Claiborne recounts a wine-soaked parade of haute cuisine staples, like oysters, caviar, lobster and truffles, foie gras with aspic, and sweetbread parfait, all of which he determined was not worth the price tag of $4,000 (the equivalent of about $18,000 today, and for which he paid just $300).

The review, "Just a Quiet Dinner for Two in Paris: 31 Dishes, Nine Wines, a $4,000 Check," ran on the front page on November 14, 1975. Nearly a thousand letters poured in to the *Times* in response, most of them condemning Claiborne's extravagance at a time when New York City was mired in crisis, fiscal and otherwise. Described in Claiborne's obituary as his "most notorious gastronomic adventure," he reportedly said as he walked out of the restaurant, "You know what was so amazing about that meal? I don't really feel that stuffed."

As I left a four-hour meal at the Grill, one of New York City's most opulent and critically acclaimed restaurants, I was similarly unsatisfied, but instead of hungry, I felt unsettled. The Grill is the magnum opus of Major Food Group, a brash New York post-

Recession empire built on absurdly expensive theme restaurants like Carbone, an Italian American fantasia that has since descended on Las Vegas and Hong Kong, and the Polynesian, one of its most recent ventures, an attempt at the perfect tiki bar. The unsettled feeling wasn't because of the price tag, which was $600 for two people—not uncommon in fine dining restaurants in New York City. (Dinner for two at Eleven Madison Park now runs up to $1,100.) It wasn't because of the food, either. The Grill's interpretations of midcentury American dining at its peak were technically flawless—a foie gras appetizer that paired silky seared livers with an herbaceous onion sauce was staggering, as was the larded squab with smoky, sweet orange preserves.

It was something else. As I reoriented myself on 52nd Street after dinner, looking at the golden glow of the dining room faintly reflected on the gray office buildings across the street and the row of black town cars with drivers waiting outside, replaying the four hours I spent inside, I realized that fully enjoying the Grill requires partaking in the luxurious nostalgia that it peddles—the fantasy of feeling like one of the wealthiest New Yorkers of the 1960s. The servers outfitted in white suit jackets designed by Tom Ford wheeling around silver gueridons and tableside flambé stations, the antiquated garde-manger station filled with towering displays of fresh fruit and vegetables, none of which you can eat—it was all designed to invoke the surreal sensation of being inside the most important restaurant in the country during the height of American global power. Every seat at the square bar was occupied as bronze rods dangled menacingly over drinkers' heads and bartenders dashed back and forth in perfectly starched uniforms. The volume of the music and the conversation between diners was high, the tone lighthearted but standoffish. The atmosphere was disorienting—it was a party, but what were we celebrating?

Shortly after the Grill opened in spring 2017, critics were falling over themselves to proclaim their love for this restaurant and its historical allusions. In the *Times*, Pete Wells hailed it as "confident, theatrical, retro, unsentimental, sharp and New Yorky," noting how it turns the "increasingly empty formality" of white-tablecloth service "into theater, or a game that everybody can get in on" in a three-star review. *Eater NY*'s Ryan Sutton said it "puts everyone under a spell that they belong here" and is "as close as you get can to a perfect New York restaurant." Former *Eater* national critic Bill

Addison called it "excessive," "smashing," and one of the year's 12 best new restaurants in America. And *GQ*'s Brett Martin, who takes nearly a quarter of his review to recount his lifelong yearning to belong at the original Four Seasons—which "may never have been populist, but its Kennedy-esque aspirational vision was open to all" —declares that the Grill and its companion restaurant the Pool "are everything great about New York, a triumph of the New York a kid might dream about growing up in the hinterlands of Deep Brooklyn."

I did not feel any of the delight that most of the critics felt. Instead, I felt embarrassed by this nostalgia, and the fact that I had just participated in it. I wondered why, in New York City, one of the most diverse places in the country, I was one of two Black patrons in a dining room at one of the best-reviewed restaurants of the past year on a Friday night; I imagined how those reviews might have been different if any of them had been written by a person of color.

While for some, Kennedy-era Manhattan is an inspirational time, calling to mind gleaming buildings and uncut optimism, for others, it represents a bleak period of misery and oppression. The original Four Seasons opened in the space in 1959, five years before the Civil Rights Act was passed, meaning I might not have been able to eat where the Grill now stands; in fact, it's hard to imagine that this space would have been quick to welcome Black diners even after the act was passed. Or that its designer, the famed architect Philip Johnson, would want them there, given his history as a Nazi sympathizer. This is a context I cannot push to the back of my mind when dining.

The critical success of the Grill speaks to the origins of modern restaurant criticism—of which Claiborne himself is the patriarch, even devising the *Times*'s star system—which was largely to tell upper- and middle-class, implicitly white New Yorkers where to spend their money on their next night out. As a student of food criticism and restaurant goer, I've often thought about how being a Black woman impacts my dining experience, and wished that more critics understood that experience.

From being asked for a drink by white patrons to being told a different wait time for a table (or told there are none at all), restaurant dining rooms too often act in accordance with the same racial hierarchy as the rest of the world. I've been cut in front of as if I didn't exist and been grabbed by a diner who thought I was ignoring her when she wanted another drink, or whatever she felt she needed at the moment. I've been handed the dessert wine menu at a bar because the bartender assumed I liked sweet wines, and been asked, "Have you had a negroni before?" when ordering one—and even after assuring them that yes, I had, still suffered through a lecture explaining the concept of bitter flavor profiles. Experiences like these are constant reminders to people of color that they're an "other" in dining spaces.

Even my first visit to the Grill was a reminder that my skin didn't fit in with the rest of the clientele. After I'd angled in between groups of men in suits to order a Hemingway daiquiri with aged El Dorado rum, the bartender looked at me sideways and asked, "What do you do?" I lied and said I work in consulting. Apparently, I didn't fit the profile of a Grill patron, or an aged-rum drinker. "You want to have the guy coming to the Four Seasons who has the ripped jeans," the landlord, real estate mogul Aby Rosen, once told the *New Yorker,* and yet in my sweater and jeans, I was methodically scanned up and down by the people around me.

In those moments, I want to ask the bartender why he responded to my drink order with a question about what I do for a living, just loudly enough to be heard by everybody around us, so they'd know what I'd experienced. But, as many Black diners know, being in a dining space can often mean choosing between being ignored, interrogated, or assaulted. From being attacked while asking for silverware to being questioned for simply sitting at a table, there are plenty of ways in which restaurant experiences can quickly become unsafe for Black diners. I suspect that the critics who loved the Grill have never had to negotiate these same realities.

Months after visiting the Grill, I ate at Henry at Life Hotel by JJ, a Pan-African restaurant by chef Joseph "JJ" Johnson, formerly of Minton's and the Cecil in Harlem. The compact, handsome restaurant is in a generic hotel lobby near Madison Square Park, outfitted in dark woods with a low ceiling that makes the space feel like a basement. The menu is the culmination of years of travel and deep research on the African diaspora and its impact on the world's cuisines. Here, Africa's spices and cooking techniques are applied to ingredients from all over the world. The continent's impact visible in dishes with global inspirations, animated like a breeze picking up dry leaves in autumn: lamb kebabs are served with kimchi and roti bread on the side, while shrimp and pork dumplings are presented on a bed of fragrant yellow curry.

Henry's atmosphere felt like the New York that I see in my day-to-day life, reflecting the city's racial, ethnic, and age diversity. Current *Times* critic Pete Wells also noticed it. "On many nights Brown faces and white faces, topknots and braids, headscarves and headbands, sit side by side, giving Henry more the appearance of a restaurant in Harlem than of one just off Herald Square," he wrote in the one-star review. His remark that Henry has the "appearance of a restaurant in Harlem" is meant to give the reader some context for the feel of the dining room, but reminded me of a Yelp review affirming a restaurant's authenticity by noting the race of the clientele; it implies that a dining room composed largely of Black diners is out of place in a Midtown Manhattan neighborhood, even though some 24 percent of the city's residents are Black.

Wells also noted Henry's "seamless playlist of hip-hop and R&B" that "unspools" over the course of dinner, but for me it was an audible reminder that this is a Black chef's restaurant—not a restaurant that is playing Black music for effect or ambiance, but showcasing the actual soundtrack of Johnson's life, and the lives of many Black Americans who grew up in the 1990s and early 2000s.

A restaurant like Henry, with a Black chef running a kitchen exploring the often overlooked and undervalued imprint that Africa has left on cuisines around the world, should be celebrated. Not only is a restaurant of its kind still far too rare in this city, but its success would inevitably pave a smoother path for other Black chefs. Henry appeared on Wells's annual list of New York's best new restaurants, but the city's critics have otherwise been largely silent on it. It raises the question of how critics decide which restaurants to fete—and why so infrequently, the kinds of restaurants they choose are ones that are comfortable for someone like me.

Everyone has a culinary baseline, a set of flavors or foods they're intimately familiar with as the result of their background. These baselines aren't only racial, they're cultural and geographical and can shift over the course of a person's lifetime. Conversely, we all have culinary blind spots—cuisines or ways of eating that we're not familiar with. The implied comfort critics found at the Grill, jux-

taposed with their discomfort at—or disregard for—Henry high-
lights the existing critical establishment's overwhelming whiteness,
and how its gaze favors restaurants that speak to that experience.
This fact has been acknowledged by many food writers. "Where
are all the Black restaurant critics?" Nikita Richardson asked in a
Grub Street op-ed. For *Philadelphia,* Ernest Owens recounted how, in
a city where Black people are a plurality, the food scene is trapped
in "a self-perpetuating cycle" where "white writers write for mostly
white audiences and cover mostly white-owned restaurants that ca-
ter mostly to white people," driven in part by increasing gentrification. With some notable exceptions, women have historically been
few and far between: in a 2014 article, then–*LA Weekly* restaurant
critic Besha Rodell wondered why there are so few female food
critics, noting that there were twice as many male critics at the
time. As far as I can tell, there has never been a Black food critic at
a major publication or food section of a newspaper. (The culinary
historian Jessica Harris did have a stint reviewing restaurants at the
Village Voice, alongside Robert Sietsema, between 1998 and 2002.)
    But there's some hope. If the end of 2017 marked the begin-
ning of the critical establishment taking a good, long look at who
gets covered, 2018 was the year that it began asking in earnest who
gets to be a critic, and who they're reviewing restaurants for. With
the loss of Pulitzer Prize–winning food critic Jonathan Gold of the
Los Angeles Times, and the retirement of the stalwart (and occasionally ethically dubious) critic Michael Bauer at the *San Francisco
Chronicle,* new openings emerged for critics in two of the country's
most vital food cities. Tejal Rao was named the first *New York Times*
California restaurant critic; Soleil Ho was named Bauer's replacement at the *Chronicle;* and the *Los Angeles Times* picked up two writers to take over Gold's food criticism duties, Patricia Escàrcega of
Phoenix New Times, alongside *Eater*'s Addison.
    It's a good start. Sure, the restaurant-criticism establishment re-
mains mostly white, but three women of color filling roles that
were traditionally reserved for white people does create some optimism about the future of the genre, in part because all three
have written about chefs and communities of color deftly. Hopefully their coverage will expand the world of restaurant criticism
in meaningful ways. But there's more that can be done: There are
still too few Latinx writers in food media, and the fact that there
isn't a visible Black food critic with a culinary baseline rooted in

Black foodways reviewing American restaurants and adding to the discourse is shameful—speaking all too clearly to how closely food media has fallen in line with the lack of diversity in newsrooms across the country. And to move the conversation even beyond the male-female discrepancy noted by Rodell, nonbinary writers should also have the opportunity to add their experiences to the canon as critics.

"Until there's a diversity of voices in the world of restaurant criticism, chefs are going to feel that only one point of view is being represented," Rodell wrote in 2017. I would add that readers also notice. The homogenous old guard, focusing its coverage on fine or "elevated" dining—and the select restaurants outside of those spheres that it has chosen to hold up in order to maintain the pretense of a fair shake—while often disregarding everyday Caribbean, Asian, South American, Mexican, and African restaurants, sends distinct messages to white readers (here are places you'll like) and readers of color (your spaces don't deserve coverage beyond a cheap-eats section). Restaurant criticism is fundamentally cultural criticism and just as our society isn't a monoculture, our restaurant critics shouldn't reflect one.

Wanting to see if I missed something, I made one last visit to the Grill. The hosts let me know that there was a private event in the main space—but the Pool Lounge was open, so I could have a drink there. I was led through the Grill, which is the only way to get to the Pool. The dining room tables had been removed, and in their place was a cocktail party, men in black ties and women in floor-length black dresses, scattered amid loud music. Servers and support staff weaved their way through the crowd, balancing platters of champagne flutes and canapés. The gueridon parked behind the stair railing looked abandoned. As I walked through the hallway to the Pool, I asked if the guests were celebrating a wedding or a birthday. The hostess turned to me and said coolly, "It's actually a memorial service."

CYNTHIA R. GREENLEE

A Real Hot Mess: How Grits Got Weaponized Against Cheating Men

FROM *Vice*

IN HER POEM "Grits," Angela Jackson's anonymous woman narrator stays up all night, seething while stirring a pot of grits she's planning to throw on a man, her man. Searingly hot, the grits would stick "on both his faces."

Jackson's poem pulsates with an untold backstory of betrayal real or perceived—and an act of violence the "she" may or may not commit. Jackson paints a conflictual portrait of a woman unraveling yet rational enough to plot. She's stirring up a strike against a lover.

He means enough to her that his supposed duplicity keeps her angry. His absence keeps her awake, doing the impossible of keeping even long-cooking grits creamy for hours. The sticky, grainy mess will cling to his skin. She means to maim and mark him, so there will be no mistake that he's unfit for fidelity or other partners.

The poem, published in Jackson's 1998 collection *And All These Roads Be Luminous,* is part of a larger history of grits becoming a weapon in the hands of southern, mostly Black, women.

As Erin Byers Murray, author of *Grits: A Cultural and Culinary Journey Through the South,* notes, grits "aren't always comfort. In some cases, they're traumatic. Or even worse, used to cause pain." Within southern African American culture particularly, the throwing of grits is often a woman's tool of rage and domestic warfare.

Because this humble breakfast staple seems a novel instrument of vengeance and a well-known incident involved legendary soul singer Al Green, the idea of grits as a weapon has worked its way into Black film, literature, music, and a fair share of legal cases.

And it has a specific context. It's usually framed as a particularly resourceful revenge, an extreme "scorched-skin" campaign waged against an unfaithful or abusive male partner. An October 1977 *Jet* magazine article whose headline asked "Should People Be Told About Their Cheating Spouses?" led with this: "'If I ever caught my old man cheating,' a pretty Chicago wife sneered, 'I'd probably give him a late-night bath in hot grits and honey.'" Some relationship guides aimed at Black Christians mention attack by grits as a possible outcome when feelings turn sour. "When your mate feels violated, expect anything," advised one, including "broken car windows, scratches all over your face, or even hot grits covering your body sticking to you as the hot water scorches your skin."

Food is about relationships and power: who cooks for whom, who can leave the table without cleaning, who picks the strawberries, who pockets the profits. And not all relationships are healthy. The food served for pleasure can also serve as punishment. Take the origin story of Prince's hot chicken in Nashville. Family lore has it that the chicken got its mouth-scalding heat from a girlfriend who objected to the late-night shenanigans of her partner. When he requested her special fried chicken after carousing without her, she slathered it in cayenne pepper, battered it, and fried it. The story has the apocryphal patina of a much-told tall tale —but if true, someone liked revenge served blindingly hot and with ample pepper.

But it's Al Green's story of being on the receiving end of tossed grits that may be most responsible for pop culture representations of harm by hominy. It's almost as much of his legend as his songs that described the unpredictability of love, which will make you both do right and do wrong.

On October 18, 1974, the crooner had stripped naked and was preparing to bathe, when his new lover, Mary Woodson, entered the room and doused his back with a pot of hot grits.

Egg-sized blisters erupted on his skin, but Green was saved by the quick thinking of another woman who was also in the house, heard his screams, and pushed him under the shower's cooling water.

Shortly before the bathroom scene, Woodson had asked the

singer about his marital intentions. The two had only known each other for several months, but Woodson may have been uncomfortable about the other women in Green's life—and the other woman right there in the house. Then 28, Green was slim of hip, wide of smile, and never wanted for female company.

For his part, Green thought Woodson was "a real woman, not like all the giggling girls who flocked around me on the road." She was moody but head-turningly beautiful, self-possessed enough not to chase him, and therefore attractively mysterious. According to Green, he evaded the marriage question while Woodson slowly stirred a pot of water and told him, out of the blue, she would never hurt him. Soon after, he was writhing in grits-induced agony. Woodson fled the room. She fatally shot herself in another part of his eight-bedroom Memphis estate, leaving a suicide note in her purse.

The unusual weapon and Green's fame made the story a media sensation and the troubled Woodson a one-dimensional punchline. "Al Green" became a part of the cultural lexicon and an actual verb entry in Urban Dictionary. I've heard men half-jokingly warn other men that if they don't shape up, they too might "get Al Greened" by a female partner.

Woodson had a history of self-destructive behavior and psychiatric care. She was a wife and mother who left behind a family, and she'd swallowed sleeping pills and slit her wrists days before her death. The story of Mary Woodson struck *An American Marriage* author Tayari Jones so much that just this month—almost 45 years after Woodson's death—the author referenced Woodson in response to a tweet that asked, "Who is a woman, who growing up, you always thought was a public joke but upon getting older you realized her story wasn't so funny after all?"

A Woodson-inspired character makes a brief appearance in Jones's novel *Silver Sparrow;* the book's Mary met the narrator and her family before the fateful, fatal night with the novel's Al Green. Dressed in a homemade (but chic) pink pantsuit, the Mary of Jones's novel came to Atlanta for a church conference and had her hair curled in a salon by the narrator's mother, Laverne. Sitting in the chair, Mary talked about this "man I got" who sang with a healing touch, and she cuddled the feverish then-five-year-old narrator. Mary promised to stay in touch after getting to Memphis, but the narrator's father nixed that, saying "there was something wild in her face." In Jones's telling, Mary threw the grits at the novel's Al Green figure the next day.

Green's hot grits encounter left him with second-degree burns, mourning Mary, and struggling to make sense of what happened. But it may have also inspired disgraced singer R. Kelly who, like Green, has made a career on blending the sacred and the sexual.

In his 1998 album *R.*—which sold more than 12 million copies and included the anthem "I Believe I Can Fly"—the song "Down Low Double Life" tells a story of a man with "doggish ways." Two women ultimately band together against him after the "damn Caller ID" outed his philandering.

Next thing the song's subject knew, according to an interlude in the song, his former paramours assaulted him while asleep, "woke me up pourin' hot grits." The song is quintessential R. Kelly when he's not in bump-and-grind mode. It's in his other register: the ratchet confessional. In this case, it's the tale of a hapless man who can't help himself. He just falls in and out of love and lust with multiple women. He's both victim and responsible for this sticky situation.

But how do we understand the women on the other side of this equation, those who seized a common pantry item—and, with it, power? How do we understand their violence, female anger, and the responses that often downplay their grits-throwing as merely a funny thing that happened? Popular references vacillate between portraying them as women pushed too far by male mistreatment, blatantly unhinged, or a particular kind of "crazy" that has little to do with actual mental health issues. Throwing grits at a male partner can be gendered justice, a weapon of the weak when that woman has been that man's punching bag.

I remember a long-ago kitchen conversation about a distant relative who had Al Greened her husband. The reactions varied. Kinfolks guffawed, hid chuckles, stared at the table silently. One—recently "saved and bathed in the blood of Jesus"—acknowledged that the husband in question was a "pretty-boy" pissant who fathered outside children, gambled away the grocery money, and had left his wife with a black eye. Still, his alley-cat morals didn't mean he deserved to have his earlobe melt into his neck. But even Sanctified Cousin didn't go hard in his defense, and the consensus around the dinner table was that the grits-tossing was the creamy, searing coda to a relationship that had long been an irredeemable hot mess.

By throwing grits at a no-good male partner, Black women became a female version of the "crazy nigger." Explained by Nathan McCall in the modern-classic masculinity memoir *Makes Me Wanna Holler,* this term applied to someone with an "explosive temper, who took no flak from no one—man, woman, or child. He would shoot, stab, bite, or do whatever he could to hurt somebody who disrespected him . . . We admired craziness as an esteemed quality, something to be admired, like white people admire courage. In fact, to our way of thinking, craziness and courage were one and the same." While McCall's "crazy culture" attached to urban young men who would fight over a salty look, a sneaker smudge, or bona fide insult, the grit-throwing woman earned a particular prestige when she abandoned the boundaries of "normal" behavior. People feared, admired, and wondered at her, but thought twice before crossing into her path.

The power—or fearful respect—to be gained from tossing grits could draw other consequences: spreading conflict to family and friends, negative responses in social circles, retaliation and injuries if her aim missed the target, media attention, and legal woes. Alexis Staton, a Maryland woman accused of burning her husband with hot grits in 2015 (which she later said was not "done deliberatedly" [*sic*] and was a response to his emotional, financial, and physical abuse), lost her job and her children faced taunts at school, though she was found not guilty of assault and reckless endangerment. Despite the notion that grits-throwing is a woman's crime of retribution, grits can be wielded by men—not just against them—and in situations of mutual aggression. A year earlier, 60-year-old Edward Holley of Orlando, Florida, dumped "scolding [*sic*] hot greasy grits" on a neighbor with whom he'd fought the night before. Thirty percent of the victim's body was burned, and Holley was charged with attempted second-degree murder. The jury had to decide if malevolent grits-tossing met the standards for conviction: intent to commit the action, whether it was "imminently dangerous," and showed a "depraved mind."

The imminent danger of hot grits also meant they missed a potential recent film appearance. Tiffany Haddish, describing a monologue that didn't make it into her hit film *Girls Trip,* listed all the things she'd do to a man who wronged her friend: drugging him and burning a message into his penis, or resorting to hot grits. "Universal said they were afraid women would actually do this shit. So they didn't put it in there 'cause they didn't want to get sued."

Tyler Perry had no such reservations. In 2006 hot grits made a cameo in the Tyler Perry film *Madea's Family Reunion*. When engaged Lisa confesses that her fiancé has been hitting her, Madea shells out advice—mainly to turn grits, a stock pot, and a cast-iron skillet into an arsenal. A woman has to work with what she has, says Madea. Madea urged Lisa to invite her partner-perpetrator to the table with a sweet morning greeting and bubbling grits on the stove. "And when it starts to boil like lava . . . throw it right on him." And if that weren't enough to make her point (or disable him), Lisa could follow up with a cast-iron skillet wielded the way Venus and Serena Williams powered their racquets. Dressed in a bathrobe, Tyler Perry as Madea engaged in a quick, fluid two-step and mimicked the tennis stars' movements.

"That's called grit ball."

BURKHARD BILGER

Open Wide

FROM *The New Yorker*

IN A LABORATORY in Denver, on a decommissioned US Army base, a baby sits in a high chair with two electrodes attached to his chest. To his left, on a small table, a muffin tin holds four numbered cups, each filled with a green substance. On the walls and the ceiling, four cameras and an omnidirectional microphone record the baby's every burble and squawk, then transmit them to a secure server in an adjacent room. What looks like a window with blinds, across the room from the baby, is in fact a two-way mirror with a researcher behind it, scribbling notes. The baby's mother takes a spoonful of the first sample and lifts it to the baby's mouth, and the experiment begins.

Building 500, as this facility was formerly known, has the looming hulk of an Egyptian temple: it was once the largest man-made structure in Colorado. When it opened, in 1941, four days before the attack on Pearl Harbor, threats to American safety were much on the government's mind. (After the war, President Eisenhower spent seven weeks on the eighth floor, recuperating from a heart attack.) The Good Tastes Study, as the baby experiment is called, is in a similar spirit. The two electrodes on the baby's chest will monitor his heart rate and how it fluctuates with his breathing. A third electrode, on the sole of the baby's foot, will measure his "galvanic skin response," or how much he's sweating. Together, they'll indicate whether the green substance is triggering a fight-or-flight response. Does the baby sense danger?

The enemy in question is kale. The four cups are all filled with raw kale leaves whipped into a smooth purée, or slurry, as food researchers call it. One sample is plain, another sweet, another sweeter still, and the last one salted. Sugar and salt can mask the bitterness in kale, but this baby isn't fooled. No matter which sample he's offered, he grimaces and turns his head, purses his lips, and swats the spoon away. The more his mother tries, the grumpier he gets, till he kicks his foot so hard that he jostles the electrode, disrupting the signal. "It's just a thing that happens," Susan Johnson, the director of the study and a professor of pediatrics at the University of Colorado, told me. "Completely throws off the galvanic skin response. If you can find a body part that's *not* in motion, let me know."

Most babies could use a dose of kale: a half cup has more than a day's worth of vitamins A, C, and K. The only problem is that they hate it—or so parents and baby-food manufacturers seem to assume. Two years ago, when Johnson launched the study, she sent her graduate students to find some commercial baby foods made from pure kale or other dark-green vegetables. They couldn't find any. The few that did exist were mixed with fruit. "I sort of blew it off at first," Johnson told me. "I just sent them out again and said, 'Try harder.'" They went to Kroger, Walmart, Whole Foods, and Sprouts; they scoured the organic markets in Boulder, then widened their search to the internet. Still no luck. The closest thing they could find was a Polish product made with Brussels sprouts. "That's when I started to get less frustrated and more interested," Johnson said.

Food preferences are a chicken-and-egg problem. Do we choose them or do they choose us? The Good Tastes Study was designed to tease such mysteries apart. Over the next six months, 106 babies will pass through Building 500 and try the samples. Afterward, two experts in human expression will scrutinize their faces on the videos. They'll divide their features into zones of activity and classify every twisted lip and wrinkled nose according to a Facial Action Coding System. The system can sort adult expressions into emotional categories: Happiness, Sadness, Surprise, Fear, Anger, Disgust, and Contempt. But baby faces are too pudgy for such specificity, Johnson says, so she'll settle for positive, negative, and neutral. (When a baby makes a gesture known as "the rake" and claws the kale off his tongue, that's negative.) She'll correlate those responses with the electrode readings, compare them with the babies' reactions to a control substance (oatmeal), and then circle back to see how the parents reacted to their children's reactions.

Baby food shouldn't be this hard. After a few hundred thousand years of raising children, humans ought to have this part down. No food has been more obsessively studied, no diet more fiercely controlled, no dining experience more anxiously stage-managed. Yet we still get it wrong. On any given day, a quarter of American toddlers eat no vegetables. When they do eat them, the most popular choice is french fries. Why don't babies know what's good for them? And why don't we?

When my kids were young and peevish and a carrot could cause a revolution—when Ruby loved oatmeal but hated Cream of Wheat, and Hans loved Cream of Wheat but hated oatmeal, and Evangeline wanted no breakfast at all; when every dinner was like the Yalta Conference and the table like enemy terrain, booby-trapped with vegetables that could go off in your face—I took courage from Calvin Schwabe.

Schwabe was a man not easily disgusted. A veterinary epidemiologist at the University of California, Davis, he specialized in parasitic worms that get passed from dogs and wild animals to people and end up in their liver, lungs, and brain. When Schwabe moved to Davis, in 1966, after a decade studying tapeworm infestations in Lebanon and Kenya, he found the local culture a little tame. He was famous for taking grad students to ethnic restaurants and chiding the chefs for not using authentic ingredients. He hosted dinners of grilled guinea pig and deep-fried turkey testicles.

Squeamishness is more than a minor character flaw, Schwabe believed. It's an existential threat. Even in America, people go hungry every day although they're surrounded by perfectly nutritious food. Pets, for instance. "Some 3,500 puppies and kittens are born every hour in the United States," Schwabe wrote in *Unmentionable Cuisine,* his cookbook of taboo foods, published in 1979. "The surplus among them represents at least 120 million pounds per year of potentially edible meat now being totally wasted." *Unmentionable Cuisine* is a work of calculated outrage, but it's not *A Modest Proposal.* It's a practical guide, Schwabe wrote, for the not-too-distant day when people may have no choice but to eat stewed cat (page 176) and beetles in shrimp sauce (page 372). If we were all just a little less finicky, we could feed the world.

It's a sensible argument, but then food preferences are rarely amenable to sense. Our tastes are us, we like to think. We were born hating lamb or fermented fish, even if half the world loves nothing better. And it's true that everyone experiences food differently. The woman beside you on the bus may have three times as many taste buds as you do, and different genes regulating those tastes. Depending on which version of the TAS2R38 gene you have, you may be highly sensitive to bitter foods, mildly sensitive, or not sensitive at all. People with dense, hypersensitive taste buds are often called supertasters, and are said to represent about a quarter of the population. Another quarter, with sparse, insensitive taste buds, are called nontasters, and the rest fall somewhere in between.

But it's not that simple. Supertasters don't always live up to the name—in some studies, they react to food just as regular tasters do—and genetic effects tend to fade. Children who are hypersensitive to bitterness are often especially fond of sugar. But that predilection disappears in adults, while the taste for bitterness grows. Being a finicky eater makes evolutionary sense for a toddler, lumbering around sticking things in his mouth. Better to spit them out if they don't taste familiar. But we learn to pick our poisons, and then to love them beyond reason. We go from Pabst to IPA, milk chocolate to dark, latte to espresso, homing in on the bitterness we once avoided. "Our biology is not our destiny," Julie Mennella, a biopsychologist at the Monell Chemical Senses Center, in Philadelphia, told me. "We're omnivores, and there is a lot of plasticity in the brain." Taste begins as nature and ends as nurture.

The index at the end of *Unmentionable Cuisine* is a gallery of horrors, or a good bedtime story, depending on the child: "Bat, baked," page 209; "Donkey brains," page 165; "Dormouse, stuffed," page 208. Schwabe presents his book as a collection of culinary taboos, but it's really the opposite: a celebration of what people *will* eat. Some Chinese love earthworm broth, and Zanzibaris feast on white-ant pie; the French have been known to eat eels with sea-urchin-gonad sauce, and some Hawaiians have a taste for broiled puppy. Human beings will eat damn near anything, it seems. You just have to start them young.

Late one afternoon in August, in a suburban kitchen in Scarsdale, New York, I watched a woman named Saskia Sorrosa roast beets for a baby-food recipe. Beets are kale's dark twin in the baby-food family. Something about their loamy sweetness, the taste of iron and manganese that seeps through them like runoff from a rusty pipe, turns children off. "I used to use a little magical thinking," Sorrosa said. "When my girls were little, I'd tell them that if they eat beets they'll make rainbow poop." Slender and tan, in a denim shirt and black jeans, Sorrosa moved about the kitchen with an easy efficiency. She peeled and chopped the roots, spread them on a cookie sheet with some fresh fennel, and drizzled them with olive oil. She did the same with a tray of asparagus and leeks, then put the trays in the oven. "But they also learned pretty quickly that there was only one meal. That was that. If they didn't eat it, there was no dinner."

Sorrosa is the founder and CEO of Fresh Bellies, a line of organic baby meals that Walmart and Kroger began carrying this summer. Seven years ago, when she made her first baby food, she was 33 years old and a vice president of marketing for the National Basketball Association. She had a six-month-old girl and could find nothing in stores to feed her that wasn't insipid or sweet. "So I'd come home from work and make the menu for the week," she said. "Two or three flavors, purée and freeze, then the same thing again two days later. I wasn't just making peaches. I was making peaches with lavender, figuring out which vegetables to cook with onions and which ones with garlic. It was like having a second full-time job."

Born and raised in Ecuador, Sorrosa speaks with her hands and in a rapid, ebullient English with no trace of an accent. Her father was a general manager for Del Monte in Guayaquil, then a banana farmer and exporter. He could afford to send his three daughters to an international school. Sorrosa came to the United States at 17 to study communications at George Washington University, found work in Miami and New York, and eventually married a childhood friend. "My friends said it was like dating your brother," she said. After their second daughter was born, two years after the first, Sorrosa quit her job and launched her business. She rented a professional kitchen, hired a chef who'd worked for Mario Batali, and began selling her baby food at farmers markets up and down the Hudson. Within three months, she was making as many as two thousand jars a week. This year, Fresh Bellies will produce half a million. Next year, the company should quadruple that number.

Baby food is in the midst of a golden age. With the rise of two-income families, home delivery, and ever pickier eaters, the global market has grown to $9 billion a year, 16 percent of it in the United States. Nine out of ten Americans have eaten commercial baby food for some period of time. Happy Baby, Tiny Organics, Once Upon a Farm, and dozens of other brands have joined in a scrum for the boutique market, over the bodies of fallen competitors like Bohemian Baby. One baby-food delivery service, called Yumi, promises to introduce babies to "over 80+ ingredients" in "the most nutrient-dense purees available." Its lineup includes kiwi chia pudding and baby borscht: "Superfoods for Superbabies."

Sorrosa has a simpler goal. She wants her children to eat the way she ate as a child. "In Ecuador, we had whatever the adults were having—it was just puréed and given to babies," she said. "I learned to eat spicy young." On weekends, friends and neighbors would descend on her parents' farm for buffets of ceviche and sancocho soup (a beef broth with mashed plantains and lime juice), braised goat stew, and shrimp in peanut sauce. All of which found its way into Sorrosa's mouth as she hung from her mother's hip.

"Palate training" is the buzz phrase for this, though it makes babies sound a bit like interns at a wine bar. We learn to eat what we're given to eat, and that education begins before we're born. When a pregnant woman eats a green bean, its flavor winds its way into the amniotic fluid around her fetus, and later into her breast milk. "Carrots, vanilla, alcohol, nicotine, mint—I've never found a flavor that didn't get through," Julie Mennella told me. Those tastes, and the colors and textures of things that contain them, come to signify food in babies' minds. Children whose mothers ate potatoes with garlic while pregnant, a study in Ireland found, are more likely to enjoy potatoes with garlic ten years later.

By now, Sorrosa's kitchen was filled with the smell of roasting vegetables, earthy and sweet. She took the trays from the oven and let them cool, then puréed the beets and fennel with an herb stock made with oregano from her garden. She was doing the same with the asparagus and the leeks when her daughters came tumbling in, wearing summer dresses and pink headbands. Sorrosa handed them bags of beet chips and freeze-dried red peppers to eat. When I asked what their favorite foods were, Alexa, the five-year-old, tilted her head and scrunched her eyes. "Chicken nuggets? Hamburgers?" Her mother laughed and waved her off. "We *never* eat chicken nuggets," she said. Then she took a plate and spooned the two purées on it, bright green and red like traffic lights, and handed it to me.

This was cheating, of course. No commercial baby food could be so fresh. To keep for weeks on a shelf, food has to be pressure-cooked at 250 degrees, or simmered at lower temperatures and spiked with an acid to help fend off bacteria. Fresh Bellies takes the second approach. Its We Got the Beet flavor is tart with lemon juice and much rougher on the tongue than the suave purées she'd given me. It's also three times as expensive as most baby food and has to be kept refrigerated. Still, it's recognizable as food in a way that the gray sludge in jars often isn't. And it has no added sugar or fruit. "You could mix it with chickpeas to make a really delicious hummus," Sorrosa said, and she was right. This was baby food for grownups.

Sorrosa wasn't teaching her girls to eat as she did in Ecuador. She was teaching them to eat as she does now, in Scarsdale, with cookbooks by Ottolenghi and the Barefoot Contessa on the counter. Her girls were contented omnivores, as she intended. But what part of their training was essential to their good health, and what part was just teaching them to be foodies like their mother? "I like Chop't salad!" Isa, the seven-year-old, told me, trying to cover for her sister's chicken-nugget comment. "And chicken-noo-dle ramen!" Sorrosa gave her the side-eye. "Ramen?" Then her face brightened. "Oh, you mean at Momofuku! You do love that."

Babies are creatures of fashion. They may not know what fashion is, but they're under our control, so we dress them as we like and feed them what we want. Their diets distill our anxieties. In the 19th century, this meant breast milk for a year or until the first molars appeared. In the 1930s, with the rise of "scientific motherhood," it meant formula at first, then cereal at seven or eight months. It meant jars of overcooked carrots in the 1950s, in the heyday of industrial food, and homemade purées in the 1970s. Babies have been early adopters of organic, low-carb, gluten-free, vegan, and hypoallergenic diets. But if the latest trend is to feed them what they'll eat as adults, we may be betting on the wrong horse. Our own diets seem to change every five years. Who's to say what their diet will be?

Fruits and vegetables are the best proof of that fickleness. Until the early 20th century, they were a suspect food, the cultural historian Amy Bentley writes in *Inventing Baby Food*. Raw fruit was thought to cause fever, based on medical theories that dated back to the second-century Greek physician Galen of Pergamum. Vegetables were seen as sources of dysentery and diarrhea. (The real problem was the polluted water used to wash them.) When canned fruits and vegetables were sold, it was mostly in apothecaries, as laxatives. Only the discovery of "vitamines," so named by the Polish biochemist Casimir Funk, in 1912, restored their reputation. "Nowadays it has become a race between physicians and nutritionists to see who dares to feed vegetables and solid food the earliest," a pediatrician at the Mayo Clinic wrote in 1954. "Vegetables have already been fed in the first month. We can now relax and see what it is all about."

What it was about was business, abetted by bad medicine. Between 1921, when a restaurant manager named Harold Clapp made the first commercial baby food, in Rochester, New York, and 1960, the baby-food industry swelled into a quarter-billion-dollar business. In that same period, the average age at which babies were fed solid food dropped from seven or eight months to less than two. Formula and "patent foods" were better than breast milk, pediatricians and advertisers claimed. Formula never ran out, and baby food could be enriched to suit an infant's needs. "For Baby's Sake, Stay Out of the Kitchen!" a Gerber ad insisted in 1933. Science could provide what mothers could not.

They weren't wrong. Babies of that era were often anemic, so they needed food fortified with iron. But that was because physicians insisted on clamping their umbilical cords immediately after birth. This kept blood from flowing from the placenta, depriving the baby of up to a third of its blood supply. Instead of nursing at their mother's breast, babies were carted off and given formula, which kept the mother's milk from coming in. It was a self-perpetuating cycle, and it kept spinning long after children grew up. Just as eating broccoli as a baby can teach you to love it as an adult, eating foods full of sugar, salt, starches, and preservatives can give you a taste for those things later on. It's palate training on an industrial scale.

Babies can get fat when fed solid food too soon. Before the age of five months, they're often too weak to refuse a meal, and adults, in their way, follow suit. "Industrializing the food supply was a win for most people," Bentley told me. "It created safe, affordable, shelf-stable food that only rich people used to be able to eat. The problem is that, when so much food is available, the rules around it disintegrate. We can afford to eat like cavemen now or to be gluten-free. We can eat anything, anywhere, anytime, and the really delicious stuff is not that great for you. So now we aren't dying of disease or hunger. We're dying from consuming too much."

The beaming faces on baby-food jars can hide quantities of unhealthy additives and worse, Ralph Nader told Congress in 1969. Seven years earlier, Rachel Carson had found that chemical fertilizers could work their way into the fruits and vegetables in baby food. A year after that, a study found that rats fed a baby-food diet developed hypertension. A series of contamination scandals followed: rodent excrement in dry baby food, cockroach fragments in Beech-Nut jars, chips of enamel paint and high levels of lead in many others. "One of the enduring characteristics of the food industry is its penchant to sell now and have someone else test later," Nader said. Even dog food was more clearly labeled.

The backlash was furious but brief. If the scientific mothers of the 1930s wanted baby food untouched by human hands, the natural mothers of the '70s wanted only handmade food. After a half century of being pushed around by doctors and industry, they were ready to "take mothering back," Bentley writes. Pressing a button on a blender was easier than forcing squash through a sieve, and a spate of new cookbooks offered advice for the trickier parts. "Peel the banana," a recipe for "Banana" in *Making Your Own Baby Food* explained, "and mash it in a dish with a fork."

A third of all baby food is now homemade, yet the baby-food industry is bigger than ever. Its new products have more vegetables and fewer additives. They are better labeled and more cleanly processed (though a recent study found trace quantities of heavy metals in nearly all the baby foods it tested, probably from pesticides and airborne pollutants). Gerber even has certified dietitians, lactation experts, and sleep coaches on call for free. But the true attraction is still convenience. Grinding your own carrots is a drag, even with a Baby Bullet blender, and your child may like the stuff in jars better anyway. "We are concerned with the technical task of mass feeding," Gerber's director of research, Robert A. Stewart, concluded in 1968, after dismissing the notion that the company's use of sugar, salt, modified starch, and MSG was bad for babies. "The quickest way to fail in such mass feeding is to prepare a nutritional product in a form that the consumer will not eat."

The taste-testing center for the Gerber Products Company is in a town I may not name, in a facility I've been forbidden to describe in detail. It's a kind of baby black-ops site. "Do you know where you're going?" my driver asked, when he arrived in a Lincoln town car. "I know the address. But do you know what the business is?" Gerber has been conducting taste tests since the 1950s. At first, the samples were sent to panelists by mail; then the tests were moved to a hotel in Fremont, Michigan, where the Gerber factory is situated. But the company worried that the results were skewed: many of the panelists owed their jobs to Gerber. So the tests were moved to this town which I shall not name, in a state that will likewise go unspecified. "They rented out a church basement for a while," Sarah Smith-Simpson, a chipper, speed-talking principal scientist with Gerber's Consumer Sensory Insight division, told me. "But they kept getting bumped out by funeral lunches."

We were waiting for the babies to show up. Gerber runs about 150 taste tests a year—since this facility opened, in 1996, babies have tried more than 150,000 individual servings. As we watched, nine mothers and one father filed in with babies on their hips. They took their places in cubicles furnished with high chairs and desktop computers. Then a cart full of white ramekins was wheeled in. Half the ramekins were filled with a pale-yellow purée; the other half had a purée that was closer to beige. Across from me, a moonfaced girl in a white stegosaurus jumper, identified only as Judge No. 7, grunted and kicked her legs. She turned and gave me a long, level stare, then blew a raspberry in my direction.

For the next 15 minutes, she and the other babies would taste the two samples and their parents would rate their reactions on the computer. It was the Good Tastes Study without electrodes. Only instead of kale the babies were eating applesauce.

There aren't many things that babies like better than applesauce. The two samples were subtly different—one was made from a single apple variety, the other from four—but they were equally sweet. And sugar is the great override button of infant taste. A few drops can calm a baby's heart, release opiates in her brain, and settle her neural activity into a pleasurable pattern. Adults in taste tests reach a bliss point at about five teaspoons of sugar per cup of water. Babies prefer twice that amount. This test, in other words, was a no-brainer. It was like asking third graders if they want to go to Disneyland. Really? How about Harry Potter world? Judge No. 7 was already pounding her tray for more.

Gerber would have it no other way. The company has dominated the baby-food industry almost from the day, in 1927, when Dorothy Gerber, tired of mashing peas in her kitchen, asked her husband if he couldn't do a better job of it at his canning factory. Between 1936 and 1946 alone, Gerber's business grew by 3,000 percent. The company now claims roughly two-thirds of the baby-food market, and has the highest consumer loyalty of any brand in America. Fremont is nestled among apple orchards and vegetable fields near Lake Michigan, where the winds off the water cool the ripening fruit and help it "set sugar" in the summer. There is a baby-food festival every July, with crawling competitions and baby-food-eating contests, and a harvest festival in September. From the sky-blue water tower at the center of town to the image of the iconic Gerber baby in the lobby (clearly too young to be eating solid food), everything seems to belong to the same happy kingdom. When I visited, this fall, the Gerber employees I interviewed seemed incapable of a negative thought. They'd all fed Gerber products to their children or grandchildren, apparently, and always with impeccable results: every child healthy, every mealtime harmonious, every dinner sweet.

That is not most parents' experience. In 2002 Gerber commissioned a survey of children's eating habits in more than 3,000 American households. The rate of childhood obesity had tripled in 30 years, and the survey confirmed the reasons in sobering detail. American babies were drinking soda as early as seven months. They ate a third too many calories, often from chips and fries. One in five ate no green vegetables daily, and one in three no fruit. The picture has improved a bit since then—babies now breastfeed a little longer—but the overall pattern holds. American toddlers are more likely to eat dessert than plants.

Judge No. 7 had had enough. She signaled this fact by grabbing the spoon from her mother's hand, slapping it to her forehead like a salute, and shouting "Baaaaa!" She'd eaten both dishes clean. "They like what they like," Smith-Simpson said, after the parents had filed out of the room, sated babies back on their hips.

We were standing in an observation room next door, looking out at the testing area through a two-way mirror. On Gerber's old nine-point tasting scale (it has since switched to seven points), an eight or above was a home run—cause for a joyous announcement in Fremont. Vegetables averaged six and a half. "I don't know that anyone likes Brussels sprouts or kale the first time," Smith-Simpson said.

We know how to solve this problem. To learn to like a vegetable, children have to try it again and again, the psychologist Leann Birch found more than 40 years ago. Sometimes it takes 10 tries or more. But who wants to take that advice? Who wants to watch a baby toss a turnip across a room 5 times, much less 10? "Most of our research shows that parents will buy one container and give it three or four times, but they won't buy it again," Smith-Simpson told me. Good eating habits are the one skill that parents don't mind their children giving up on, Saskia Sorrosa told me: "When they're learning to ride a bike, they fall down a hundred times. Learning to read takes years. But when they're learning to eat it's 'Oh, well, you didn't like it the first time. Don't bother.'"

Taste tests like Gerber's miss the point, Sorrosa believes. Babies have no idea what's good for them. If we want them to eat like adults, their food should taste good to adults. Yet Sorrosa can't escape the logic of the market, either. The beet-fennel purée that she made for me was delicious, but she couldn't risk it on a supermarket shelf. Beets are polarizing enough on their own, she said. "Add fennel and you have two things that people either love or hate." It's the basic conundrum of baby food: If it sells, it's probably not best for babies. If it's best for babies, it probably won't sell.

Gerber doesn't add sugar to most of its purées anymore, but it's there just the same. The vegetables are almost always mixed with fruit—apple-blueberry-spinach, pear-zucchini-mango—or naturally sweet. "Production carrots like these grow bigger and set more sugar than the ones you get in a store," Chris Falak, one of Gerber's agricultural-team leaders, told me when we checked on a carrot crop outside Fremont. "They'll get even sweeter after a week of sunny days and cool nights." Of the more than 500 baby foods with vegetables that Susan Johnson's graduate students surveyed for the Good Tastes Study, nearly 40 percent listed fruit as a first ingredient; another quarter listed red and orange vegetables first. Only 1 percent were mostly dark-green vegetables.

The American diet is like a broken bridge, Johnson says. It's missing a span of simple, savory baby foods that can lead to healthy eating habits. "There's nothing wrong with fruit. But fruit in my dark-green vegetables? Who thought that was a good idea?" Getting children across the bridge has never been easy, but in a culture that always plays to their weaknesses it can seem impossible. American toddlers now eat an average of seven teaspoons of sugar a day, according to the Centers for Disease Control—more than the recommended allowance for adults. Even baby food made with a single, unsweetened ingredient may taste nothing like the real thing. Babies raised on the pressure-cooked bananas in jars, one study found, were no more likely than others to enjoy the fresh fruit.

The observation room had a second one-way mirror, which looked into a small working kitchen. "We wanted to figure out what parents do at home—how they store the product, feed it, and prepare it," Smith-Simpson said. Then she pushed a button and the room began to revolve like the grand-prize booth on a game show. A minivan was now parked where the kitchen used to be. "The car is the second most used environment," she said.

If convenience to a housewife meant not having to cook baby food, convenience to a working parent means not having to serve it. Drivers can't spoon-feed babies in a car seat, but they can hand them a tube of banana puffs and let them feed themselves. The baby-food industry, having lost some of its youngest customers —the recommended age for starting solid food has crept back up to six months—has expanded its audience on the other end. That has led to a proliferation of new "delivery systems," including squirt bottles and squeeze tubes and bags of dehydrated veggie chips. Babies once weaned from jars at 12 months now sip from pouches well into their toddler years. Half of American children under three use them.

The idea, as usual, came from the military. The baby foods of the 1950s and '60s were often based on foods developed for American soldiers in World War II. Their powdered, concentrated, and prepackaged ingredients were easy to serve and close to imperishable. What could be better for baby? And today's pouches are direct descendants of the Army's foil-packed field rations. If you want to see the future of baby food, look in a foxhole.

"War fighters are a weapons system. We fuel them with food," Stephen Moody, the director of the US Army's Combat Feeding Directorate, told me, when I visited his labs in Natick, Massachusetts. Square-built and direct of speech, with ears like miniature satellite dishes, Moody runs a team of 87 chemists, biologists, food scientists, and support staff, developing field rations for all five branches of the military. "We are building the fuel for that war fire," he said. This seemed a world away from babies eating applesauce. But Moody's goals were a lot like Gerber's: mobility, nutrition, taste. The tinned beef and soy biscuits of World War II have given way to a food court's worth of flavors: buffalo chicken with brown rice, beef goulash with smoked paprika, mango-chipotle salmon. Toss a foil pack into a plastic sack with some salt water, add a tea bag of iron and magnesium powder, and the resulting chemical reaction will heat the meal to 100 degrees in 10 minutes. The pack can survive for three years at 80 degrees and withstand a thousand-foot drop from a C-17 cargo plane. Yet the chicken-burrito bowl I tasted was better than most fast food. Even the rice had kept its shape and bite, thanks to a special variety that had taken months to source.

"It's only nutritious if they eat it," Moody said, echoing the Gerber scientists of the 1960s. The soldiers in his field tests are a lot like the babies in taste tests. They get tired of eating the same dish. They refuse to eat some things even when hungry. They have limits to what they'll do for a meal. "We always go to war with the perfect rations for the last war," Moody said. "We are trying to get ahead of that." Today's military is focused on counterinsurgency and mobile expeditionary squads—the equivalent of families in minivans, and similar concerns apply. How heavy is my backpack? What's the most nutritious snack bar? What's the simplest self-serve container? Three meals' worth of standard field rations weigh just under five pounds. "First strike" rations for expeditionary forces weigh about three pounds. By microwaving foods in a vacuum or bombarding them with sound waves, Moody's team has managed to reduce their weight and volume by an additional 30 percent, while improving their flavor.

The logical end to all this is personalized nutrition: to each according to his body chemistry. Field rations vary from 3,600 calories for ordinary soldiers to 6,000 for Army rangers or Arctic ski patrols. "You wouldn't want to put the same thing in a fighter jet that you put in a tank," Moody said. The next step is to tailor the rations with nutrients for specific tasks: tyrosine for improved cognition, anthocyanins to repair muscles, calcium to thicken bones. (Millennial recruits are prone to stress fractures, Moody said, their frames having gone soft from too much screen time.) One day soon, soldiers will come back from a patrol, download data from their smartwatches, and 3D-print pills of the nutrients they've lost. The baby version won't be far behind.

The two fields come closest to converging in the cockpits of spy planes. U-2 pilots need to keep a pressurized helmet on at all times, so they can't use a spoon or a fork. To keep them nourished for flights of up to 12 hours, the Combat Feeding Directorate has designed what look like oversized tubes of toothpaste. Stick the nozzle in a socket on the dashboard and it heats up like a cigarette lighter; stick it in your helmet and you can squeeze the hot food into your mouth. "When we first developed them, we did a lot of surveys," Jill Bates, the directorate's sensory coordinator, told me. She squeezed two lines of food onto a plate, one beige and the other cream-colored. "And we realized that the pilots wanted more texture and mouthfeel in there. The idea that they were having a meal—not just grown men eating puréed meat."

The lines did look lumpier than expected, but I wasn't prepared for the taste. I'd been imagining something like Plumpy'Nut, the nutritional paste given to starving children. Yet if I closed my eyes and forgot about the tube, my first taste was of apple pie—or a reasonable simulacrum, with bits of crust and real fruit. The second line tasted like a luxurious mac and cheese. It was made with real Gouda and truffle oil, Bates explained, and tiny beads of pastina pasta: "That's the only kind that can squeeze through." Like the other tube foods they'd developed—tortilla soup, key lime pie, polenta with cheese and bacon—these were dishes meant to do more than nourish. They were designed to trigger sense memories: to call to mind a kitchen in Iowa, as a pilot circled the Syrian desert at 70,000 feet.

It's a lesson Americans learn early and never seem to forget—that even a replica of a replica of a thing can soothe the heart. That a rough facsimile is often enough. It's why we have Velveeta and margarine and orange juice from concentrate, protein shakes and Soylent drinks and superfood smoothies, made for runners and hikers or just people in a hurry. We're all eating baby food now.

My children have long since grown up and can feed themselves. The strange things I forced on them as kids—goat kefir gets mentioned more often than I'd like—seem not to have stunted them too badly, or twisted their palates into unseemly shapes. Two of them even like beets. Still, after a few months in the crosscurrents of baby-food research, I couldn't help having second thoughts. Did I feed them right? Are their dietary foibles my fault? Would some magic combination of Swiss chard and tempeh, grass-fed beef and organic dragon fruit have made them stronger?

Food should be a comfort to us, but it's just as often a torture. And so, one morning this fall, hoping to clear my head of theories and countertheories and get a hint of how other babies eat, I went to an African farm stand in Maine. Portland has been a haven for immigrants for more than 40 years, beginning with Vietnamese and Cambodians in the 1970s. In the past 10 years, a stream of refugees have arrived from Sudan, Somalia, and the Democratic Republic of the Congo, among other countries, and a scattering of African markets have popped up to serve them. This stand was the brainchild of a group called Cultivating Community, which trained immigrant farmers to grow African produce in Maine. The Somali Bantu man who supplied the vegetables had leased an acre southeast of Lewiston, where he grew the crops these mothers missed most: amaranth greens, African corn, bitter eggplant.

By the time I arrived, a line of women had formed, most of them with babies in slings or strollers. Mariam, the good-natured Djiboutian who ran the stand, had told some of the mothers that I was coming, so a group of them stood to one side, eyeing me curiously, their hands on their hips or holding bags of greens. Four were from the Congo, one from Angola, and one from Somalia; all were dressed for going out, in elaborately plaited wigs and weaves and carefully applied makeup. We talked for a while about what they feed their babies, and how it differs from what their older children ate in Africa—they'd all immigrated in the past two years. Then I made plans to watch three of them cook for their children. "But only if you buy the ingredients!" a feisty Congolese woman named Rachel, with long copper braids, told me. "This takes time, you know!"

Rachel was 29 and had studied mathematics in Kinshasa. When she fled the Congo, two years ago, after a government crackdown on dissidents and student protesters, she had an 8-year-old boy and a 5-year-old girl, and she was pregnant. The only visas that she and her husband could get were for Ecuador, so they flew to Quito with their children, and made their way north, country by country, on foot and by bus, until they reached Laredo, Texas, and were granted temporary asylum. Now here they were in Maine, on an alien continent. The climate was so cold that it seemed frankly hostile, and the government was less and less inclined to let them stay. The least she could do was feed her children some food from home.

The next day, I picked Rachel up at her apartment, in North Portland, and we went shopping at a Sudanese market in the East End. While I wandered among sacks of fufu flour and canary beans, bottles of palm oil and sorrel syrup, Rachel hitched her daughter Soraya onto her back with a blanket. Soraya was a year old now, with bright eyes and a look of plump, irrepressible health. She watched as her mother threw a head of garlic and some yellow onions into her cart, then picked out an especially fearsome-looking dried catfish, black from smoke. Together with the amaranth leaves and eggplant she'd bought at the farm stand, they were the key ingredients in one of her favorite Congolese dishes, *lenga-lenga*.

"Even just this, with some fish and tomatoes, *c'est formidable*," Rachel told me, back at her apartment. She was slicing a green pepper into a pan of onions and whole garlic cloves that were sautéing on the stove. She added peeled and cubed eggplant and some sliced leeks, then checked on the amaranth leaves boiling beside them, soft as lamb's-quarters. Across the room, Soraya was slumped on the couch. She was watching a cartoon of a mother cradling her child, singing, "Hush, little baby, don't say a word." Rachel glanced over at her, then mashed the softened eggplant against the side of the pot with a wooden spoon. She poured the sautéed vegetables into the boiling greens, dropped in two bouillon cubes and the smoked catfish, boned but not skinned, and cut in two whole tomatoes. Then she covered the pot and set it to simmer.

*

Feeding children isn't molecular biology; it just feels like it sometimes. The perfect diet is a target that's both moving and receding, its bull's-eye shrinking in the distance. The Recommended Dietary Allowances for calories and nutrients, first issued by the National Research Council in 1941, were deemed too permissive in 1994. The latest versions, called Dietary Reference Intakes, also include adequate, average, and tolerable nutrient levels—three more numbers for parents to keep in mind. And every year seems to bring more supplements to obsess over: probiotics, phytonutrients, antioxidants, adaptogens. "We've got solids down to a science," the Yumi baby-food website promises. If only.

No doubt there's always something better for babies to eat. But they're resilient creatures, for all their flab. Any good, varied diet will get them through, and the components aren't hard to figure out: a dark-green vegetable, an orange vegetable, a carbohydrate, and a protein for iron and B vitamins. A single egg or half a cup of milk, two or three times a week, can be the difference between a healthy child and a malnourished one, Mutinta Hambayi, a senior nutritionist with the World Food Program, in Rome, told me. "One mother said to me, 'When you have a mouse hole and there are seven babies in there, I can feed one to my child every day!' They are called hunger foods, but they are not. They are foods that countries have adapted to eating." In Zambia, where Hambayi grew up, people eat caterpillars; in Kenya, termites; in Uganda, flying ants; in Cambodia, spiders. "People find it disgusting, but I'm from a landlocked country," Hambayi said. "I had the same reaction when I saw prawns."

Babies do have some sense of what's good for them, it turns out. "Self-weaned" infants, who dispense with purées and just gnaw on their parents' food, tend to be slimmer and healthier than those raised on baby food. But only if their parents eat healthy meals themselves. And there's the catch. The average American's diet is so abysmal, Amy Bentley told me, that most babies are better off eating commercial baby food: "They'll get more and a greater variety of fruits and vegetables than those fed the family meal." To learn to feed our children, we need to learn to feed ourselves.

Rachel's *lenga-lenga* was like no baby food I'd ever seen. It was full of onions and garlic and bitter green pepper. It had mashed eggplant and leeks that could give a baby gas. It was salty from the bouillon—the rest of the family would be eating it, too—and far from sweet. By the time it was done cooking, it was a thick green porridge, pungent with smoked fish and sulfurous plants. It made kale look like Christmas candy. And yet, when Rachel brought a bowl of it over to Soraya on the couch, she bounced up and down and clapped her hands.

"With really young babies, it's not about liking or not liking," Susan Johnson had told me. "If they want to eat, they'll eat." That's the most striking finding of the Good Tastes Study. In video after video, the babies grimace or purse their lips after the first taste of kale. But when offered a second spoonful, they eat it anyway. "It's amazing that they do, but they do," Johnson said. "There seems to be this window of opportunity between six and nine months— maybe even twelve months—where they're just interested in food. And that predisposes them to healthy eating. They're like baby birds. It doesn't even matter if they like it. They just try it."

Soraya coughed a little and glanced at the TV. She shook her head and clutched at an empty Cheetos bag on the couch. The spoon was floating toward her now, filled with that smelly, familiar stuff from the bowl. She looked up at her mother with wide, inscrutable eyes, and slowly opened her mouth.

LAURA HAYES

Fare Access: DC Restaurants Could Do More to Welcome Diners with Disabilities

FROM *Washington City Paper*

TRUE OR FALSE: If a customer who uses a wheelchair cannot access the tables in the bar area of a restaurant because the only choices are barstools and high-tops, the restaurant should offer the customer a table in the dining room and the same happy hour prices available at the bar.

True. "Restaurants are required to modify their policies and procedures as needed to serve patrons with disabilities as equal to those without disabilities," according to DC Office of Disability Rights Director Mathew McCollough.

But restaurants don't always respond tactfully. "Sometimes I have to negotiate," says Kelly Mack, a DC resident who uses a wheelchair. "Some places will do it, others are less friendly about it. Sometimes it feels like more effort than it's worth. You want different people in your venue. It's surprising the resistance I've gotten."

Other local diners with disabilities report interactions with restaurant employees that range from disappointing—not receiving any eye contact—to egregious—staffers calling them a "fire hazard" or a "liability."

Accessibility is more than whether a doorframe is wide enough for a wheelchair. It's equally about the hospitality diners with disabilities receive when they come in for a meal, including whether employees are nimble in accommodating them so they can have the same experience as other diners.

One in four US adults—61 million people—have a disability that impacts major life activities, according to a 2018 Centers for Disease Control and Prevention report. The most common disability type, mobility, affects one in seven adults. As of 2017, there were at least 75,783 people with disabilities living in DC.

Patrons with disabilities are protected from discrimination under Title III of the Americans with Disabilities Act, which took effect in 1992 and oversees places of public accommodation. They're double protected under the DC Human Rights Act of 1977. The ADA requires that new construction be accessible and mandates that restaurants built before the law went into effect remove barriers where "readily achievable." The subjective term creates room for restaurant tenants and building owners to argue they can't swallow the cost of a sizable renovation, such as retrofitting a building with an elevator.

DC is a historic city where old buildings abound. Some restaurants, such as those on the second floor of a rowhouse, may never be able to serve a customer with a mobility disability. But the lion's share of restaurants can—they have the opportunity to create memorable meals and ensure that the infrastructure in place is in good working order.

City Paper spoke with local residents with mobility, hearing, and vision disabilities to better understand what it's like to navigate DC's dining scene. We found a wide gap between what restaurants can achieve and what happens in practice, but also a few local businesses that have done excellent work in prioritizing inclusiveness.

When Mack dines out, attitude is everything. "They don't have to be perfectly accessible, but as long as they're welcoming and don't make a fuss about my wheelchair," she says. "Some places I go aren't really accessible. I have to go somewhere else to use the restroom. But I go there because I love them and they're welcoming."

Mack would be less likely to return to a restaurant whose employees communicate only with her companions, likely because they're nervous. It irks her when they ask her husband questions that she's better equipped to answer. "I know I'm in a wheelchair. It's not a surprise. I can talk about it."

Many of the diners *City Paper* spoke with are like Mack. They play favorites. If they find a restaurant that's accessible and welcoming, they're likely to come back and tell their friends. One of Mack's new go-to restaurants, for example, is Barcelona Wine Bar in Cathedral Heights.

But when people with mobility disabilities stray from their usual spots, they face a daunting number of concerns: Can I get up to and through the door? Can I maneuver around inside? Are there tables that I can transfer to or tables at the right height for my wheelchair? Can I get to the restroom? Will I be able to shut the stall?

Cara Liebowitz, a DC resident who uses a wheelchair, expects to be able to dine anywhere but her outings often reveal that's not possible. "I'm part of the ADA generation," she explains. She was born after the law first passed in 1990. "I've grown accustomed to things being accessible, so it shoots me in the foot sometimes. I assume they'll be accessible and don't think about the possibility that they won't be."

Even one step leading into a restaurant can be a deal-breaker. So can the width of the doorframe. Some restaurants with one or two steps unfold portable ramps. They sell for as little as $89 online. Other restaurants have an alternate entrance, but that isn't always ideal.

"A lot of times, especially at a fancy restaurant, there will be a sign that says 'Accessible entrance around the back,'" Liebowitz says. "It'll be in a shady corner by the dumpsters. It says, 'Ring a bell and someone will assist you.' Maybe if you're lucky someone will answer. Then they'll say, 'Tell us when you want to leave.' That makes me feel like a prisoner." Sometimes the alternate entrance winds through the kitchen.

Once inside, restaurants can be hard to navigate if they're jammed with tables. "Servers have told me, 'You have to move, you're in the way,'" Liebowitz says. "They've told me I'm a fire hazard. That's happened to me more than once."

Before diners with mobility disabilities try a new restaurant, they use whatever resources they can to discern if the building is accessible. There's a dearth of useful information online and no fact-finding method is perfectly reliable.

When there's no accessibility information on a restaurant's website, Liebowitz loads Google Maps' street view to hunt for steps. If she's lucky, a vehicle won't be blocking the image of the doorway. When a friend invited her to brunch a couple of weeks ago, they said they had looked on Google and thought the place was accessible. "I got there and the place had a step," Liebowitz says. "My friend felt really badly about that. Luckily we were able to go to an accessible restaurant down the street."

Calling a restaurant can reveal more information, but not every host understands all the facets of accessibility. *City Paper* called 50 restaurants that had available tables on Resy to inquire if they were accessible or accessible enough for a wheelchair user to enter. Ten didn't pick up, illuminating another pitfall—restaurants don't always answer the phones.

Some were eager to share their plan, however complex, of getting a patron who uses a wheelchair inside. Others requested advance notice. A couple made stipulations like "first floor only." And a handful were surly, stressing how it would be a "really tight squeeze." An individual who answered the phone at Beuchert's Saloon said, "There's one step up at the threshold. Then it's all one floor. I won't pretend to know people's abilities."

Six admitted they weren't accessible, including Obelisk, which cited being "grandfathered in" since it's in an older townhouse. The ADA does not have a provision to "grandfather" a facility. A restaurant must remove barriers when it is readily achievable no matter when it was built.

Only 1 of the 34 restaurants that self-identified as accessible posted pertinent information online: "Kyirisan has a wheelchair accessible entrance and restroom," the website reads. "Our outdoor dining area also is wheelchair accessible. Since some of our tables are booths or high-top tables, and therefore not accessible, please note in your reservation if you need an accessible table."

Information about accessibility is absent from local reviews, too. Readers have asked *Washington Post* critic Tom Sietsema about mobility issues at least twice in the past six years during his online chats. On January 8, 2014, a reader asked: "Tom, can we assume that if an accessibility issue is not flagged in your review of a restaurant it is 'wheeled mobility' accessible?'"

Sietsema replied: "While I like to give readers a sense of an establishment's design (pros and cons, including noise levels) I think it's up to anyone with a special request to make sure he or she can enjoy the restaurant. That means calling a restaurant ahead of any visit, asking to speak to someone in charge and being clear about your needs. It's the same strategy I suggest for anyone with dietary or other issues. Some restaurants are better equipped than others to make you happy."

This struck a nerve with Mack, who emailed Sietsema. "Basic accessibility for people with disabilities has now been required for more than 20 years," she wrote. "I do not consider my disability a 'special request.'"

Again on January 30, 2019, a reader asked Sietsema if he would consider including accessibility information in his reviews. "Because of mobility issues, we find that many of the places you review are impossible to access," the reader explained. Sietsema wrote back: "It's something I've thought about, and would like to include, but also wonder how much reporting I'd have to do, and how discretely I could say, measure doors, etc."

No local publication is off the hook. Accessibility information is also missing from *Washingtonian* reviews and opening announcements or "first look" stories in *City Paper, DCist,* and *Eater.*

More information would only encourage diners with disabilities to dine out with greater frequency. "There's this stereotype that we're sad pitiful people who sit at home collecting benefits," Liebowitz says. "We contribute to the economy like everyone else. If you're not accessible or your attitude isn't welcoming, you're losing business . . . I hate having to frame it in terms of business." A 2018 American Institutes for Research study found that people with disabilities have disposable income totaling $490 billion.

Accessibility is only going to become more pressing, according to Kristin Duquette, a DC resident and former Team USA swimmer (paralympic) who uses a scooter. "Disability is the biggest minority population in the world," she says. "The longer we're living with the advancement of technology a lot more people are going to be disabled at some point in their life. Some restaurants, whether consciously or subconsciously, are making decisions that negate a huge consumer population."

Restaurants with accessibility features like an elevator can improve the experience for all, according to Duquette. "More able-bodied people will use it out of convenience," she says. "It's beneficial for everyone."

Duquette describes a pair of experiences at Kirwan's on the Wharf. "The first time was for happy hour and I thought because the area was so new, it would have more of an inclusive structure but it didn't," she says. When *City Paper* called Kirwan's to inquire if the restaurant was accessible, an employee responded, "No, not really. Only if the person can get out of their wheelchair. And if they do that they can only sit at a two-top on the first floor."

The next time Duquette visited was for an event. It was on the second floor and there is no elevator. While she couldn't join the party, she says the manager made sure her experience "was great under the circumstances."

Owner Mark Kirwan didn't install an elevator for two reasons. First, the ADA does not require elevators in facilities under three stories or with fewer than 3,000 square feet per floor. Second, he says, "We would have lost a lot of space and we wouldn't have been able to make what we needed to pay the rent." Kirwan also says his managers are trained to ask private-function organizers to notify them if any guests have accessibility concerns.

When there are barriers to entry, restaurants must bend to accommodate diners so they can have the same experience as others. When Duquette went to meet friends for dinner at Daikaya Izakaya, she realized it was on the second floor and there wasn't an elevator. She could enter the first-floor ramen shop, however. "They moved another party and put us in our own space on the first floor and gave us the opportunity to order food from the second floor," she says.

Duquette also requires plastic straws to drink. "Because of my disability, it's a lot easier for me to use a straw," she says. "Paper straws disintegrate. I can't not bite on the straw. I love the environment. I love turtles. I get it. But I can't get into this restaurant, and on top of that you want me to carry around my own straw?"

She requested one in a restaurant recently and was told they're illegal. While DC's plastic-straw ban took effect this year, businesses that provide straws to the public must provide single-use plastic straws as a reasonable accommodation under the law.

Kings Floyd, a DC resident and power-chair user, has grown accustomed to asking for accommodations. She found a Chinese restaurant she likes but can't get inside. "It's in a historically preserved three-story walk-up," she says. "You can't reasonably charge me a delivery fee because I can't get into your restaurant. That's an accommodation. I'm allowed to access the food and service provided at your restaurant."

Floyd's request was met, but what happens when someone with a disability encounters an inaccessible restaurant? There's no agency that enforces the ADA. The only recourse is to file a complaint with the Department of Justice and incur legal fees or file a complaint with the DC Office of Human Rights for free.

"Most of these restaurants are trying," says Dana Fink, a DC resident and wheelchair user. "There definitely are some that aren't. Ones that have one tiny step down into the building, that's such an easy fix. There's just no recourse unless you want to sue them and I don't have the energy to sue every restaurant in DC."

Fink and others consider it a law with no teeth. "The burden of proof is on you," she continues. "You have to make a case that [a modification] is readily achievable." She's filed complaints with DOJ. "It typically doesn't resolve—most of mine take a year to hear back."

OHR enforces local and federal human rights laws. You don't have to be a DC resident to file a complaint, but the discrimination must have occurred in the District. In fiscal year 2017, OHR received 16 complaints regarding places of public accommodation that cited disability. That doesn't mean they were restaurants. Retail stores, hotels, and theaters are a few other places of public accommodation. In fiscal year 2018, OHR received 13 complaints.

"Being accessible is a factor of doing business," Fink says, equating it to fire safety and food safety measures. "These are all things that come with having a business. I don't know why accessibility gets filtered out."

Practical accommodations differ for diners with varying degrees of hearing and vision, but in many cases, staff would be better equipped to address needs with more robust education and training.

When DC resident Dr. Denise Decker dines out, her guide dog, Wonder, sits quietly next to her chair. She wears a harness to broadcast she's working. Service dogs are protected under the ADA, but not every restaurant knows what to expect. "Because of restaurant turnover and staff training and all the things managers and owners have to do, some staff don't know how to handle it," she says. "They might think, 'No dogs allowed!'"

She wants restaurants to know that Wonder has gone through specialized training. "I don't want people to be afraid and I don't want her training to be damaged by people wanting to feed or play with her."

If a restaurant has concerns, they're permitted to ask Decker two questions by law: Is this a service dog? What service does this dog provide? They cannot ask to see identification or ask for the dog to demonstrate the skill. Decker sings a familiar tune. "Staff should address me directly since I'm holding the harness," she says. "[Avoiding communicating with me] doesn't happen every day, but more than you would think."

Some diners who are blind or low vision don't use a guide dog, such as Arlington resident Mark Reumann. He reads braille and notes that not all restaurants have braille menus, and when they do, they're often out of date.

There are two ways Reumann finds out what's for dinner. First, he can ask a server to read the menu out loud. Second, he can navigate to a restaurant's website where he can use screen-reading technology. There's one potential barrier. "Some use PDFs, which are pictures and not accessible at all," he says. "Make sure menus are part of the website. Or, if it's a PDF, make sure it's text."

The other tricky point comes when it's time to pay. "Most places, when they bring the bill, they'll tell the diner what the total is," he says. "We've had a couple people put the bill down and quietly sneak away. Indicate that you've put the bill down and tell the blind diner what the total is."

DC has one of the largest deaf communities in the country because of Gallaudet University. Keith Doane graduated from the school and is now one of three cofounders of Catalyst+ LLC, a consulting firm that helps businesses and organizations support deaf employees, serve deaf customers, and design spaces according to DeafSpace guidelines. DeafSpace includes more than 150 architectural elements that are deaf-friendly.

Ample light is the biggest priority for diners who are deaf or hard of hearing. Dining companions need to be able to see each other to sign or gesture. "The eyes become the most important sensory input one can have in this society," he explains. He'll look for tables that are spotlighted. Sometimes he'll make specific table requests at the host stand.

When it comes to ordering, Doane's first ask is that servers not be afraid. "We all are accustomed to breaking down barriers," he says. He'll use his index finger to point to items on the menu and if there's a need for more information, such as how he'd like his burger cooked, he'll use his smartphone to type or a pen and paper. "I tried mouthing 'medium rare,' once, but the server thought I said 'medium well,'" he explains. "I hate when communication short-circuits and I get an overcooked hamburger."

Gesturing is also welcome. "We don't expect anyone to be fluent in ASL," he says, referring to American Sign Language. But learning the sign for "thank you" goes a long way. Doane also wants restaurants to know not all people who are deaf are the same. Some, like Doane, were born deaf and learned ASL. Others lost their hearing with age or because of an illness.

A number of DC restaurants and bars made accessibility a priority during their build-outs. Liz Cox, the taproom manager at Red Bear Brewing Company, says the owners set out to be one of the most accessible businesses in DC when they opened this year. Two sections of the bar are at the ADA's recommended height. So is the food pickup window and 75 percent of table seating. Two of the four restrooms are ADA bathrooms.

One of the brewery's bartenders, Jamie Sycamore, is a sign language interpreter by day, making it easy for him to interface with customers who sign and train other staff on the basics. And, Cox says, they're making strides in securing braille menus.

"People doing new construction can definitely achieve this," Cox says. "Was it a little extra work? Yes. But it was a massive undertaking no matter which way you look at it. What's a couple extra steps to make sure that it's friendly? With new construction there's no excuse."

That's how Drink Company CEO Angie Fetherston felt when Columbia Room moved to its new location—a second-floor space in Blagden Alley—in 2016. Even though they would be ADA compliant without an elevator because of square footage, putting one in was nonnegotiable. "The elevator was a big fight," she says. "We almost broke our lease over it."

Columbia Room's website is one of the unicorns that posts accessibility information. "Please let us know any access issues in advance for your reservation if you can or tell the door person," it reads. "We have an elevator, ramps, and an access-positive attitude toward our colleagues, friends, and family with disabilities."

Fetherston says she couldn't imagine telling former regulars with mobility disabilities they couldn't frequent the new location. "We had a longtime regular in a motorized wheelchair come through and tell us the points that are difficult to navigate," she says. "That's how we do it. We ask for help. Bars are where community happens, so we have to make it open to anybody who would like to come."

Michael Mason is the studio director at design firm Hapstak-Demetriou+. He's worked on buzzworthy DC restaurants including Rose's Luxury, Bread Furst, and Convivial. When he meets with clients before shovel meets gravel, he has to educate them about ADA compliance.

"Some are very savvy about it," Mason says. "It's a conversation that we're happy to have with them. Some people ask why they need to provide this. Some people push back against it a little here or there, but usually once we walk them through it, they're excited to be a part of it."

He helps them understand that it's not just to escape a bad Yelp review. "We can make arguments that differently abled diners spend billions of dollars in restaurants every year . . . from a dollars-and-cents perspective, it's important to accommodate everyone."

While not every restaurant may have the means to put in an elevator, lifts that can bring a wheelchair user from one level of a restaurant to another are more approachable. Mason ballparks their price at $12,000 to $15,000.

When a restaurant does have infrastructure in place, such as a lift or an elevator, it behooves them to ensure they're functional. "A lot of restaurants will use elevators for storage," Liebowitz says. "I'm sharing the elevator with a cart full of dishes or a garbage can."

The last time the city formally reached out to restaurants about accessible dining was in 2014. OHR called the campaign Accessible DC. They canvassed restaurant-heavy neighborhoods, and also distributed to restaurant owners a short guidebook that covers best practices for both creating a welcoming atmosphere and building a physically accessible space. It included a checklist for restaurants to determine where they stand.

But hundreds of restaurants have opened in the DC area over the past five years, and many older restaurants have changed hands.

An OHR spokesperson says they hope to offer a joint workshop with the Office of Disability Rights in August or September.

In the meantime, some Washingtonians have been leading grassroots movements related to accessibility.

Actor and disability advocate Andy Arias runs a group called DC Universal Pride that focuses on disability and LGBTQ issues. It meets at the DC Center for the LGBT Community the second Saturday of every month. "We talk about everything from dating, love, and relationships, but our main focus is the lack of accessibility in DC for the disabled community."

He feels people with disabilities are particularly "invisible" in the LGBTQ community. "People think we don't go out," he says. "I get patted on the head all the time when I go clubbing and people are like, 'You're so brave.' I'm like, 'What? How am I brave? I'm just living my life. Brave is dealing with your ass.'"

Arias describes a recent evening at a bar when an owner was hesitant to let him upstairs because he didn't want to be liable if he fell. "He wasn't talking to me, he was talking to my friend," Arias recounts. "Look sweetie, I've been in this body a long time. I can deal with this." Two men carried him up three flights.

While Arias can't do much about venues with multiple staircases, he's identified an area where he hopes to make inroads. He calls it the One Step Away campaign. It asks businesses to eliminate the one or two steps that lead up to their doors. "That's the whole thing about the campaign—if you try to move forward then we're cool."

And here's why he thinks it matters.

"You're either going to get in a horrible car accident or age into disability," Arias says. "I hate to be that real with people, but that's the truth. It's not like disability is never going to touch you because, surprise, it is. Then you're going to be like, 'Holy shit, I should have cared more about accessibility.'"

Best Practices

Keep a list at the host stand that denotes which tables are accessible and bullet points to describe a restaurant's accessibility features should someone call. Use a reservation system that allows customers to make notes about accessibility.

If the main entrance isn't the accessible entrance, have signage directing patrons to the accessible entrance.

Doorways should have a minimum clear opening of 32 inches with the door open 90 degrees, measured between the face of the door and the opposite stop. Wider is even better.

Ask before you help, touch someone, or touch someone's mobility device.

Communicate directly with the patron with a disability.

Servers should keep a pen and paper handy should a customer need to communicate in writing.

Tables should be spaced far enough apart for patrons using mobility devices to pass through.

Accessible tables have a surface height of no more than 34 inches and no less than 28 inches above the floor. If seating is fixed (booths), 5 percent of tables should still be accessible.

At least one seating area that people with disabilities access must provide the same services and environment as other inaccessible areas when readily achievable.

Consider including accessibility information on your restaurant's website.

Service animals may accompany customers with disabilities into restaurants. Emotional-support animals are not protected by the ADA.

At least one accessible restroom must be available when readily achievable. It should be large enough for a wheelchair, have grab bars, low counters, and low sinks.

Requiring a driver's license as the only acceptable document for proof of age discriminates against people with vision disabilities. Make an exception to accept another form of ID with age.

Sources: Americans with Disabilities Act, Disability Rights Education & Defense Fund, DC Office of Human Rights

Kitchen Shift

FROM *The New Yorker*

FOR AMERICANS LIVING through turbulent times, Canada can seem like a refuge. The Montreal chef David McMillan figures it doesn't hurt for Canadians to have a getaway plan, too. Since 2012 he's owned a lakeside cabin in the Laurentian Mountains, accessible only by boat. It's equipped with solar power, fishing rods and rifles, and enough dried provisions to last a year. McMillan, who has three young daughters, told me, "If anything is weird, I could grab everybody and head up there." The cabin was an inspiration for *Joe Beef: Surviving the Apocalypse*, McMillan's second cookbook with Frédéric Morin, his partner in five Montreal restaurants, including Joe Beef. Published late last year, and cowritten with Meredith Erickson, a cookbook author who was one of Joe Beef's first servers, the new book is in part a tongue-in-cheek survivalist's manual, with instructions for building a subterranean bunker, making hardtack, and growing endive in darkness. By "apocalypse," the authors mean a range of modern ills, from the "constant noise" of social media to the threat of nuclear war. "We don't want to just survive," Erickson writes. "We want to live it out in full Burgundy style." To that end, the book also collects more than a hundred of the chefs' recipes, including a tater-tot galette, sweetbreads cooked with charcoal and licorice, and a rendition of *jambon persillé*, a Burgundian charcuterie of ham suspended in parsleyed jelly.

Joe Beef, which opened in 2005, is McMillan and Morin's first and best-known restaurant. It specializes in ambitious but unfussy French cooking—no white tablecloths, no minimalist dishes sprinkled with microgreens or gold leaf. Situated in the former industrial neighborhood of Little Burgundy, near the Lachine Canal, the restaurant has the feel of a ragtag bistro, with vintage furniture and stuffed animal heads mounted on the walls. The menu, written only on chalkboards, in French, is defined by exuberant immoderation, a blend of the haute and the gluttonous. On a given night, it might include a traditional foie-gras torchon or a sandwich of foie gras on white bread; tartare of raw duck, venison, or horsemeat; and a hulking strip steak topped with cheese curds —a Québécois staple—or fat links of *boudin noir.* Often, it includes dishes that aren't French at all: skate schnitzel, porchetta, barbecued ribs cooked in the backyard smoker. Diners willing to spend at least $100 apiece can forgo ordering and let the kitchen stuff them with a dozen courses of its choosing. The food writer John Birdsall once published an ecstatic piece on the site First We Feast titled "I Puked at Joe Beef and It Made Me a Better Man."

For a long time, McMillan and Morin made a point of living the experience that they were selling. McMillan was known for drinking with his customers, and then downing bottles of wine long after dinner service was over. The chefs' spirit of extravagance helped make Joe Beef a success. In 2007 they opened Liverpool House, two doors down, to accommodate Joe Beef overflow; four years later they expanded Joe Beef into an adjacent space, doubling its capacity. And a couple of years after that, they opened a wine bar, Le Vin Papillon, two doors down from Liverpool House. Today they employ 150 people. But their ethos of excess proved unsustainable. In an essay for *Bon Appétit,* in February, McMillan wrote, "The community of people I surrounded myself with ate and drank like Vikings. It worked well in my twenties. It worked well in my thirties. It started to unravel when I was forty. I couldn't shut it off."

One day in January of last year, Morin and several employees and friends staged an intervention for McMillan at Joe Beef. McMillan had always thought of addiction as a weakness, not a disease. But he agreed to go to rehab, and his monthlong stay there, he wrote, provided a "crash-course in alcoholism, wellness, and the language of sobriety." When he got out, he continued to attend AA meetings. Morin, who is married with three kids, realized that he also had a problem. Several months after McMillan got sober, he stopped drinking, too.

One morning not long ago, I went with McMillan and Morin

to their latest venture, McKiernan Luncheonette, across the canal from Joe Beef. They opened it, last September, with Derek Dammann, the chef-owner of Maison Publique, a gastropub in town —one of many local establishments that feel made in Joe Beef's image. Housed in a former textile mill, McKiernan is the largest of their restaurants, and the only one to serve breakfast and lunch. It offers dishes in McMillan and Morin's maximalist style: a grilled cheese as big as a skateboard; a $120 *côte de boeuf.* There is also lighter, café fare, such as clam chowder and buffalo-milk yogurt with granola. When we arrived, the kitchen staff were slicing baguettes for *jambon beurre.* McMillan said, laughing, "Five of the best chefs in Montreal, making seven-dollar sandwiches!"

He and Morin are both in their forties but they are physical opposites, a Québécois Asterix and Obelix. Six feet three and heavily tattooed, McMillan is Joe Beef's front man—charismatic, obscenely quotable, as inconspicuous as a grizzly bear. Morin is smaller and more circumspect, with an aquiline nose, a pronounced French-Canadian accent, and a sly sense of humor. In the early years of Joe Beef, Morin spent most of his time in the kitchen; McMillan readily admits that Morin is the better cook. As the business has grown, both have moved into supervisory roles, stopping by the restaurants frequently but leaving their staff to handle day-to-day tasks. Since getting sober, both have lost a significant amount of weight.

Until very recently, debauchery was considered inescapable in some corners of the restaurant industry. Anthony Bourdain, in his 2000 memoir, *Kitchen Confidential,* enshrined the perception of cooks as hard-driving misfits, and of kitchens as places generally populated by "a thuggish assortment of drunks." Mario Batali, who in 1998 opened Babbo, his flagship restaurant, in New York, made his prodigious appetites a defining part of his image, along with his ponytail and orange Crocs. Batali was one of the world's most admired chefs, known for rhapsodizing about the pleasures of Italian specialties such as lardo and *bucatini all'amatriciana.* That changed in December of 2017, when, in reports by *Eater* and the *Washington Post,* multiple women accused him of sexually harassing or assaulting them. At one of his late-night party spots, the West Village gastropub the Spotted Pig (where he was an investor), he and Ken Friedman, a co-owner, drank heavily and subjected women to unwanted verbal and physical advances, according to

the *Times*. Suddenly, Batali's proud intemperance was considered
in a new light—as emblematic of a kind of ugly behavior that had
been allowed to flourish in the industry for too long. (Both Batali
and Friedman denied some of the allegations. In March, Batali
sold his share of his restaurant group. Friedman remains an owner
of the Spotted Pig.)

For diners who are attracted to brash culinary celebrity, Joe
Beef became no less a destination than Babbo or David Chang's
Momofuku Noodle Bar, which opened, in New York, a year before
Joe Beef. Chang has called Joe Beef his favorite restaurant in the
world; both he and Bourdain, another fan, became friends of Mc-
Millan and Morin. Bourdain, who committed suicide last year, had
been open about abusing heroin and crack cocaine early in his
career, and about eventually getting clean. But he never gave up
drinking, and he struggled with depression. After he died, a tox-
icology report found only trace amounts of alcohol in his system.
Still, Morin said that Bourdain's death was a factor that made him
question his own relationship with alcohol: "It surely couldn't have
helped him, that's the most I feel qualified to say."

McMillan and Morin are not the first high-profile chefs to get
sober in recent memory. Michael Solomonov, who owns Zahav, the
acclaimed Israeli restaurant in Philadelphia, began treatment for
crack-cocaine addiction and alcoholism a decade ago. Sean Brock,
best known for the restaurant Husk, in Charleston, wrote last April
about quitting drinking and taking up a new "self-care" regimen
that included meditation and Reiki. Brock and Solomonov are just
two of many chefs who now serve nonalcoholic cocktails at their
restaurants. In "The Rise of the Sober Chef," a First We Feast story
from 2015, Solomonov noted that admitting you're an alcoholic
"is less of a taboo than it was ten years ago—even in the kitchen."

Before McMillan and Morin gave up drinking, Joe Beef was
an occasionally volatile and abusive work environment; they are
adamant that sobriety has made them more responsible bosses.
Both are evangelists by nature. Where they once promoted un-
bridled hedonism, they've now become unlikely crusaders against
the excesses of restaurant culture. McMillan said, "I believe clearly
now that you can make a decision to go into the service industry
and have a healthy life, a happy life, as a waiter, a sommelier, or a
cook."

*

McMillan and Morin grew up in Montreal, not far from each other, and both developed an early interest in French cooking. Morin watched Jacques Pépin and Julia Child on TV; McMillan recalls his mother bringing home a book by the Lyonnaise chef Paul Bocuse. After high school, both began working in restaurants, and, later, attended cooking school. At the time, there was little glamour in being a chef. "We went into cooking like you go into plumbing or electricity," McMillan said.

They didn't know each other well until 1999, when they found themselves working together at the Globe, a restaurant and supper club in downtown Montreal. McMillan was the chef de cuisine and Morin was his sous chef. The Globe had been an excellent French restaurant, they told me, but it began catering to a late-night crowd who cared little about the food. "They dressed the waitresses like sluts, in little pink tight dresses," McMillan said. "They did bottle service. The restaurant was frequented by the Mafia and motor-cycle gangs and drug dealers, vodka drinkers, DJ culture. Sodom and Gomorrah." In 2004 Morin took over the kitchen while Mc-Millan oversaw the opening of a sister restaurant, Rosalie. McMillan, overworked and drinking too much, had what he has called a "little breakdown." "We were so burned out," Morin said. "We were both on antidepressants." They wondered if they should get out of the industry altogether.

At the time, modernist chefs like Ferran Adrià, in Spain, and Charlie Trotter, in Chicago, were in vogue, but McMillan and Morin retained their passion for traditional French food. After shifts at the Globe, they ate at L'Express, one of Montreal's few remaining old-school bistros, where the ceilings are painted yellow to match stains from the cigarette smoke that once filled the dining room, and each meal begins with a server delivering to the table a jar of cornichons and a pot of mustard. McMillan and Morin still consider it a perfect restaurant. They also admired a new generation of chefs who'd opened small, idiosyncratic restaurants in the United States and in Canada: Gabrielle Hamilton, who had, Morin said, the temerity to put Triscuits on the menu at her tiny New York restaurant, Prune; Martin Picard, whose Montreal tavern, Au Pied de Cochon, served the kind of snout-to-tail cooking that was gaining popularity at the time, with a Québécois spin, including a famous foie-gras poutine.

On their days off, McMillan and Morin often hung out in Little Burgundy—then a backwater neighborhood of greasy spoons, thrift shops, and art deco buildings like the home of Atwater, one of Montreal's sprawling indoor markets. One morning, the owner of a café on Notre-Dame Street West mentioned that he was closing his business, and offered them cheap rent on the dingy space. McMillan, Morin, and Allison Cunningham, a server at the Globe (who later married Morin), decided to go in on it together. They fixed up the 26-seat dining room, putting in wainscoting and a bar made from a farmhouse floor. Out back, they planted a garden and installed a smoker. They named the restaurant after Charles "Joe Beef" McKiernan, the proprietor of a rowdy nineteenth-century Montreal tavern.

McMillan and Morin served raw seafood and French classics such as Dover-sole meunière and *pâté en croûte*. Morin devised a creamy, lardon-studded lobster spaghetti, now a Joe Beef staple. They found a supplier of horsemeat, an ingredient that they describe in their first cookbook, *The Art of Living According to Joe Beef*, as "the great divide between Anglophone and Francophone." There was an intimacy to the dining room: McMillan shucked oysters at the bar and kibitzed with customers. The occasional rude or disruptive guest was invited to leave. Within six months, the restaurant was booking tables a month in advance.

McMillan and Morin attribute much of their success to the support of Chang and Bourdain. In a 2013 episode of his TV series *Parts Unknown*, Bourdain spent a sybaritic few days with McMillan and Morin in and around Montreal. They staged a six-course meal in an ice-fishing shack on the frozen St. Lawrence River. It included Glacier Bay and Beausoleil oysters, oxtail consommé over foie gras, chilled lobster à la Parisienne with shaved truffles, wild hare in a sauce of its own blood, Époisses cheese smeared on bread, and a layer cake called a marjolaine. They smoked Cuban cigars and drank white burgundy and Chartreuse. Later in the episode, on a trip to Martin Picard's Cabane à Sucre Au Pied de Cochon, outside Montreal, Morin opened a bottle of sparkling wine with a hammer.

McMillan's greatest passion, apart from French cooking, was natural wine, a movement—until recently based almost entirely in France—to produce wines using organic or biodynamically grown grapes, no additives, and minimal processing. In 2015 he helped Vanya Filipovic, Joe Beef's wine director and a partner in Le Vin

Papillon, start an import business, turning his restaurants into a hub of natural wine in North America. But his oenophilia became a cover for his accelerating alcoholism. When McMillan first went to rehab, he said, he'd look at other addicts and think, "Oh, no, no, I'm not like you losers. I have a *natural-wine* problem."

McMillan made intermittent efforts to drink less and to go to the gym. In 2013 he had gastric bypass surgery. He lost 180 pounds in the following years, but he continued to drink heavily. Max Campbell, a bartender and server who has worked at Joe Beef for more than a decade, told me that, each night, when McMillan came into the restaurant, "I'd open one, two bottles, three bottles, I don't know." McMillan would make the rounds in the dining room, pouring wine, calvados, and champagne for customers and for himself. Sometimes Campbell had to make excuses for McMillan's drunken behavior; one night, he drove him home in McMillan's own car. Meredith Erickson told me, "David changed from being the guy who everyone wanted to circle around, and listen to the stories, to a guy where everyone was just, like, 'I'm feeling really uncomfortable, because you're not acting like the guy we love right now.'"

Several current and former Joe Beef employees told me that they'd felt pressure to drink. After hours, McMillan would herd staff members to the bar across the street and buy them beers and shots of whiskey. In the summer, Campbell said, "we'd all sit outside on the terrace and we'd drink beer until the keg ran out." Emily Ekelund, a former employee, started working as a busser at Joe Beef in 2011, and was eventually promoted to bartender. In 2014 she left the job to focus on getting sober. When she returned, a year and a half later, to work at Le Vin Papillon, it was with certain stipulations—she'd no longer close the bar or work past midnight. "I needed to get myself out of that environment in order to stop drinking," she said.

According to a 2015 report by the Substance Abuse and Mental Health Services Administration, the food-service and hospitality sectors have among the highest rates of alcohol and drug use of any industry. Morin said that he thinks drinking is responsible for most of "the anger and the pressure and the abuse" in professional kitchens. As a young chef, he witnessed several bad fights in kitchens, including one that had to be broken up by the police. McMillan told me, "Everybody that I worked for, all my mentors, were

screamers. I've been hit multiple times in the kitchen." Morin recalled once throwing a pan of bacon onto the floor after a line
cook accidentally tossed out fresh fish. McMillan said, "Joe Beef
is the nicest restaurant I've ever worked at. But have I screamed
at people? Yes, I have. Have I punched people? Fucking yeah. I've
never hit a woman."

McMillan sometimes abetted what a former employee called
"bullshit frat-boy stuff." He used homophobic slurs, and he once
gave a cook a glass of chicken blood to drink, telling him that it
was his "mother's strawberry wine." Afterward, McMillan gave him
whiskey, to kill the salmonella. "He was fine, he was drunk," he
told me. "That's boys being bad in the kitchen." In a 2014 profile by Lesley Chesterman, a Montreal food critic, in the Swedish
food magazine *Fool*, McMillan bragged about how he greeted female customers: "My new line is, 'You're so hot I would chase you
through the forest with an ax.'" And yet McMillan doesn't believe
that he acted inappropriately toward women, in part because his
longtime partner (now ex) Julie Sanchez, was a server at Joe Beef
for many years. Filipovic and Erickson, who worked at the restaurant until 2010, both told me that they were always treated with
respect. A former bartender, Sarah Reid, told me, without animus,
that McMillan slapped her butt on several occasions after he'd
been drinking. At the time, she considered it a sign that he was
pleased with her work. "We're all brainwashed in this culture," she
said, adding, "I don't want to demonize Dave and say that he is
the problem." (McMillan denies ever slapping Reid. "Even in my
drinking, I remember everything," he said.)

Last June, in an article in the *Globe and Mail,* Reid and 20 other
women detailed allegations of sexual harassment and assault
against Norman Hardie, one of Canada's leading winemakers, and
a friend and associate of McMillan and Morin. (Hardie denied
many of the allegations.) A week later, a former Joe Beef busser
—who is trans and uses the pronoun "they"—claimed, in a string
of Instagram posts (later deleted), that, in 2016, when they were
working in the restaurant, the chef de cuisine groped their geni-
tals. The busser, who declined to comment on the incident, wrote
that they complained to a manager, who did little in response; they
left the job the following day. They decided to come forward on
social media after reading the Hardie exposé, which noted that

McMillan had cut ties with the winemaker and quoted him saying, "I'm horrified and disappointed in Norman." McMillan was distancing himself from one abuser, the employee wrote, while "he employs and supports" another.

The chefs declined to discuss the incident with me, but, in an article published last year, in *Eater Montreal*, McMillan acknowledged that the groping had occurred; the chef de cuisine was "extremely remorseful," he said. McMillan added that he hadn't been in the restaurant during the incident, and blamed alcoholism for making him an inattentive boss. The busser wasn't able to appeal to him for help, he said, "because I was stuck drinking somewhere." He told me, of that period, "I went to work and I wondered who I was going to drink with, when I was going to drink, what winemaker was in town, what wines are we selling—wine, wine, wine, wine, wine, wine, wine. Meanwhile, some chef at some other restaurant has just made someone cry for the fifth time. And, instead of addressing it, I would get someone else to address it. I was a coward."

McMillan told me that, in rehab, he was advised to find a new line of work. "I have no other skills or education apart from this business, so I was in a very awkward position," he said. "I thought I was going to work in a grocery store, to be honest." Instead, he started working kitchen shifts again, at Elena, an Italian restaurant co-owned by his friend Ryan Gray, a former Joe Beef sommelier who had got sober a few years earlier. After McMillan returned to his restaurants, three months later, he found that the staff welcomed his and Morin's sobriety. "The kids," as McMillan calls them, now party less, and often choose sparkling water or kombucha instead of beer at the end of a shift. Since the publication of his *Bon Appétit* piece, McMillan said, he receives messages every day, from industry people all over the world, seeking advice on how to get sober. At McKiernan Luncheonette, on Sunday nights, one of their employees hosts recovery-group meetings in the dining room, which McMillan, Morin, and a number of their staff attend. The group has a name, inspired by the French culinary term *mise en place:* Remise en Place—to put back in place.

Some members of Montreal's food community found the *Bon Appétit* article inspiring; others found it self-serving. McMillan and Morin are shrewd stewards of their restaurants'—and their own

—reputations, and their sobriety can seem like a marketing maneuver: by making a show of reforming their ways, they are taking
credit for addressing problems that they long helped to perpetuate.

Several former Joe Beef employees told me it was obvious that
Hardie, the winemaker, had been mistreating women since long
before the allegations against him were made public. "Did Norman Hardie objectify women in my presence? Yes," McMillan said.
The incident that Sarah Reid described to the *Globe and Mail*—
Hardie putting his hand up her shirt and down the back of her
pants—took place at an event that McMillan attended. Still, he
maintains that he wasn't aware of the extent of the abuse until
he got a phone call about the paper's investigation while he was
in rehab. He sees himself as a teller of hard truths about the industry. "Some of my peers are furious at me for speaking about
the Norman Hardie stuff," he said. "Some of my peers are furious
at me for speaking about alcohol." Ekelund, the former Joe Beef
employee, told me, "It's very easy to take sobriety and make it the
righteous thing that you're doing." She added, "Making yourself
look good publicly is not making amends."

This past February, a Canadian TV personality, Anne-Marie
Withenshaw, tweeted, and later deleted, a message that seemed
directed at McMillan: "It's interesting how some chefs now flashing their sobriety as a badge of manhood used to relentlessly bully
(and use homophobic slurs which I won't) the ones trying to quietly get/stay sober a decade ago." McMillan tweeted, in response,
"I am imperfect absolutely. I was and am a product of the environment I was brought up in and in the twilight of my career am
committed to change." Withenshaw told me that she didn't wish
to elaborate on the comment, and added that she meant to call
attention to a problem bigger than any one chef or restaurant. A
few people I spoke to declined to discuss Joe Beef out of fear that
it could damage their careers. Yasmin Hother Yishay, who worked
for Joe Beef briefly in 2015, developed a podcast, the following
year, about incidents of labor violation and abuse in Montreal's
restaurants, including the groping at Joe Beef. It was never finished, she told me, because not enough people were willing to
go on the record. "Alcoholism is a huge part of that industry, but
that's not even the problem," she said. "It's a space where men can
roam free."

*

One evening, I met McMillan, Morin, and Erickson for drinks and hors d'oeuvres at Le Vin Papillon. McMillan and Morin's first two restaurants have often been described as "masculine." Liverpool House is decorated with photographs of tractor trailers and serves some of the same dishes as Joe Beef. (In 2017 Prime Minister Justin Trudeau had dinner there with Barack Obama; Ariel Schor, the restaurant's chef de cuisine, reported that Obama "was surprised at the size of our portions.") Le Vin Papillon has an aesthetic that McMillan regards as more feminine, with whitewashed floors and walls, and paintings of its namesake *papillons*, or butterflies, on the wall. The food is lighter, too. "I realized one day, sitting at Joe Beef, that there were beautiful, responsible women and men who were eating only the appetizers and drinking responsibly by the glass," McMillan told me, over a plate of house-cured ham. "I built Vin Papillon with an image of how Vanya and Meredith ate and drank. They wouldn't come to Joe Beef and crush a magnum with two steaks."

Last year McMillan and Morin opened a second wine bar, Vin Mon Lapin, with Filipovic and her husband, where they serve an omelet filled with lobes of fresh sea urchin and a *salade rose*, made with radicchio, pink endive, and delicate curls of foie gras. Until a recent staffing change at Vin Papillon, the kitchens at both wine bars were run by women. But Filipovic, who oversees the front of the house at Joe Beef and the two bars, told me that she doesn't like the masculine-feminine distinction. She thinks of the lighter fare at Vin Papillon and Vin Mon Lapin as part of a natural evolution. "We all kind of got older and stopped being able to deal with eating like that all the time," she said.

For dinner, we went to Joe Beef, where we sat on the back patio, beneath a giant metal lobster. A parade of dishes began to arrive from the kitchen: raw oysters, razor clams, and scallops on shaved ice; crackly brown croquettes stuffed with "smoked meat," the Montreal cousin to pastrami; tender tripe in a fragrant consommé; rosy slabs of roast beef. Filipovic poured Erickson and me a different wine for each course. McMillan, who was drinking non-alcoholic beer, listened attentively to her descriptions and sniffed a few glasses. Morin, who was given a diagnosis of celiac disease in 2010, after years of stomach problems, drank only water. He said that the condition hasn't interfered with his work: much of Joe Beef's menu—raw seafood, meat and potatoes—is gluten-free.

The food was as decadent as ever—"It's not broken, I'm not gonna fix it," McMillan said—but he and Morin told me that they've become less interested in putting truffles and foie gras on everything. Morin recalled reading a biography of Julia Child, in which she describes a dinner of a few large oysters, an entrée of fish, and a slice of Brie de Meaux for dessert. "The simple French menu, the one that I now find most appetite-whetting—I used to consider it boring," he said. "But a part of sobriety is learning to deal with boredom, which in time you realize is more like simplicity." Both he and McMillan ate modestly; more than one platter was returned to the kitchen largely untouched. At one point, a customer stopped by the table.

"You guys look great!" he said to McMillan and Morin.

"Ah, we've been wearing makeup, more and more makeup," Morin replied. "We're still dark on the inside."

McMillan remains proudly chauvinistic about Montreal's dining scene. "I had two eighteen-year-old girls from Laval"—a suburb of Montreal—"the other day, who were having a meal at Joe Beef before going out to a nightclub, and they were having deer liver medium rare," he said. "Show me a restaurant in Manhattan that has deer liver, and then show me two eighteen-year-old girls from New Jersey eating it—and loving it—medium rare."

Lately, McMillan has been spending much of his time at his cabin, where he takes his daughters fishing and foraging for mushrooms. He recently bought a farm, near the border of Vermont, which he plans to eventually turn into a restaurant. He also started a natural-wine label, working with vintners in Ontario. His chefs will drive for hours to buy a single bag of whitefish caviar; it would be a shame to let customers pair their food with a commercial Chablis. "Our job is putting two things inside your body, food and wine," he said. "One has to go with the other." When he needs to taste a new bottle, he sips and spits. He acknowledged that advocating for sobriety and for wine at the same time might sound contradictory: "There's always going to be someone who says, 'Yeah, but you're only a year sober, shut the fuck up, you're a rookie, you could fuck up any day.' I go, 'Yeah, no, sure, I might, but for now I'm not, so fuck you.'"

McMillan and Morin have not eliminated all their workplace liabilities. The chef de cuisine who groped the busser is now a co-owner of one of their other restaurants. (McMillan told *Eater* that the chef has "proven by his actions that he's a good man.") Only one woman currently works in the Joe Beef kitchen. A front-of-house employee, Kellie Stupert, told me that she was verbally abused by a male coworker last summer, but that McMillan immediately reprimanded him. "He told me that he was on my side, that they had my back," she said. "You can't really ask for anything better than that." McMillan believes it's inevitable that such issues arise in a company as big as theirs. But he now has "zero tolerance for homophobia, zero tolerance for misogyny, sexism," he said, adding, "It sounds hypocritical, because I'm sure people you've talked to have said, 'Yeah, it's rich coming from him.'"

Stephanie Cardinal, who worked for four and a half years at Le Vin Papillon, first as a sous chef and then as the chef de cuisine, said that McMillan and Morin were supportive when, last year, she worked to get sober. McMillan took her with him to AA meetings, even if they were held during her shifts. Still, she struggled with the demands of the job. She helped with the opening of Vin Mon Lapin, then returned to Le Vin Papillon. This past winter, fearing that she was burning out, she sat down with McMillan and Morin to discuss her situation. "Rather than telling me, 'Yes, you should stay at Vin Papillon,' or 'Yes, let's open up a restaurant together,' they told me, 'Steph, you're twenty-eight,'" she said. "'If you stay here at Vin Papillon, you're going to find yourself a year from now hitting that same wall.'" In March, with McMillan and Morin's encouragement, she left her job to figure out what she wanted to do next. She said, "Letting me go is the nicest gift they've ever given me."

KAITLYN TIFFANY

Lean Cuisine Doesn't Want to Be Part of Diet Culture Anymore. Does It Have a Choice?

FROM *Vox*

MY MOM DRANK SlimFast when I was a kid, and my mom keeps the freezer packed with Lean Cuisine now. On a recent trip home, I ate Santa Fe–style rice and beans or classic five-cheese lasagna for lunch every day without noticeably depleting the pile of boxes.

She doesn't *always* eat these things, and I've never heard her express any particular conflict when she chooses to. She was young during the diet-obsessed '80s, a time when women were told flat-out to be thin, which was dangerous and cruel and a tragic waste of women's energy and creativity, but also, maybe, at the very least clear. There was—despite the toxicity—something a lot less contorted for the generation that could just walk calmly through the family barbecue with a meal-replacement shake, explaining that they were in the mood to drop a few pounds.

My mom was raised on women's magazines, and I was raised on women's blogs. The latter tried to undo the criminal handiwork of the former, but it could only offer up a much more complicated recipe for happiness as replacement.

Lean Cuisines, obviously, are bad. Lean Cuisines are diet culture, insisting that 250 calories is enough for a dinner, and the name "Lean Cuisine" is understood by the Food and Drug Administration as a "nutrient content claim," so Lean Cuisines are required by the government to be "lean" (less than 10 grams of fat, 4.5 grams or less of saturated fat). But that leanness doesn't even translate to health, especially in the way we think of it now; as nutritionist Laura Silver explains, Lean Cuisines are mostly white pasta or meat, with potatoes and without nearly enough vegetables. At the very least, Lean Cuisine's parent company Nestlé is bad—known for looking for loopholes in water laws in economically depressed cities, an idea most of us probably could not even have come up with in a Mad Libs of scams.

Maybe, in some circles, Lean Cuisine is most famous for the Vine in which Guy Fieri throws a signed Lean Cuisine into a crowd. That would be nice. But in other circles, Lean Cuisine is famous for a sexy jingle about "satisfaction" and men stuffing towels in their mouths to avoid screaming at thin women's hot bods. Lean Cuisine has more or less successfully pivoted its branding to "wellness"—it's contorted around the body-positivity movement and done what it needed to in order to survive—and resumed making lots of money. But the product remains Lean Cuisine.

Throughout the 1970s and '80s, the Food and Drug Administration led a shockingly noble war on dieting products. In 1977 it issued a broad warning about liquid-protein weight-loss products —including the popular drink Metrecal—and in 1978 pulled many of them from stores after they were connected with close to 70 deaths (mostly due to heart irregularities after consumers lost dangerous amounts of weight). In 1982, the *New York Times* reported, the agency made starch blockers illegal, "rounded up millions of [the] pills and bulldozed them into landfills." Asked for comment by the *Times* on the prevalence of weight-loss sauna suits and waistbands, an FDA spokesperson said, "You could wake up slimmer, but you might also wake up dead."

But, as I'm sure you know, this didn't exactly work. The 1980s was the decade of villainizing fat and cholesterol, and by the middle of it, the field was dominated by the familiar players: Weight Watchers, Lean Cuisine, and SlimFast, the meal-replacement shake that launched the same year Metrecal tanked. It was a $10 billion global industry, and more than 60 percent of American women were participating. The pie was so big, the major companies were more than happy to share it: Lean Cuisine provided Weight Watchers points conversions on its packaging; SlimFast was suggested to replace only breakfast and lunch, leaving dieters the option of a Lean Cuisine dinner.

Lean Cuisine launched in 1981 as Stouffer's "healthy" sub-brand. One of its first taglines was "You'll love the way it looks on you," which is a joke because the whole point of Lean Cuisine is that you won't see it on you. In fact, you'll begin to disappear! By 1983 Lean Cuisine was so popular that grocery stores suffered frequent Lean Cuisine shortages, and Lean Cuisine wisely ran print ads apologizing for not being able to keep up with our insatiable hunger for leanness.

That year, the competition in the frozen-food business became absolutely vicious. Lean Cuisine sold an estimated $300 million worth of its 14 meal options, and an executive from competitor Swanson told the *New York Times* that companies were "hurling trees and mountains at each other to take over," which is a confusing metaphor but I assume means that people were being aggressive. According to the *Times*, which cited various industry analysts, the rapid growth in the market was due almost exclusively to "the younger, more affluent, more health conscious and sophisticated shopper," a group that includes "the nation's growing population of working women."

The microwave dinner—which has never quite gone out of style and remains a standard pop culture signifier of the put-upon go-getter eating alone over the sink—was for dieters, and dieting was for women, and the diet microwave dinner was for ambitious women, who didn't have very much time to spare but needed to be thin, and these things bubbled and spun under a 700-watt bulb until they were one hot, gooey mess.

From 1983 to 1988, the *Times* reported, sales of low-calorie frozen dinners rose 24 percent, nearly twice as much as typical frozen meals. Lean Cuisine was blunt about its appeal, and told the paper that the product was specifically for "young women on a diet or concerned about their appearance."

This is not the world we live in now—or it's not the words we use to describe it. "'Dieting' was now considered tacky. It was anti-feminist. It was arcane. In the new millennium, all bodies should be accepted, and any inclination to change a body was proof of a lack of acceptance of it," Taffy Brodesser-Akner writes in her landmark report on the revitalization of Weight Watchers (a year before it decided to go by WW alone). "People were now fasting and eating clean and cleansing and making lifestyle changes, which, by all available evidence, is exactly like dieting," she adds.

In June 2015 Lean Cuisine brand manager Chris Flora told *Ad-Age* that "diets are dead" and that his company wanted "to show that we are truly shifting away from diet." In other words, Lean Cuisines would still be lean, because they are mandated by decades of tradition and by the gaze of the government (which has pierced the company before), but women should not feel that this is on purpose, or the point. Lean Cuisine sales had dropped 20 percent over the previous two years, Bloomberg had recently reported, and Flora admitted that the company had effectively shut down its advertising operations for more than a year while trying to figure out what it could or should say about food and women and what they want and what they can have.

In July 2015 the company launched its Feed Your Phenomenal campaign. The first TV ad showed a Boston delivery nurse coming home from a night shift and eating a Lean Cuisine mac and cheese. Soon after, Lean Cuisine put a scale in Grand Central Station and asked women to put not their bodies but the things they cared about on it. For example, a college degree. A divorce. Their young daughters. (Wait, what?) "The new Lean Cuisine—here to feed what really matters to you," went the tagline, which, while less objectively offensive than "You'll love the way it looks on you," also makes no sense.

Though Lean Cuisine has been criticized for focusing its marketing so heavily on women, it can't exactly be blamed. The men of Silicon Valley are dieting now too, but they call it "intermittent fasting." (They call meal-replacement shakes "meal-replacement shakes," except in their case, almost nobody assumes they are speaking in code about wanting to shuck 5 to 10 pounds.) They are not trying to "lose weight" so much as they are trying to become hyperproductive pieces of muscle machinery in drop-crotch pants. In 2019 Soylent chief executive Bryan Crowley told the *New York Times* that Soylent Squared, the company's new 100-calorie "mini-meal" in the shape of a square, was designed in part to "bring more females into the fold."

(SlimFast's meal-replacement bars are 200 calories, and its

snack bars are 100 calories. Dieters are encouraged to follow a 3-2-1 plan, which includes three 100-calorie snacks, two 200-calorie meal replacements, and one actual meal per day.)

Even if it wanted to, Lean Cuisine would have a hard time tearing itself away from its origins completely: modern wellness has demanded that everybody be "healthy" insofar as they are functional, and "optimized" insofar as they look fit, which is negligibly different from telling them to be thin.

And that healthy posture is a little more complicated for Lean Cuisine. Silver, a Brooklyn-based dietitian and nutritionist certified by New York University, says most Lean Cuisines aren't balanced meals: "Almost all of these Lean Cuisine dinners are between two hundred and three hundred calories, which is just not enough food for a meal." They are largely refined pasta, and when they do have vegetables, the portion size is too small.

On top of that, the idea that the cholesterol a person consumes in their food has any effect on the levels of cholesterol in their body has been debunked for at least 15 years, so the low-cholesterol promise of Lean Cuisine is pretty much pointless. "Even the low-fat part of it—we can't categorically say that fat is bad for you, it's not," Silver says. "It matters where it comes from. There's certainly a difference in getting our fat from extra-virgin olive oil or avocados or nuts versus superprocessed foods."

Though you could obviously supplement a Lean Cuisine with your own sides, Silver suggests the damage is already done: "It makes no sense that it should be the same portion size for a petite teenage girl and a middle-aged man who weighs two hundred and fifty pounds. Of course it's not going to be the right portion for both people, but both people might go into it thinking it *should* be the right portion for them and wind up feeling unsatisfied and then feeling like, what's wrong with me here?"

In 2004 I was 11, and Lean Cuisine had a slate of TV commercials that were slightly different but all centered on a group of four female friends—just like *Sex and the City!* Three friends, looking glum, low-energy, and thin, would say what they'd eaten recently. "I licked the butter off a piece of toast," for example. The fourth woman—peppy, carefree, thin—would describe a rich, complicated-sounding meal with many delicious components. "I had grilled chicken in a creamy three-cheese sauce with crisp broccoli and red peppers," for example. Three jaws go slack with jealousy and horror. "It was, uh, one of those new dinners from Lean Cuisine," the woman clarifies.

When I was a teenager, magazines were packed with "Thanks, Lean Cuisine" print ads, which said things like "Thanks for my skinny jeans" and "Behind every successful woman is her microwave."

In 2013, when I was in my second year of college, in a *Jezebel* post titled "Sad Singletons Go Hungry After 500,000 Lean Cuisines Recalled Because They Are Full of Glass," Lindy West laid out the website's general stance on Lean Cuisine, writing, "If you think about it, broken glass is a fantastic weight-loss supplement! Just try absorbing calories when your stomach and esophagus are riddled with holes!" I'm sure I laughed at this, and agreed that Lean Cuisine was disgusting and antifeminist and therefore not for me.

Later, when I graduated and moved to New York, I ate it daily. This was, I hoped, just a personal choice, another idea I had been coached on by women's blogs and *Sex and the City* reruns. I'm the sort of person who thinks almost all food tastes fine—"I have a Protestant suburban church-dinner palate!" I often shout when other people discuss restaurants—and I find Lean Cuisine familiar and reassuring. If I wanted to eat comforting, cheap, not particularly healthy food that was less likely to make me gain weight than other comforting, cheap, not particularly healthy foods, who was I hurting?

Then again, what is a personal choice? The great tradition of dieting in America is one of the advertising industry's most emphatic victories: Lucky Strike used to sell smoking cigarettes as a way to avoid eating ("Reach for a Lucky instead of a sweet!"), and three generations of women ate Ayds diet candy—the active ingredient was originally an oral anesthetic, numbing the tongue so it couldn't experience flavor. The pressure to be thin is not something I can remove from myself, or others, regardless of what a formerly-known-as-diet company may say about itself now.

Nate Hill, the marketing director for Lean Cuisine, provided information for this story via email. "Lean Cuisine focuses on helping women live their best lives by encouraging every woman to define what that means for herself," he wrote to me, asked about the company's recent advertising strategy. When I wondered if Lean Cuisine had ever contemplated a name change—along the lines of Weight Watchers, to distance itself from the 1980s diet era it was born in—he replied, "We've had discussions over the years about the brand name and it's always come back to the fact that Lean Cuisine is a leading brand that consumers know, love, and count on to deliver great-tasting meals."

But just a few years ago, when the company was desperate, Lean Cuisine executives were more candid about the situation they'd found themselves in. In 2016 Jeff Hamilton, president of Nestlé Prepared Foods, publicly estimated that Lean Cuisine had lost more than $400 million in sales in the previous five years.

"Consumers were embarrassed to be in line with boxes of Lean Cuisine," Hamilton told a marketing trade journal. "We had become a diet food for skinny white women."

They reversed course by deleting the word "diet" from all of their marketing and redesigning the Lean Cuisine box—typically stark white and medicinal-looking—to be warm and friendly, implying hearth and carbohydrates, like an advertisement for Panera Bread. The new box won the grand prize at the first Nielsen Design Impact Awards, which are not for *good* packaging or product design, exactly, but for packaging or product design that results directly in a revenue spike.

In presenting the award, Nielsen said simply, "The design makeover helped drive a sales increase of $58 million in the year following the redesign compared to the year prior—a significant amount for a large brand innovating in the declining frozen food category."

Lean Cuisine's brand refresh has worked the way the company hoped, in that its sales rebounded and it is widely known that it is trying to put less emphasis on dieting—a successful public relations campaign. But Lean Cuisine talking less about weight loss doesn't mean that Lean Cuisine is talked about any less by people who care about weight loss. A product is a product. It doesn't matter what you say about it if that doesn't actually change what ends it's used for.

In my cursory searches of Reddit and Tumblr, in hopes of finding some millennial or Gen Z opinions on Lean Cuisine, it took mere seconds to wind up looking at subreddits dedicated to eating fewer than 1,200 calories a day (the moderators ask that everyone include their starting weight, current weight, and goal weight in the badge next to their username), or pro-anorexia and "thinspo" tags with strange spellings to get them past Tumblr's content filters. The people in these spaces are not buying Lean Cuisine because it's on sale, and they are not even a little bit joking.

Lean Cuisine is still Lean Cuisine. You search for it and you find thinspo blogs. You eat it and you still feel hungry.

Last summer, Lean Cuisine launched its #ItAll campaign, which was about women having it all. "What does having it all mean to you?" The company asked women to answer the question privately and then in front of their friends, at which point, a beautiful woman confronted them on camera to point out the discrepancies between their answers. Privately, one woman said she didn't want kids, and in front of her friends, she said she wanted three. Another was interested in a career in marketing all of a sudden, when she wasn't before.

In the final ad, each woman laughs an open-mouthed laugh, flashing perfect teeth, and the point of the experiment is never quite addressed—likely because, if it were, it would be impossible not to associate these low-calorie "wellness" meals with a similar sort of duplicity, as flimsy and sweaty as so many pieces of microwaved plastic wrap.

JOSÉ R. RALAT

The Demand for "Authenticity" Is Threatening Kansas City's Homegrown Tacos

FROM *Eater*

LUIS SILVA DIDN'T settle in Kansas City to work on the railroad. But he did move because of it.

By the time Silva, an immigrant from Guadalajara via Omaha, arrived in 1922 to sell insurance, Mexican workers accounted for more than 85 percent of the Kansas City–area railroad labor force, according to the Kansas Historical Society. For decades, his fellow *mexicanos* had traveled to the metropolis to work for companies like the Atchison, Topeka and Santa Fe Railway (aka the Santa Fe) and in meatpacking plants like Armour and Company, where they toiled alongside generations of Italians who had long dominated the industries. Before that, there were the vaqueros, who drove cattle northward from Texas and whose cowboying skills were recounted in "El Corrido de Kiansis," a Mexican folk song that dates to the 1860s.

Silva forged a successful career. But in 1958 he saw a new opportunity and opened Spanish Gardens Taco House. On the restaurant's menu were enchiladas, tamales, chili, and a regional specialty that developed as a result of the proximity of the area's Italian and Mexican communities: fried tacos topped with a ketchup-like "taco sauce" and Parmesan cheese.

Tacos reflect and represent their time and place. In the early 20th century, immigration from the Middle East to Puebla, Mexico, led to the creation of tacos árabes, cooked on the vertical spit known as a trompo; that gradually morphed into Mexico City's iconic taco al pastor. More recently in the United States, market demand, population shifts, and ingredient availability gave rise to the Korean taco in Los Angeles, which was given a national platform by Roy Choi and his Kogi BBQ food truck in 2008.

Similar forces were instrumental in creating the Kansas City taco in the mid-20th century. Asked how her father came to use Parmesan, Jean Silva Miller says that "it was the cheese that was around." But even though the Parmesan-covered taco was born of Mexican immigrants, becoming a local staple of Mexican restaurants in Kansas City, Missouri, today, demand for more "authentic" Mexican food threatens to wipe it out.

The Silvas seasoned the ground meat filling simply—salt, pepper, garlic, red chile powder—and cooked it before spooning it onto corn tortillas. Next, they folded the tortilla and sealed it with toothpicks to prevent the meat from spilling out during the frying process.

"I pinned hundreds of those each day at the restaurant," Silva Miller says.

The tacos were fried with the toothpicks, which were removed before serving. Up to this point, there isn't much difference between the fried tacos of Kansas City and Mexican tacos dorados (literally, "golden tacos").

They're not so different from the first taco recipes published in the United States at the turn of the 20th century, either. But then come the garnishes: lettuce, salsa, and a flurry of Parmesan. "My dad would buy big blocks of the cheese," Silva Miller says. "My hand would go round and round, grinding and grinding all day."

Silva Miller still makes them like that today. However, she no longer cooks them at the restaurant. After opening a second location, Spanish Gardens Taco House expanded into the food-manufacturing business, adding Spanish Gardens Foods, which produced jars of taco sauce and spice mixes at a Kansas City factory near the original restaurant location. Both restaurants closed soon after. Silva Miller's son, Andrew, now oversees production at the company.

Silva's taqueria didn't invent deep-fried Parmesan-topped tacos. Local legend says Los Corrals, which opened in Kansas City in 1949, was the first Mexican restaurant to serve them. In-a-Tub opened in 1957, the year before Spanish Gardens, though it now uses the sort of bright-orange cheese powder you'd find in boxes of stove-top mac and cheese, rather than grated Parmesan.

The popularity of crunchy, toothpick-sealed Kansas City tacos only rose throughout the 1960s and '70s. Humdinger Drive-In —down the street from Los Corrals—began dishing out burgers, milkshakes, Italian sandwiches, and tacos in 1962. About the only thing that's changed is the addition of a flashy food truck. Augustin and Teresa Medina opened La Fonda El Taquito in 1972 as a postretirement venture. (In 1999 the restaurant relocated from its original 20-seat diner to spacious Westside digs; it's co-owned by the couple's daughters, Maria Medina Chaurand and Sandra Medina.) Kansas City native John Ponak opened his place, Ponak's Mexican Kitchen & Bar, in 1975. These restaurants had other specialties riffing on Mexican dishes—carnitas remains a popular menu item at La Fonda El Taquito, while Spanish Gardens, the restaurant, specialized in chili—but the Kansas City taco was and continues to be the common denominator.

Manny's Mexican Restaurant, one of the most prominent Kansas City Mexican eateries still selling the Kansas City taco, didn't arrive until 1980. When Manny Lopez, a second-generation railroad worker, and his wife, Vivian, first opened their restaurant, there were only five dishes on the menu. One was spaghetti and meatballs. Another was the Mucho Tacos, a plate of tacos based on a Lopez family recipe created by Manny's mother, Lucy, during leaner times.

"My grandmother made tacos with peas and with potatoes," says David Lopez, the general manager and a second-generation owner-operator of Manny's, "because if ever ground beef got expensive —which it tended to—maybe my grandma and grandpa couldn't afford to get as much ground beef."

But there was plenty of Parmesan cheese. "The Parmesan was cheap and around," Lopez says. It should be noted that another Parmesan taco existed in California at the same time as the Kansas City–style taco. Jimboy's Tacos, based in Sacramento, has been selling its version, with a Parmesan-encrusted tortilla, since 1954. Neither Lopez nor Jean Silva Miller say their parents were aware of Jimboy's when their families' restaurants opened. "All of our recipes originate from how my grandma made her food," Lopez says.

I first came across Kansas City–style tacos in Dallas, at a pop-up in the parking lot of a home goods and design store. The tacos, served by Lisa Martinez as Tacos & Art, were snappy, with light ground beef kicked off by salty, tangy grated Parmesan. On my plate, they looked like crunchy, cheesy grins. I ordered more before finishing my first.

For Martinez, who moved to Dallas from Kansas City for her daughter's education, those tacos are a tangible reminder of home. Her aunt began to sell them in 1985 at P.R.'s Place, the Kansas City bar her grandfather, Pat Rios, opened in 1974 in the neighborhood of Westside. "They're made the same way she made them for me when I was growing up," Martinez says. "Come Sunday or Monday, all us ladies, and my uncle sometimes, but mostly women, we used to all sit around the table at my grandmother's house and stuff tacos for like three hours. We would stuff about hundreds and hundreds of tacos."

When it comes to the current state of the taco at P.R.'s Place, Martinez's voice softens. Although they continue to sell out of tacos and the business still has its steadfast regulars, fewer people line up for tacos at her family's bar these days. "It's not the same," she says. "[Kansas City tacos] take time to prepare. You must have the right corn tortillas, seasoned meat, and toppings. A lot of places want to sell fast tacos."

Andrew Miller has also noticed the steady downturn in the popularity of the Kansas City taco. "There aren't a lot of restaurants that make them anymore," he says. "Everyone's making street tacos or wants to use eighty ingredients in their tacos."

Lopez also sees a growing preference for trendy dishes over the comfort of the Kansas City taco, pinning its decline in part on the viral nature of media like Yelp reviews that claim the taco is not truly Mexican.

"All the Yelpers and Food Network fans across the country have put their 'knowledge' on things they have zero experience in culturally or emotionally," he says. "Access to Twitter or Yelp does not make you an expert on how my grandparents made our food."

This next chapter in Kansas City's Mexican cultural and culinary community is in line with national trends in Mexican food —high regard for craft and history, a hyperfocus on Mexican cuisine's regionality, and well-intentioned but ill-informed presumptions of "authenticity" that come at the expense of Kansas

City's own Mexican identity and its native taco. Simply put, the Kansas City taco isn't cool anymore, even as tacos are more popular there than ever before, cooked by Americans and Mexicans alike.

Taking a cue from Mexican meat markets, Bichelmeyer Meats, a German-style butcher that's been around for more than 70 years, offers taco options on Saturdays like carne asada, lengua, and barbacoa. Beach bum–themed Tiki Taco serves vegan barbecued jackfruit tacos under a thatched awning.

And February of this year saw the opening of Guy Fieri's Dive & Taco Joint. It's a modern taco shop outfitted with an American roadhouse-inspired design, tacos al pastor, "Boulevard ginger-lemon-glazed pork tacos (with chipotle, sweet onion, grilled pineapple-serrano salsa, cilantro, cotija and an avocado-tomatillo salsa)," and potent drink specials like the "KC Ring of Fire (tequila with a hot sauce pellet that sinks to the bottom)."

Yoli Tortilleria is among the pioneers of the new Mexicanization of Kansas City. Established in 2017 by Marissa Gencarelli, a native of Sonora, and Mark Gencarelli, her Kansas City–born and raised husband, Yoli supplies tortillas made with non-GMO blue, red, white, and yellow corn to greater Kansas City–area restaurants, newfangled taquerias, and specialty food shops. They are also available at Yoli's stand at the Overland Park Farmers Market in Overland Park, Kansas, where small-batch bags of tortillas infused with the likes of squid ink or chiles sell out by 10:00 a.m.

Shortly after moving to Kansas City, Marissa Gencarelli went to Manny's—"the Parmesan taco place," as she calls it—for the Mucho Tacos platter. The pride in and the love for the tacos didn't go unnoticed by Gencarelli.

"[Adapted versions of traditional Mexican tacos] are a reflection of culture and traditions adapting to new environments," she says. "You use what you got, you adapt. They hold a special place in my heart."

Regional expressions of the taco—be they modern interpretations or the Kansas City taco—don't need to be relegated to the realm of nostalgia as contemporary Mexican trends rise. Barbecued jackfruit tacos and tacos imported from Flavortown can succeed without edging out the locally established specialty.

But some longtime purveyors of the Kansas City taco are concerned they'll need to relinquish culinary territory in the face of an evolving Mexican-food landscape. "There is a crossroads coming," David Lopez says before adding a positive note. "True comfort food will never go away. There are people in this beautiful country who appreciate and need that comfort to help put a smile on their faces. That is why we do what we do."

JOE FASSLER

The Man Who's Going to Save Your Neighborhood Grocery Store

FROM *The Counter/Longreads*

IN 2014 RICH Niemann, president and CEO of the midwestern grocery company Niemann Foods, made the most important phone call of his career. He dialed the Los Angeles office of Shook Kelley, an architectural design firm, and admitted he saw no future in the traditional grocery business. He was ready to put aside a century of family knowledge, throw away all his assumptions, completely rethink his brand and strategy—whatever it would take to carry Niemann Foods deep into the 21st century.

"I need a last-great-hope strategy," he told Kevin Kelley, the firm's cofounder and principal. "I need a white knight."

Part square-jawed cattle rancher, part folksy CEO, Niemann is the last person you'd expect to ask for a fresh start. He's spent his whole life in the business, transforming the grocery chain his grandfather founded in 1917 into a regional powerhouse with more than 100 supermarkets and convenience stores across four states. In 2014 he was elected chair of the National Grocers Association. It's probably fair to say no one alive knows how to run a grocery store better than Rich Niemann. Yet Niemann was no longer sure the future had a place for stores like his.

He was right to be worried. The traditional American supermarket is dying. It's not just Amazon's purchase of Whole Foods, an acquisition that trade publication *Supermarket News* says marked "a new era" for the grocery business—or the fact that Amazon hopes to launch a second *new* grocery chain in 2019, according to a recent report from the *Wall Street Journal*, with a potential plan to scale quickly by buying up floundering super-markets. Even in plush times, grocery is a classic "red ocean" in-dustry, highly undifferentiated and intensely competitive. (The term summons the image of a sea stained with the gore of count-less skirmishes.) Now, the industry's stodgy old playbook—"buy one, get one" sales, coupons in the weekly circular—is hurtling toward obsolescence. Today, with new ways to sell food ascendant, legacy grocers like Rich Niemann are failing to bring back the customers they once took for granted. You no longer need gro-cery stores to buy groceries.

Niemann hired Kelley in the context of this imminent doom. The assignment: to conceive, design, and build the grocery store of the future. Niemann was ready to entertain any idea and invest heavily. And for Kelley, a man who's worked for decades honing his vision for what the grocery store should do and be, it was the opportunity of a lifetime—carte blanche to build the working model he's long envisioned, one he believes can save the neigh-borhood supermarket from obscurity.

The store that resulted is called Harvest Market, which opened in 2016. It's south of downtown Champaign, Illinois, out by the car dealerships and strip malls; 58,000 square feet of floor space mostly housed inside a huge, high-ceilinged glass barn. Its bulk calls to mind both the arch of a hayloft and the heavenward jut of a church. But you could also say it's shaped like an ark, because it's meant to survive an apocalypse.

Harvest Market is the anti-Amazon. It's designed to excel at what e-commerce *can't* do: convene people over the mouthwater-ing appeal of prize ingredients and freshly prepared food. The proportion of groceries sold online is expected to swell over the next five or six years, but Harvest is a bet that behavioral psychol-ogy, spatial design, and narrative panache can get people excited about supermarkets again. Kelley isn't asking grocers to be more like Jeff Bezos or Sam Walton. He's not asking them to be ruth-less, race-to-the-bottom merchants. In fact, he thinks that grocery stores can be something far greater than we ever imagined—a place where farmers and their urban customers can meet, a crucial link between the city and the country.

But first, if they're going to survive, Kelley says, grocers need to start thinking like Alfred Hitchcock.

*

Kevin Kelley is an athletic-looking man in his mid-50s, with a piercing hazel gaze that radiates thoughtful intensity. In the morning, he often bikes two miles to Shook Kelley's office in Hollywood —a rehabbed former film-production studio on an unremarkable stretch of Melrose Avenue, nestled between Bogie's Liquors and a driving school. Four nights a week, he visits a boxing gym to practice Muay Thai, a form of martial arts sometimes called "the art of eight limbs" for the way it combines fist, elbow, knee, and shin attacks. "Martial arts," Kelley tells me, "are a framework for handling the unexpected." That's not so different from his main mission in life: he helps grocery stores develop frameworks for the unexpected, too.

You've never heard of him, but then it's his job to be invisible. Kelley calls himself a supermarket ghostwriter: his contributions are felt more than seen, and the brands that hire him get all the credit. Countless Americans have interacted with his work in intimate ways, but will never know his name. Such is the thankless lot of the supermarket architect.

A film buff equally fascinated by advertising and the psychology of religion, Kelley has radical theories about how grocery stores should be built, theories that involve terms like "emotional opportunity," "brain activity," "climax," and "mise-en-scène." But before he can talk to grocers about those concepts, he has to convince them of something far more elemental: that their businesses face near-certain annihilation and must change fundamentally to avoid going extinct.

"It is the most daunting feeling when you go to a grocery-store chain, and you meet with these starched-white-shirt executives," Kelley tells me. "When we get a new job, we sit around this table— we do it twenty, thirty times a year. Old men, generally. Don't love food, progressive food. Just love their old food—like Archie Bunkers, essentially. You meet these people and then you tour their stores. Then I've got to go convince Archie Bunker that there's something called emotions, that there are these ideas about branding and feeling. It is a crazy assignment. I can't get them to forget that they're no longer in a situation where they've got plenty of customers. That it's do-or-die time now."

Forget branding. Forget sales. Kelley's main challenge is redirecting the attention of older male executives, scared of the future and yet stuck in their ways, to the things that really matter.

"I make my living convincing male skeptics of the power of emotions," he says.

Human beings, it turns out, aren't very good at avoiding large-scale disaster. As you read this, the climate is changing, thanks to the destructively planet-altering activities of our species. The past four years have been the hottest on record. If the trend continues —and virtually all experts agree it will—we're likely to experience mass disruptions on a scale never before seen in human history. Drought will be epidemic. The ocean will acidify. Islands will be swallowed by the sea. People could be displaced by the millions, creating a new generation of climate refugees. And all because we didn't move quickly enough when we still had time.

You know this already. But I bet you're not doing much about it—not enough, at least, to help avert catastrophe. I'll bet your approach looks a lot like mine: worry too much, accomplish too little. The sheer size of the problem is paralyzing. Vast, systemic challenges tend to short-circuit our primate brains. So we go on, as the grim future bears down.

Grocers, in their own workaday way, fall prey to the same inertia. They got used to an environment of relative stability. They don't know how to prepare for an uncertain future. And they can't force themselves to behave as if the good times are really going to go away—even if, deep down, they know it's true.

In the 1980s you could still visit almost any community in the United States and find a thriving supermarket. Typically, it would be a dynasty family grocery store, one that had been in business for a few generations. Larger markets usually had two or three players, small chains that sorted themselves out along socioeconomic lines: fancy, middlebrow, thrifty. Competition was slack and demand—this is the beautiful thing about selling food—never waned. For decades, times were good in the grocery business. Roads and schools were named after local supermarket moguls, who often chaired their local chambers of commerce. "When you have that much demand, and not much competition, nothing gets tested. Kind of like a country with a military that really doesn't know whether their bullets work," Kelley says. "They'd never really been in a dogfight."

It's hard to believe now, but there was not a single Walmart on the West Coast until 1990. That decade saw the birth of the "hypermarket" and the beginning of the end for traditional grocery stores—Walmarts, Costcos, and Kmarts became the first aggressive competition supermarkets ever really faced, luring customers in with the promise of one-stop shopping on everything from Discmen to watermelon.

The other bright red flag: Americans started cooking at home less and eating out more. In 2014 Americans dined out more than in for the first time on record, the culmination of a slow shift away from home cooking that had been going on since at least the 1960s. That trend is likely to continue. According to a 2017 report from the USDA's Economic Research Service, millennials shop at food stores less than any other age group, spend less time preparing food, and are more likely to eat carryout, delivery, or fast food even when they *do* eat at home.

But even within the shrinking market for groceries, competition has stiffened. Retailers not known for selling food increasingly specialize in it, a phenomenon called "channel blurring"; today, pharmacies like CVS sell pantry staples and packaged foods, while 99-cent stores like Dollar General are a primary source of groceries for a growing number of Americans. Then there's e-commerce. Though only about 3 percent of groceries are currently bought online, that figure could rocket to 20 percent by 2025. From subscription meal-kit services like Blue Apron to online markets like FreshDirect and Amazon Fresh, shopping for food has become an increasingly digital endeavor—one that sidesteps traditional grocery stores entirely.

A cursory glance might suggest grocery stores are in no immediate danger. According to the data-analytics company Inmar, traditional supermarkets still have a 44.6 percent market share among brick-and-mortar food retailers. And though a spate of bankruptcies has recently hit the news, there are actually more grocery stores today than there were in 2005. Compared to many industries—internet service, for example—the grocery industry is still a diverse, highly varied ecosystem. Forty-three percent of grocery companies have fewer than four stores, according to a recent USDA report. These independent stores sold 11 percent of the nation's groceries in 2015, a larger collective market share than successful chains like Albertsons (4.5 percent), Publix (2.25 percent), and Whole Foods (1.2 percent).

But looking at this snapshot without context is misleading—a little like saying that the earth can't be warming because it's snowing outside. Not long ago, grocery stores sold the vast majority of the food that was prepared and eaten at home—about 90 percent in 1988, according to Inmar. Today, their market share has fallen by more than half, even as groceries represent a diminished proportion of overall food sold. Their slice of the pie is steadily shrinking, as is the pie itself.

By 2025, the thinking goes, most Americans will rarely enter a grocery store. That's according to a report called *Surviving the Brave New World of Food Retailing*, published by the Coca-Cola Retailing Research Council—a think tank sponsored by the soft drink giant to help retailers prepare for major changes. The report describes a retail marketplace in the throes of massive change, where supermarkets as we know them are functionally obsolete. Disposables and nonperishables, from paper towels to laundry detergent and peanut butter, will replenish themselves automatically, thanks to smart-home sensors that reorder when supplies are low. Online recipes from publishers like Epicurious will sync directly to digital shopping carts operated by e-retailers like Amazon. Impulse buys and last-minute errands will be fulfilled via Instacart and whisked over in self-driving Ubers. In other words, food—for the most part—will be controlled by a small handful of powerful tech companies.

The Coca-Cola report, written in consultation with a handful of influential grocery executives, including Rich Niemann, acknowledges that the challenges are dire. To remain relevant, it concludes, supermarkets will need to become more like tech platforms: develop a "robust set of e-commerce capabilities," take "a mobile-first approach," and leverage "enhanced digital assets." They'll need infrastructure for "click and collect" purchasing, allowing customers to order online and pick up in a jiffy. They'll want to establish a social media presence, as well as a "chatbot strategy." In short, they'll need to become Amazon, and they'll need to do it all while competing with Walmart—and its e-commerce platform, Jet.com —on convenience and price.

That's why Amazon's acquisition of Whole Foods Market was terrifying to so many grocers, sending the stocks of national chains like Kroger tumbling: it represents a future they can't really compete in. Since August 2017 Amazon has masterfully integrated e-commerce and physical shopping, creating a muscular hybrid that represents an existential threat to traditional grocery stores. The acquisition was partially a real estate play: Whole Foods stores with Prime lockers now act as a convenient pickup depot for Amazon goods. But Amazon's also doing its best to make it too expensive and inconvenient for its Prime members, who pay $129 a year for free two-day shipping and a host of other perks, to shop anywhere else. Prime members receive additional 10 percent discounts on select goods at Whole Foods, and Amazon is rolling out home grocery delivery in select areas. With the Whole Foods acquisition, then, Amazon cornered two markets: the thrift-driven world of e-commerce and the pleasure-seeking universe of high-end grocery. Order dish soap and paper towels in bulk on Amazon, and pick them up at Whole Foods with your grass-fed steak.

Traditional grocers are now expected to offer the same combination of convenience, flexibility, selection, and value. They're understandably terrified by this scenario, which would require fundamental, complex, and very expensive changes. And Kelley is terrified of it, too, though for a different reason: he simply thinks it won't work. In his view, supermarkets will never beat Walmart and Amazon at what they do best. If they try to succeed by that strategy alone, they'll fail. That prospect keeps Kelley up at night— because it could mean a highly consolidated marketplace overseen by just a handful of players, one at stark contrast to the regional, highly varied food-retail landscape America enjoyed throughout the 20th century.

"I'm afraid of what could happen if Walmart and Amazon and Lidl are running our food system, the players trying to get everything down to the lowest price possible," he tells me. "What gives me hope is the upstarts who will do the opposite. Who aren't going to sell convenience or efficiency, but fidelity."

The approach Kelley's suggesting still means completely overhauling everything, with no guarantee of success. It's a strategy that's decidedly low-tech, though it's no less radical. It's more about people than new platforms. It means making grocery shopping more like going to the movies.

Nobody grows up daydreaming about designing grocery stores, including Kelley. As a student at the University of North Carolina at Charlotte, he was just like every other architect-in-training: He wanted to be a figure like Frank Gehry, building celebrated skyscrapers and cultural centers. But he came to feel dissatisfied with the culture of his profession. In his view, architects coldly fixate on the aesthetics of buildings and aren't concerned enough with the people inside.

"Architecture worships objects, and capital-A architects are object makers," Kelley tells me. "They aren't trying to fix social issues. People and their experience and their perceptions and behaviors don't matter to them. They don't even really want people in their photographs—or if they have to, they'll blur them out."

What interested Kelley most was how people would *use* his buildings, not how the structures would fit into the skyline. He wanted to shape spaces in ways that could actually affect our emotions and personalities, bringing out the better angels of our nature. To his surprise, no one had really quantified a set of rules for how environment could influence behavior. Wasn't it strange that advertising agencies spent so much time thinking about the links between storytelling, emotions, and decision-making—while commercial spaces, the places where we actually go to buy, often had no design principle beyond brute utility?

"My ultimate goal was to create a truly multidisciplinary firm that was comprised of designers, social scientists, and marketing types," he says. "It was so unorthodox and so bizarrely new in terms of approach that everyone thought I was crazy."

In 1992, when he was 28, Kelley cofounded Shook Kelley with the Charlotte, North Carolina–based architect and urban planner Terry Shook. Their idea was to offer a suite of services that bridged social science, branding, and design, a new field they called "perception management." They were convinced space could be used to manage emotion, just the way cinema leads us through a guided sequence of feelings, and wanted to turn that abstract idea into actionable principles. While Shook focused on bigger, community-oriented spaces like downtown centers and malls, Kelley focused on the smaller, everyday commercial spaces overlooked by fancy architecture firms: dry cleaners, convenience stores, eateries, bars. One avant-garde restaurant Kelley designed in Charlotte, called Props, was an homage to the sitcom craze of the 1990s. It was built to look like a series of living rooms, based on the apartment scenes in shows like *Seinfeld* and *Friends,* and featured couches and easy chairs instead of dining tables to encourage guests to mingle during dinner.

The shift to grocery stores didn't happen until a few years later, almost by accident. In the mid-'90s Americans still spent about 55 percent of their food dollars on meals eaten at home—but that share was declining quickly enough to concern top corporate brass at Harris Teeter, a Charlotte-area, North Carolina–based grocery chain with stores throughout the southwestern United States. (Today, Harris Teeter is owned by Kroger, the country's second-largest seller of groceries behind Walmart.) Harris Teeter execs reached out to Shook Kelley. "We hear you're good with design, and you're good with food," Kelley remembers Harris Teeter reps saying. "Maybe you could help us."

At first, it was Terry Shook's account. He rebuilt each section of the store into a distinct "scene" that reinforced the themes and aesthetics of the type of food it sold. The deli counter became a mocked-up urban delicatessen, complete with awning and neon sign. The produce section resembled a roadside farmstand. The dairy cases were corrugated-steel silos, emblazoned with the logo of a local milk supplier. And he introduced full-service cafés, a novelty for grocery stores at the time, with chrome siding like a vintage diner. It was pioneering work, winning that year's Outstanding Achievement Award from the International Interior Design Association—according to Kelley, it was the first time the prestigious award had ever been given to a grocery store.

Shook backed off of grocery stores after launching the new Harris Teeter, but the experience sparked Kelley's lifelong fascination with grocery stores, which he realized were ideal proving grounds for his ideas about design and behavior. Supermarkets contain thousands of products, and consumers make dozens of decisions inside them—decisions about health, safety, family, and tradition that get to the core of who they are. He largely took over the Harris Teeter account and redesigned nearly 100 of the chain's stores, work that would go on to influence the way the industry saw itself and ultimately change the way stores are built and navigated.

Since then, Kelley has worked to show grocery stores that they don't have to worship at the altar of supply-side economics. He urges grocers to appeal instead to our humanity. Kelley asks them to think more imaginatively about their stores, using physical space to evoke nostalgia, delight our senses, and appeal to the parts of us motivated by something bigger and more generous than plain old thrift. Shopping, for him, is all about navigating our personal hopes and fears, and grocery stores will only succeed when they play to those emotions.

When it works, the results are dramatic. Between 2003 and 2007, Whole Foods hired Shook Kelley for brand strategy and store design, working with the firm throughout a crucial period of the chain's development. The fear was that as Whole Foods grew, its image would become too diffuse, harder to differentiate from other health food stores; at the same time, the company wanted to attract more mainstream shoppers. Kelley's team was tasked with finding new ways to telegraph the brand's singular value. Their solution was a hierarchical system of signage that would streamline the store's crowded field of competing health and wellness claims.

Kelley's view is that most grocery stores are "addicted" to signage, cramming their spaces with so many pricing details, promotions, navigational signs, ads, and brand assets that it "functionally shuts down [the customer's] ability to digest the information in front of them."

Kelley's team stipulated that Whole Foods could only have seven layers of information, which ranged from evocative signage 60 feet away to descriptive displays 6 feet from customers to promotional info just 6 inches from their hands. Everything else was "noise," and jettisoned from the stores entirely. If you've ever shopped at Whole Foods, you probably recognize the way that the store's particular brand of feel-good, hippie sanctimony seems to permeate your consciousness at every turn. Kelley helped invent that. The system he created for pilot stores in Princeton, New Jersey, and Louisville, Kentucky, were scaled throughout the chain and are still in use today, he says. (Whole Foods did not respond to requests for comment for this story.)

With a carefully delineated set of core values guiding its purchasing and brand, Whole Foods was ripe for the kind of visual overhaul Kelley specializes in. But most regional grocery chains have a different set of problems: they don't really have values to telegraph in the first place. Shook Kelley's approach is about getting buttoned-down grocers to reflect on their beliefs, tapping into deeper, more primal reasons for wanting to sell food.

Today, Kelley and his team have developed a playbook for clients, a finely tuned process to get shoppers to think in terms that go beyond bargain-hunting. It embraces what he calls "the theater of retail" and draws inspiration from an unlikely place: the emotionally laden visual language of cinema. His goal is to convince grocers to stop thinking like Willy Loman — like depressed, dejected salesmen forever peddling broken-down goods, fixated on the past and losing touch with the present. In order to survive, Kelley says, grocers can't be satisfied with providing a place to complete a chore. They'll need to direct an *experience.*

Today's successful retail brands establish what Kelley calls a "brand realm," or what screenwriters would call a story's "setting." We don't usually think consciously about them, but realms subtly shape our attitude toward shopping the same way the foggy, noirishly lit streets in a Batman movie tell us something about Gotham City. Cracker Barrel is set in a nostalgic rural house. Urban Outfitters is set on a graffitied urban street. Tommy Bahama takes place on a resort island. It's a well-known industry secret that Costco stores are hugely expensive to construct—they're designed to resemble fantasy versions of real-life warehouses, and the appearance of thrift doesn't come cheap. Some realms are even more specific and fanciful: Anthropologie is an enchanted attic, complete with enticing cupboards and drawers. Trader Joe's is a crew of carefree, hippie traders shipping bulk goods across the sea. A strong sense of place helps immerse us in a store, getting us emotionally invested and (perhaps) ready to suspend the critical faculties that prevent a shopping spree.

Kelley takes this a few steps further. The Shook Kelly team, which includes a cultural anthropologist with a PhD, begins by conducting interviews with executives, staff, and locals, looking for the storytelling hooks they call "emotional opportunities." These can stem from core brand values, but often revolve around the most intense, place-specific feelings locals have about food. Then Kelley finds ways to place emotional opportunities inside a larger realm with an overarching narrative, helping retailers tell those stories—not with shelves of product, but through a series of affecting "scenes."

In Alberta, Canada, Shook Kelley redesigned a small, regional grocery chain now called Freson Bros. Fresh Market. In interviews, the team discovered that meat-smoking is a beloved pastime there, so Shook Kelley built huge, in-store smokers at each new location —a scene called "Banj's Smokehouse"—that crank out pound after pound of the province's signature beef, as well as elk, deer, and other kinds of meat (customers can even BYO meat to be smoked in-house). Kelley also designed stylized root cellars in each produce section, a cooler, darker corner of each store that nods to the technique Albertans use to keep vegetables fresh. These elements aren't just novel ways to taste, touch, and buy. They reference cultural set points, triggering memories and personal associations. Kelley uses these open, aisle-less spaces, which he calls "perceptual rooms," to draw customers through an implied sequence of actions, tempting them toward a specific purchase.

Something magical happens when you engage customers this way. Behavior changes in visible, quantifiable ways. People move differently. They browse differently. And they buy differently. Rather than progressing in a linear fashion, the way a harried customer might shoot down an aisle—Kelley hates aisles, which he says encourage rushed, menial shopping—customers zigzag, meander, revisit. These behaviors are a sign a customer is "experimenting," engaging with curiosity and pleasure rather than just trying to complete a task.

"If I was doing a case study presentation to you, I would show you exact conditions where we don't change the product, the price, the service. We just change the environment and we'll change the behavior," Kelley tells me. "That always shocks retailers. They're like 'Holy cow.' They don't realize how much environment really affects behavior."

In the mid-2000s Nabisco approached Kelley's firm, complaining that sales were down 16 percent in the cookie-and-cracker aisle. In response, Shook Kelley designed "Mom's Kitchen," which was piloted at Buehler's, a 15-store chain in northern Ohio. Kelley took Nabisco's products out of the center aisles entirely and installed them in a self-contained zone: a perceptual room built out to look like a nostalgic vision of suburban childhood, all wooden countertops, tile, and hanging copper pans. Shelves of Nabisco products from Ritz crackers to Oreos lined the walls. Miniature packs of Animal Crackers waited out in a large bowl, drawers opened to reveal boxes of Saltines. The finishing touch had nothing to do with Nabisco and everything to do with childhood associations: Kelley had the retailers install fridge cases filled with milk, backlit and glowing. Who wants to eat Oreos without a refreshing glass of milk to wash them down?

The store operators weren't sold. They found it confusing and inconvenient to stock milk in two places at once. But from a sales perspective, the experiment was a smash. Sales of Nabisco products increased by as much as 32 percent, and the entire cookie-and-cracker segment experienced a halo effect, seeing double-digit jumps. Then, the unthinkable: the stores started selling out of milk. They simply couldn't keep it on the shelves.

You'd think that the grocery stores would be thrilled, that it would have them scrambling to knock over their aisles of goods, building suites of perceptual rooms. Instead, they retreated. Nabisco's parent company at the time, Kraft, was excited by the results and kicked the idea over to a higher-up corporate division where it stalled. And Buehler's, for its part, never did anything to capitalize on its success. When Nabisco took "Mom's Kitchen" displays down, Kelley says, the stores didn't replace them.

"We were always asking a different question: What is the *problem* you're trying to solve through food?" Kelley says. "It's not just a refueling exercise—instead, what is the social, emotional issue that food is solving for us? We started trying to work that into grocery. But we probably did it a little too early, because they weren't afraid enough."

Since then, Kelley has continued to build his case to unreceptive audiences of male executives with mixed success. He tells them that when customers experiment—when the process of sampling, engaging, interacting, and evaluating an array of options becomes a source of pleasure—they tend to take more time shopping. And that the more time customers spend in-store, the more they buy. In the industry, this all-important metric is called "dwell time." Most retail experts agree that increasing dwell without increasing frustration (say, with long checkout times) will be key to the survival of brick-and-mortar retail. Estimates vary on how much dwell time increases sales; according to Davinder Jheeta, creative brand director of the British supermarket Simply Fresh, customers spent 1.3 percent more for every 1 percent increase in dwell time in 2015.

Another way to increase dwell time? Offer prepared foods. Delis, cafés, and in-store restaurants increase dwell time and facilitate pleasure while operating with much higher profit margins and recapturing some of the dining-out dollar that grocers are now losing. "I tell my clients, 'In five years, you're going to be in the restaurant business,'" Kelley says, "'or you're going to be *out* of business.'"

Kelley's job, then, is to use design in ways that get customers to linger, touch, taste, scrutinize, explore. The stakes are high, but the ambitions are startlingly low. Kelley often asks clients what he calls a provocative question: Rather than trying to bring in new customers, would it solve their problems if 20 percent of customers increased their basket size by just two dollars? The answer, he says, is typically an enthusiastic yes.

Just two more dollars per trip for every fifth customer—that's what victory looks like. And failure? That looks like a food marketplace dominated by Walmart and Amazon, a world where the neighborhood supermarket is a thing of the past.

When Shook Kelley started working on Niemann's account, things began the way they always did: looking for emotional opportunities. But the team was stumped. Niemann's stores were clean and expertly run. There was nothing wrong with them. Niemann's problem was that he had no obvious problem. There was no *there* there.

Many of the regionals Kelley works with have no obvious emotional hook; all they know is that they've sold groceries for a long time and would like to keep on selling them. When he asks clients what they believe in, they show him grainy black-and-white photos of the stores their parents and grandparents ran, but they can articulate little beyond the universal goal of self-perpetuation. So part of Shook Kelley's specialty is locating the distinguishing spark in brands that do nothing especially well, which isn't always easy. At Buehler's Fresh Foods, the chain where "Mom's Kitchen" was piloted, the store's Shook Kelley–supplied emotional theme is "Harnessing the Power of Nice."

Still, Niemann Foods was an especially challenging case. "We were like, 'Is there any core asset here?'" Kelley told me. "And we were like, 'No. You really don't have anything.'"

What Kelley noticed most was how depressed Niemann seemed, how gloomy about the fate of grocery stores in general. Nothing excited him—with one exception. Niemann runs a cattle ranch, a family operation in northeast Missouri. "Whenever he talked about cattle and feed and antibiotics and meat qualities, his physical body would change. We're like, 'My god. This guy loves ranching.' He only had three hundred cattle or something, but he had a thousand pounds of interest in it."

Niemann's farm now has about 600 cattle, though it's still more hobby farm than full-time gig—but it ended up being a revelation. During an early phase of the process, someone brought up "So God Made a Farmer"—a speech radio host Paul Harvey gave at the 1978 Future Farmers of America Convention that had been used in an ad for Ram trucks in the previous year's Super Bowl. It's a short poem that imagines the eighth day of the biblical creation, where God looks down from paradise and realizes his new world needs a caretaker. What kind of credentials is God looking for? Someone "willing to get up before dawn, milk cows, work all day in the fields, milk cows again, eat supper and then go to town and stay past midnight at a meeting of the school board." God needs "somebody willing to sit up all night with a newborn colt. And watch it die. Then dry his eyes and say, 'Maybe next year.'" God needs "somebody strong enough to clear trees and heave bails, yet gentle enough to yean lambs and wean pigs and tend the pink-combed pullets, who will stop his mower for an hour to splint the broken leg of a meadow lark." In other words, God needs a farmer.

Part denim psalm, part Whitmanesque catalog, it's a quintessential piece of Americana—hokey and humbling like a Norman Rockwell painting, and a bit behind the times (of course, the archetypal farmer is male). And when Kelley's team played the crackling audio over the speakers in a conference room in Quincy, Illinois, something completely unexpected happened. Something that convinced Kelley that his client's stores had an emotional core after all, one strong enough to provide the thematic backbone for a new approach to the grocery store.

Rich Niemann, the jaded supermarket elder statesman, broke down and wept.

*

I have never been a fan of shopping. Spending money stresses me out. I worry too much to enjoy it. So I wanted to see if a Kelley store could really be what he said it was, a meaningful experience, or if it would just feel fake and hokey. You know, like the movies. When I asked if there was one store I could visit to see his full design principles in action, he told me to go to Harvest, "the most interesting store in America."

Champaign is two hours south of O'Hare by car. Crossing its vast landscape of unrelenting farmland, you appreciate the sheer scale of Illinois, how far the state's lower half is from Chicago. It's a college town, which comes with the usual trappings—progressive politics, cafés and bars, young people lugging backpacks with their earbuds in—but you forget that fast outside the city limits. In 2016 some townships in Champaign County voted for Donald Trump over Hillary Clinton by 50 points.

I was greeted in the parking lot by Gerry Kettler, Niemann Foods' director of consumer affairs. Vintage John Deere tractors formed a caravan outside the store. The shopping cart vestibules were adorned with images of huge combines roving across fields of commodity crops. Outside the wide-mouthed entryway, local produce waited in picket-fence crates—in-season tomatoes from Johnsonville, sweet onions from Warrensburg.

And then we stepped inside.

Everywhere, sunlight poured in through the tall, glass facade, illuminating a sequence of discrete, airy, and largely aisle-less zones. Kettler bounded around the store, pointing out displays with surprised joy on his face, as if he couldn't believe his luck. The flowers by the door come from local growers like Delight Flower Farm and Illinois Willows. "Can't keep this shit in stock," he said. He makes me hold an enormous jackfruit to admire its heft. The produce was beautiful, he was right, with more local options than I've ever seen in a grocery store. The Warrensville sweet corn is eye-poppingly cheap: two bucks a dozen. There were purple broccolini and clamshells filled with squash blossoms, a delicacy so temperamental that they're rarely sold outside of farmers markets. Early on, they had to explain to some teenage cashiers what they were—they'd never seen squash blossoms before.

I started to sense the "realm" Harvest inhabits: a distinctly red-state brand of America, local food for fans of faith and the free market. It's hunting gear. It's Chevys. It's people for whom commercial-scale pig barns bring back memories of home. Everywhere, Shook Kelley signage—a hierarchy of cues like what Kelley dreamed up for Whole Foods—drives the message home. A large, evocative sign on the far wall reads PURE FARM FLAVOR, buttressed by the silhouettes of livestock, so large it almost feels subliminal. Folksy slogans hang on the walls, sayings like FULL OF THE MILK OF HUMAN KINDNESS and THE CREAM ALWAYS RISES TO THE TOP.

Then there are the informational placards that point out suppliers and methods.

There are at least a half-dozen varieties of small-batch honey; you can find pastured eggs for $3.69. The liquor section includes local selections, like whiskey distilled in DeKalb and a display with cutting boards made from local wood by Niemann Foods' HR manager. "Turns out we had some talent in our backyard," Kettler said. Niemann's willingness to look right under his nose, sidestepping middlemen distributors to offer reasonably priced, local goods, is a hallmark of Harvest Market.

That shortened chain of custody is only possible because of Niemann and the lifetime of supply-side know-how he brings to the table. But finding ways to offer better, more affordable food has been a long-term goal of Kelley—who strained his relationship with Whole Foods CEO John Mackey over the issue. As obsessed as Kelley is with appearances, he insists to me that his work must be grounded in something "real": that grocery stores only succeed when they really try to make the world a better place through food. In his view, Whole Foods wasn't doing enough to address its notoriously high prices—opening itself up to be undercut by cheaper competition, and missing a kind of ethical opportunity to make better food available to more people.

"When," Kelley remembers asking, "did you start to mistake opulence for success?"

In Kelley's telling, demand slackened so much during the Great Recession that it nearly led to Whole Foods' downfall, a financial setback that the company never fully recovered from—and, one could argue, ultimately led to its acquisition. Harvest Market, for its part, has none of Whole Foods' clean-label sanctimony. It takes an "all of the above" approach: there's local produce, but there're also Oreos and Doritos and Coca-Cola; at Thanksgiving, you can buy a pastured turkey from Triple S Farms or a 20-pound Butterball. But that strong emphasis on making local food more accessible and affordable makes it an interesting counterpart to Kelley's former client.

The most Willy Wonka–esque touch is the hulking piece of dairy-processing equipment in a glass room by the cheese case. It's a commercial-scale butter churner—the first one ever, Kettler told me, to grace the inside of a grocery store.

"So this was a Shook Kelley idea," he said, "We said yes, without knowing how much it would cost. And the costs just kept accelerating. But we're thrilled. People *love* it." Harvest Market isn't just a grocery store—it's also a federally inspected dairy plant. The store buys sweet cream from a local dairy, which it churns into housemade butter, available for purchase by the brick and used throughout Harvest's bakery and restaurant. The butter sells out as fast as they can make it. Unlike the grocers who objected to "Mom's Kitchen," the staff don't seem to mind.

As I walked through the store, I couldn't help wondering how impressed I really was. I found Harvest to be a beautiful example of a grocery store, no doubt, and a very unusual one. What was it that made me want to encounter something more outrageous, more radical, more theatrical and bizarre? I wanted animatronic puppets. I wanted fog machines.

I should have known better—Kelley had warned me that you can't take the theater of retail too far without breaking the dream. He'd told me that he admires stores where "you're just not even aware of the wonder of the scene, you're just totally engrossed in it"—stores a universe away from the overwrought, hokey feel of Disneyland. But I had Amazon's new stores in the back of my mind as a counterpoint, with all their cashierless bells and whistles, their ability to click and collect, their ability to test-drive Alexa and play a song or switch on a fan. I guess, deep down, I was wondering if something this subtle really could work.

"Here, this is Rich Niemann," Kettler said, and I found myself face-to-face with Niemann himself. We shook hands and he asked if I'd ever been to Illinois before. Many times, I told him. My wife is from Chicago, so we've visited the city often.

He grinned at me.

"That's not Illinois," he said.

We walked to Harvest's restaurant, a 40-person seating area plus an adjacent bar with a row of stools, which offers standards like burgers, salads, and flatbreads. There's an additional 80-person seating area on the second-floor mezzanine, a simulated living room complete with couches and board games. Beyond that, they pointed out the brand-new wine bar—open, like the rest of the space, until midnight. There's a cooking classroom by the corporate offices. Through the window, I saw a classroom full of children doing something to vegetables. Adult cooking classes run two or three nights every week, plus special events for schools and other groups.

For a summer weekday at noon in a grocery store I'm amazed how many people are eating and working on laptops. One guy has his machine hooked up to a full-size monitor he lugged up the stairs—he's made a customized wooden piece that hooks into Harvest's wrought-iron support beams to create a platform for his plus-size screen. He comes every day, like it's his office. He's a dwell-time dream.

We sit down, and Kettler insists I eat the corn first, slathering it with the house-made butter and eating it while it's hot. He reminds me that it's grown by the Maddoxes, a family in Warrensburg, about 50 miles west of Champaign.

The corn was good, but I wanted to ask Niemann if the grocery industry was really that bad, and he told me it is. I assume he'll want to talk about Amazon and its acquisition of Whole Foods and the way e-commerce has changed the game. He acknowledges that, but to my surprise he said the biggest factor is something else entirely—a massive shift happening in the world of consumer packaged goods, or CPGs.

For years, grocery stores never had to advertise, because the largest companies in the world—Procter and Gamble, Coca-Cola, Nestlé—did their advertising for them, just the way Nabisco helped finance "Mom's Kitchen" to benefit the stores. People came to supermarkets to buy the foods they saw on TV. But Americans are falling out of love with legacy brands. They're looking for something different, locality, a sense of novelty and adventure. Kellogg's and General Mills don't have the pull they once had.

When their sales flag, grocery sales do too—and the once-bulletproof alliance between food brands and supermarkets is splitting. For the past two years, the Grocery Manufacturers Association, an influential trade group representing the biggest food companies in the world, started to lose members. It began with Campbell Soup. Dean Foods, Mars, Tyson Foods, Unilever, Hershey Company, the Kraft Heinz Company, and others followed. That profound betrayal was a rude awakening: CPG companies don't need grocery stores. They have Amazon. They can sell directly through their websites. They can launch their own pop-ups.

It's only then that I realized how dire the predicament of grocery stores really is, and why Niemann was so frustrated when he first called Kevin Kelley. It's one thing when you can't sell as cheaply and conveniently as your competitors. But it's another thing when no one wants what you're selling.

Harvest doesn't feel obviously futuristic in the way an Amazon store might. If I went there as a regular shopper and not as a journalist sniffing around for a story, I'm sure I'd find it to be a lovely and transporting way to buy food. But what's going on behind the scenes is, frankly, unheard of.

Grocery stores have two ironclad rules. First, that grocers set the prices, and farmers do what they can within those mandates. And second, that everyone works with distributors who oversee the aggregation and transport of all goods. Harvest has traditional relationships with companies like Coca-Cola, but it breaks those rules with local farmers and foodmakers. Suppliers—from the locally milled wheat to the local produce to the Kilgus Farmstead sweet cream that goes into the churner—truck their products right to the back. By avoiding middlemen and their surcharges, Harvest is able to pay suppliers more directly and charge customers less. And it keeps costs low. You can still find $4.29 pints of Halo Top ice cream in the freezer, but the produce section features stunning bargains. When the Maddox family pulls up with its latest shipment of corn, people sometimes start buying it off the back of the truck in the parking lot. That's massive change, and it's virtually unheard of in supermarkets. At the same time, suppliers get to set their own prices. Niemann's suppliers tell him what they need to charge; Niemann adds a standard margin and lets customers decide if they're willing to pay.

If there's a reason Harvest matters, it's only partly because of the aesthetics. It's mainly because the model of what a grocery store is has been tossed out and rebuilt. And why not? The world as Rich Niemann knows it is ending.

In 2017, just months after Harvest Market's opening, Niemann won the Thomas K. Zaucha Entrepreneurial Excellence Award —the National Grocers Association's top honor, given for "persistence, vision, and creative entrepreneurship." That spring, Harvest was spotlighted in a "Store of the Month" cover feature in the influential trade magazine *Progressive Grocer.* Characteristically, the contributions of Kelley and his firm were not mentioned in the piece.

Niemann tells me his company is currently planning to open a second Harvest Market in Springfield, Illinois, about 90 minutes west of Champaign, in 2020. Without sharing specifics about profitability or sales numbers, he says the store was everything he'd hoped it would be as far as the metrics that most matter—year-over-year sales growth and customer engagement. His only complaint about the store has to do with parking. For years Niemann has relied on the same golden ratio to determine the size of parking lot needed for his stores—a certain number of spots for every thousand dollars of expected sales. Harvest's lot uses the same logic, and it's nowhere near enough space.

"In any grocery store, the customer's first objective is pantry fill —to take care of my needs as best I can on my budget," Niemann says. "But we created a different atmosphere. These customers want to talk. They want to know. They want to experience. They want to taste. They're there because it's an adventure."

They stay so much longer than expected that the parking lot sometimes struggles to fit all their cars at once. Unlike the Amazon stores that may soon be cropping up in a neighborhood near you —reportedly, the company is considering plans to open 3,000 of them by 2021—it's not about getting in and out quickly without interacting with another human being. At Harvest, you stay awhile. And that's the point.

So far, Harvest's success hasn't made it any easier for Kelley, who still struggles to persuade clients to make fundamental changes. They're still as scared as they've always been, clinging to the same old ideas. He tells them that, above all else, they need to develop a food philosophy—a reason why they do this in the first place, something that goes beyond mere nostalgia or the need to make money. They need to build something that *means* something, a store people return to not just to complete a task but because it somehow sustains them. For some, that's too tall an order. "They go, 'I'm not going to do that.' I'm like, 'Then what *are* you going to do?' And they literally tell me: 'I'm going to retire.'" It's easier to cash out. Pass the buck, and consign the fate of the world to younger people with bolder dreams.

Does it even matter? The world existed before supermarkets, and it won't end if they vanish. And in the ongoing story of American food, the 20th-century grocery store is no great hero. A&P—the once titanic chain, now itself defunct—was a great mechanizer, undercutting the countless smaller, local businesses that used to populate the landscape. More generally, the supermarket made it easier for Americans to distance ourselves from what we eat, shrouding food production behind a veil and letting us convince ourselves that price and convenience matter above all else. We let ourselves be satisfied with the appearance of abundance—even if great stacks of unblemished fruit contribute to waste and spoilage, even if the array of brightly colored packages are all owned by the same handful of multinational corporations.

But whatever springs up to replace grocery stores will have consequences, too, and the truth is that brick-and-mortar is not going away anytime soon—far from it. Instead, the most powerful retailers in the world have realized that physical spaces have advantages they want to capitalize on. It's not just that stores in residential neighborhoods work well as distribution depots, ones that help facilitate the home delivery of packages. And it's not just that we can't always be home to pick up the shipments we ordered when they arrive, so stores remain useful. The world's biggest brands are now beginning to realize what Kelley has long argued: physical stores are a way to capture attention, to subject customers to an *experience*, to influence the way they feel and think. What could be more useful? And what are Amazon's proposed cashierless stores but an illustration of Kelley's argument? They take a brand thesis, a set of core values—that shopping should be quick and easy and highly mechanized—and seduce us with it, letting us feel the sweep and power of that vision as we pass with our goods through the doors without paying, flushed with the thrill a thief feels.

This is where new troubles start. Only a few companies in the world will be able to compete at Amazon's scale—the scale where building 3,000 futuristic convenience stores in three years may be a realistic proposition. Unlike in the golden age of grocery, where different family-owned chains catered to different demographics, we'll have only a handful of players. We'll have companies that own the whole value chain, low to high. Amazon owns the e-commerce site where you can find almost anything in the world for the cheapest price. And for when you want to feel the heft of an heirloom tomato in your hand or sample some manchego before buying, there is Whole Foods. Online retail for thrift, in-person shopping for pleasure. Except one massive company now owns them both.

If this new landscape comes to dominate, we may find there are things we miss about the past. For all its problems, the grocery industry is at least decentralized, owned by no one dominant company and carved up into more players than you could ever count. It's run by people who often live alongside the communities they serve and share their concerns. We might miss that competition, that community. They are small. They are nimble. They are independently, sometimes even cooperatively, owned. They employ people. And if they are scrappy, and ingenious, and willing to change, there's no telling what they might do. It is not impossible that they could use their assets—financial resources, industry connections, prime real estate—to find new ways to supply what we all want most: to be happier, to be healthier, to feel more connected. To be better people. To do the right thing.

I want to believe that, anyway. That stores—at least in theory —could be about something bigger, and better than mere commerce. The way Harvest seems to want to be, with some success. But I wonder if that's just a fantasy, too: the dream that we can buy and sell our way to a better world, that it will take no more than that.

Which one is right?

I guess it depends on how you feel about the movies.

Maybe a film is just a diversion, a way to feel briefly better about our lives, the limitations and disappointments that define us, the things we cannot change. Most of us leave the theater, after all, and just go on being ourselves.

Still, maybe something else is possible. Maybe in the moment when the music swells, and our hearts beat faster, and we feel overcome by the beauty of an image—in the instant that we feel newly brave and noble, and ready to be different, braver versions of ourselves—that we are who we really are.

BRETT MARTIN

The Provocations of Chef Tunde Wey

FROM *GQ*

NOBODY IS QUITE sure what's going on in the event room of the Westwood Baptist Church, University Center. Not the older Black ladies from the surrounding North Nashville neighborhood, who arrive exactly on time, summoned by a mysterious postcard sent to 300 homes, like the first chapter of an Agatha Christie novel:

> Dear Neighbor,
> You are cordially invited to attend a community dinner where we will discuss how to end gentrification in North Nashville . . . Dinner is FREE and will be delicious! Don't miss the twist!

Not the young white people from farther afield, with their vacuum-sealed water bottles and social-justice 5K T-shirts, who heard about this meeting on NPR or in the local alt-weekly. Not even the pastor, who pops his head into the room, where the long folding tables are normally used for repasts and Bible-study groups, with a look of puzzlement. The fluorescent bulbs hum, the sneakers of each arrivee squeak on the linoleum floor, and those already seated squirm and murmur to each other awkwardly.

At the head of the main table sits their host: slim, bearded, 35 years old, dressed in a dark dress shirt and slacks, and in no hurry to interrupt whatever ripples of uncertainty are traveling up and down the table. A helper moves in and out of an adjacent kitchen, quietly delivering Dixie Ultra paper plates of food. On them sits a southern meat-and-three by way of Africa: a version of *efo riro,* made with cooked-down collard greens; a pottage of mashed plantains; and finally, a Nigerian take on Nashville's most famous culinary export—hot chicken. The name of this event is Hot Chicken Shit. The aforementioned "twist" is that while dinner is free for the Black residents of the neighborhood, the prices for white visitors are listed on a pledge form at their seats: $100 for one piece of chicken; $1,000 for four pieces. For a whole bird, with sides, you must donate the deed to a property in North Nashville.

Eventually the man at the head of the table speaks: "My name is Tunde Wey. I am Nigerian. I am a cook. I am here trying to sell chicken for enormous amounts of money." The plan, he goes on, is to thus end gentrification. There is laughter around the table. "I know," he says, smiling. "But the problem is outrageous. I thought I'd come up with an equally outrageous plan to fix it."

You couldn't hope for a more succinct credo to sum up the work that Tunde Wey has been engaged in over the past several years—a hybrid of political action, performance art, revolutionary rhetoric, impish provocation, and other assorted acts of public intellectualism, all built around a critique of the way we eat in America today.

Perhaps you're looking for a story about how Food Brings Us Together. About how even in These Dark Times, we can always gather around The Table to experience the healing Power of Food.

If so, I'm sorry.

Those are the kinds of platitudes that Wey, who is a prolific texter, might respond to with one of his favorite emojis: the little face laughing so hard that tears gush out of both eyes. In fact, he does not consider such comforting narratives any kind of laughing matter. He believes they are dangerous, and it's his goal, as he travels across the country, to expose and erase them.

In New Orleans, where he now lives, he opened a lunch stall at which white people were asked to pay two and a half times more for a plate of food than people of color, the rough equivalent of the income disparity between the two groups. In Ann Arbor, white customers lined up to experience the highs and lows of random wealth distribution at Wey's food truck, which utilized an elaborate algorithm to choose which diners would receive lunch for their money and which would get stuck with empty boxes. In New York and Durham and San Francisco and a dozen other cities, he's hosted dinners where the food and drink is the pretense for facilitating the kinds of conversations that Americans do their best to avoid ever having.

In the meantime, Wey, an autodidact with no formal training in either cooking or political theory, has all but run an abattoir for food-world sacred cows. In a semiregular column for the *San Francisco Chronicle,* he excoriated LocoL, chefs Roy Choi and Daniel Patterson's experiment in progressive fast food. (Unless ownership of LocoL was transferred to the poor neighborhoods it was purporting to help, he demanded, it should "leave Watts, Oakland and its other proposed communities, or shed its narrative of change.") In another column, he took on Anthony Bourdain's televised adventures in Africa. ("His usual brand of charm, which plays well in an American context, only read as imperial. His tired and standard offer of a countercultural perspective was cloying, and it dissolved—like sugar in garri—to reveal the expansive firmament of White Americanness he represents.") In the *Oxford American,* he declared that white southern chefs should stop cooking dishes derived from the African slave trade and he upbraided author and Southern Foodways Alliance head John T. Edge: "John T., you have endorsed and celebrated the appropriation of Black Southern food without consequence, and the consequences have compounded with interest," he wrote. "You have to strip yourself of the marginal benefits of this appropriation willingly, with grace, or unwillingly by force and with shame." This, mind you, was in Edge's own column, which he had invited Wey to share. And the men are friends. You might argue with any of Wey's conclusions, but there is no question that he is intent on punching up.

That Wey's absolutism and his choice of targets have endeared him to the food establishment, rather than alienated him from it —coverage of his events has all but universally glowed, and he's become a regular invitee at conferences and festivals—is a testament to the convergence of two trends: One is the ever-expanding role of the chef as thinker, talker, activist, and nearly anything else that doesn't involve standing at a stove. The other is a moment of intense self-scrutiny in the food world, one that began even before the chef and restaurant #MeToo scandals of the past year and a half—an interrogation that has come to include food's role in everything from gender and the environment to mental health and, yes, of course, race.

There has arisen a boomlet of racially focused dining experiences. They range from the subtly pedantic (Seattle's JuneBaby offers an online encyclopedia of African American culinary history) and civic-minded (the Los Angeles City Council recently sponsored 100 free dinners around the city to facilitate racial dialogue) to the high-concept (the tasting menu at Indigo, in Houston, promises a "revised reflection of what it is like eating through the 'isms' of America as a copper-colored person" and features dishes with names like Descendants of Igbo and Eradication of Appropriation) and the bordering-on-parody (chef Jenny Dorsey's "Asian in America" dinners posit sweetbreads as "the model minority of the offal world" and incorporate spoken-word poetry and virtual reality).

Of these, Wey's projects are the least forgiving and most direct. Food at his dinners is not metaphor; it is Trojan horse. There are times when it appears that food does not even particularly interest him. His hands—expressive, slender, and soft—are not chef's hands. The act of cooking has become about as central to his work as throwing a football is to Colin Kaepernick's. Indeed, if there's a model for Wey's short, incendiary career, it is Kaepernick, whose most radical transgression has been to blast away the notion that sports can be simply a realm of mindless escape. Wey wants to do the same for food.

To be sure, there's also an element of self-flagellation, if not outright radical chic, in the spectacle of white liberal foodies lining up to be dressed down at what some reviews have proudly labeled "discomfort dinners." It is a dynamic that Wey both counts on and is ambivalent about.

"White folks will consume me. They will consume my work and feel gratification for being abused or however they perceive it," he says. "But the implication that I'm here to do a service, which is to make you uncomfortable . . . That's such an egocentric response. It's not about you! What I *want* is racial equity. The discomfort is just something that happens along the way."

Wey makes an unusual firebrand. He listens more than he talks, though when he gets rolling it is in full, composed sentences. He speaks with the deliberate effort and occasional hitch of a lifelong stutterer. He dislikes confrontation—though obviously not so much as to avoid it when he feels confrontation is necessary. In a crowd, he can even seem insecure, but a significant part of his charisma comes from the rare ability to sit comfortably with being uncomfortable.

I first met Wey in 2015, during the brief, five-month period of his life when he was acting most like a traditional chef. Ironically, it was at the white-hot center of a gentrification debate in New Orleans. I live down the street from a onetime public market called the St. Roch Market that had been moribund since Hurricane Katrina. By the time it reopened, with the help of several million dollars of federal disaster-relief money, the surrounding neighborhoods, which had once been predominantly working-class African American, had come to uneasily include a significant group of white professionals, artists, and other transplants. I don't think I need to tell you to which population the resurrected St. Roch Market, a spiffy, bright food hall featuring a cocktail bar, organic grain bowls, and a nominal grocery area offering urban-farm-grown herbs, was designed to appeal. Wey was invited to open a Nigerian food stall there. He called it Lagos, which was also the name of a traveling series of pop-ups he had been staging for the past year.

Lagos is where Wey is from. He was born there, Akintunde Asuquo Osaigbuovo Ojo Wey, in 1983. He grew up in a comfortably middle-class Yoruba family; his grandfather had been second-in-command during the military junta that ruled the country from 1966 to 1979. It was a close family—Wey remembers his mother chewing particularly tough pieces of meat before passing them to her children—but also pressure-filled. Wey's parents had a plan: One of their sons would become an engineer. Another, an architect. Their daughter would become a lawyer, and Tunde would round out the set by becoming a doctor.

He grew up steeped in Black American culture: He listened to hip-hop and dressed in streetwear unsuited for the Nigerian climate. He played American video games. (Twenty years later, when engaged in a particularly heated game of Ping-Pong, he will mutter under his breath the immortal line from *Mortal Kombat:* "Finish him!") Wey was a precocious high school student, graduating at 15. Soon after, the decision was made to send him and his brothers to live with an aunt who had settled in Detroit. He kicked around community college for a few years, trying to reconcile his parents' hopes for his medical career with the fact that he had neither the interest nor the aptitude. Finally, Wey and a partner opened a space in Hamtramck to host a rotating roster of pop-ups. They called it Revolver. At some point, his visa expired, and Wey quietly slipped into the ranks of 10.7 million undocumented immigrants living and working in every state and city across the nation.

By January 2015, his Lagos pop-ups had grown popular enough to attract some national buzz. He had moved to New Orleans to be with his girlfriend and soon-to-be wife, a community organizer named Claire Nelson, and signed on to the St. Roch Market. He had enticed the *New York Times* to send a video crew to an upcoming installment of Lagos in Los Angeles.

"I thought it was going to change my life," Wey says.

It did. Because of his legal status, Wey was doing most of his traveling by Greyhound bus, thus avoiding airports. This was not a well-thought-out strategy. While his Nigerian passport allowed him to proceed through TSA checkpoints largely without incident, the bus route from New Orleans to LA took him directly through the heart of America's immigration-enforcement belt.

Almost 20 hours into the trip, not far from Las Cruces, New Mexico, Wey was sitting in the back, zoning out and listening to music. He barely noticed that the bus had rolled to a stop. When he looked up, a border-patrol officer was making his way down the aisle. Every few rows, he would stop and ask a passenger if they were a US citizen.

Should I lie? Wey asked himself as the cop got closer. He probably could. The cop was taking some of the answers he was getting at face value, only occasionally asking for passengers' papers. He certainly wasn't out at this southwestern checkpoint looking for itinerant Nigerian chefs.

"In my head, I decided to lie," Wey says. "I was going to lie."

The cop reached his row. "Are you a US citizen?" he asked.

Wey's brain said, *Lie, lie, lie.*

He told the truth.

"I don't know why," he says, puzzling over it even now. "I just didn't have the balls. I couldn't do it." Instead, he started explaining that he had been a student but his visa had expired. The cop sighed and asked him to step off the bus. He went off to check Wey's name in his computer. Standing there in the desert, Wey was suddenly overcome by chills. "I was freezing. Started shaking violently. I was thinking, It's not cold enough out here to cause this. What the fuck is happening?"

The cop returned. "I think we're just going to let the bus go," he said. "Get your stuff."

"It was the worst thing that had ever happened in my life," Wey says. "I didn't know what was on the other side of this. Am I going to Nigeria? Am I going to prison?"

Wey's unpreparedness for the eventuality of being detained was, in part, his own brand of optimistic flakiness, but it was also a necessary accommodation faced by millions every day: it's precisely because you can be picked up at any time, ending life as you know it in an instant, that it's impossible to keep that fact constantly in mind without going mad.

"What preparation could I do?" Wey says. "It was just permanent reality. It was like living with a chronic illness: constant unease."

On Wey's first night in detention, his biggest fear was physical violence. "He's going to get fucked in prison," someone whispered to Wey about a fellow detainee.

"I thought, Are they fucking people in here?! I don't want to be in this situation," he says.

The next day he was sent to a facility and housed with other detainees clad in blue jumpsuits to signify that they were nonviolent offenders. The detainees, almost all of them Hispanic, slept in huge barracks lined with bunk beds. Finally, after 20 days, Wey was brought before a judge who would decide whether he would be allowed to post bond while awaiting a hearing. "It was a moment that only happens in movies," he remembers. "I was sweating. My palms were wet. Very few people feel that feeling: when you have no control over your whole life." The judge granted bond, with a hearing set for two years later, which effectively placed Wey into a kind of limbo: not in imminent danger of being picked up or deported, but unable to reenter the country if he left or, technically, to work. Still, it was the first safe status he'd had since being a student. It was the freest he'd felt in years.

I loved Wey's okra at the St. Roch Market, cooked down to the gelatinous consistency of *Ghostbusters* slime. And I found myself nearly addicted to his *egusi* stew, a deeply funky bowl of pulverized melon seeds, tomato, and greens. But even I wasn't able to be the kind of regular customer he needed if he was going to survive. To the out-of-town visitors at whom the market was pitched, such meals were an even tougher sell, up against more recognizable Louisianan specialties. Eventually, the market's owners came to Wey and asked him to put a chicken sandwich on the menu. "I did it," he said, "but I was also like, Fuck this. I'm not here for a chicken sandwich." When the chance came to open his own freestanding restaurant on the edge of the French Quarter, Wey jumped on it. I was excited to see what he could do with a full menu and service, but it was not to be; the space fell through. And anyway, Wey was by then onto a different trail.

The Lagos dinners hadn't been explicitly political, but neither were they pitched at foodies. Wey found himself increasingly repelled by American food culture, which he found simultaneously abstract and intellectual, and seemingly *about* nothing that really mattered: "When you examined it, there was no morality there. I don't mean morality in terms of good or evil, I mean a relevant message—or a message, period—outside of food on a plate."

Meanwhile, the Black Lives Matter movement was gaining momentum. Wey began to read deeply about America's racial past and present, from W. E. B. Du Bois to Eduardo Bonilla-Silva, whose 2003 book, *Racism Without Racists,* became a particular touchstone. In it, Bonilla-Silva points a damning finger at those who know enough to know that overt racism is no longer socially acceptable but stop short of challenging the fundamental structures that keep a racist society alive. That is to say: nearly all of us.

In March 2016, at a local butcher shop called Shank Charcuterie, Wey returned to pop-ups with a series of four dinners, but this time was different: Attendees were given a reading list to study up on before arriving. At the tables were questions for discussion. Dinner included *jollof* rice, pepper soup, whole fish, and presentations from, among others, the leader of a nonprofit aimed at helping African American girls in New Orleans. In his flyer for the event, Wey had promised: "Spicy Nigerian Food. Adult Beverages. Dim Lights. Sexy Chef. Sexy Music. Sexy Guests. Honest and Respectful Conversations. A Good Ass Party." And so it proved.

"It was the beginning, and I just had people come up and talk about shit," Wey says. "I had no idea what I was doing, and I just kept doing it."

There has remained an improvisatory nature to the dinners as Wey has staged them around the country over the past three years. Some have speakers, but discussion has become the focal point.

Wey himself often says little, other than to call on people and pose
the occasional prompting question. Some of the dinners were con-
frontational, others stilted. (The BYO booze often proves to be the
most important course in this regard.) It is not unusual for there
to be tears.

For Wey, it is navigating the immediate present of the events
that matters most. He has markedly little interest in discussing
them afterward, when he is often left spent, barely leaving his
French Quarter apartment except to play pickup games of soccer.
"I give a lot of energy, and I need a lot of downtime," he says.

At one dinner in New Orleans last fall, he told a group of stunned
urban planners—all of whom surely considered themselves progressive, justice-minded activists who had sacrificed much for their
social ideals—that they should quit their jobs. It was the harshest
I'd seen him be, and the most dogmatic in his insistence that an
abstract wrong obliterated the possibility of some concrete good. I
asked how he felt about the attendees' reactions: "I'm happy with
people leaving feeling however they feel," he answered. "I feel bad
for them personally. But I also don't have the capacity to assuage
everyone's upset feelings." Later he told me, "These are all people
who have bachelor's degrees. I'm sure they'll be fine."

That it is painful and frustrating to be told that one's individual
history, feelings, and intentions mean nothing because of one's income or skin color is, obviously, precisely the point. Still, pain and
frustration are pain and frustration. A couple of years ago, Wey
took me to task for a profile I'd written for this magazine about
a white already-quite-famous southern chef who was battling an
autoimmune disease. It was, he said, an example of the media's obsession with "the minutiae of whiteness." I said I had written about
a person, not "whiteness," whatever that meant. He said that the
fact I didn't know was part of the problem. I wondered whether,
in the age of Trump, he thought this was really the best use of his
formidable skills and growing power.

"People are dying, Brett," he said.

"But not from chef profiles!" I sputtered. And of course then
he had me.

"Wouldn't you agree," he said, switching to graduate-student
mode, "that the aggregate of all these disparate reinforcements of
whiteness or white fantasy or white power and privilege creates the
conglomerate oppressive power?"

Another time, I accused Wey of hating food. I said I sometimes suspected that his indignation at foodie culture was, at least in part, a puffed-up justification for what was really a deep ambivalence about pleasure. I told him I thought it was actually his most American trait.

"I love to eat. I love to fuck. I love to sleep," he said. Of *course,* he went on, there should be places where dining is simple pleasure, where food is respite and solace. "The problem is that we have too many spaces where food is just that. We need spaces where we can eat and not think about shit, but if *all* your spaces are spaces where you eat and don't think about shit, then you're never thinking about shit!"

Finish him!

Still, anybody who has been on the receiving end of Wey's critique might reasonably find themselves asking a version of my question: Why spend so much time going after potential allies when there are so many more egregious and obvious threats and enemies?

"In critique, you have to be hyperbolic. In practice, you need to be nuanced. But one feeds the other. It's hyperbole that creates the space for the nuance," he says. "And what is the role of the critic? To state the obvious? Or to point to the hidden and understated?"

And who can say he isn't being strategic? The night after the Hot Chicken Shit event, I went by myself to a new restaurant in East Nashville. It was in every way a lovely example of today's modern, placeless, immaculately tasteful restaurant: the menu of Italo-CaliAsian New American dishes (made for sharing), the clever cocktail list, the open kitchen, the exposed ducts and unfinished walls and concrete floors that gave the extremely expensive look of a space whose contractor quit three days before finishing. It was all so *nice.* The very quintessence of *nice.* And I sat at the bar feeling a nagging disquiet, a dissatisfaction that I sensed would not go away no matter how many clam pizzas and fluke crudos and Manhattan variations I poured down my throat in an attempt to quell it. That was when I found myself cursing Tunde Wey.

Wey was dispirited in the weeks before he went to Nashville last July to conduct research for what would become the Hot Chicken Shit dinners. "I'm doing all these projects asking white people to give something up," he said, shaking his head. "And I'm realizing they aren't going to. *White people will never give anything up.*"

Then he held a preliminary series of Nashville dinners. The Music City has been booming in recent years—even before Amazon announced in November that it would open a new operations center there—and the troubles of gentrification have predictably boomed with it. The transformation of such neighborhoods as East Nashville, Salemtown, and Germantown has been all but complete for years. North Nashville, a neighborhood with deep African American roots, has not yet undergone that process, but the signs are all there that it's next up in developers' crosshairs. After he'd been in town a few weeks, Wey's tone changed. He had been meeting with local community leaders, city officials, and activists, he texted me, and he had seized on the notion of a community land trust—a strategy that was originally deployed to protect Black and poor farmers from losing their land. A CLT in North Nashville would take ownership of the area's housing stock and legally guarantee that it would remain affordable in perpetuity. In other words, Wey wanted to buy every vacant and potentially vacant residence in North Nashville.

"It's all that's occupied my brain. It's doing my head in," he texted, followed by two emoji heads exploding.

In hot chicken he found a characteristically potent entry point for the project: a uniquely Black food that has been flagrantly appropriated in recent years. Invented, the legend goes, by a vengeful lover of a man named Thornton Prince (who, instead of howling in pain, went on to perfect the dish, at Prince's Hot Chicken Shack, in North Nashville), hot chicken has become so popular in recent years that the three most famous examples in the world right now are served by a white couple inside a food court in LA's Chinatown, an Australian who was invited to serve his at last year's MAD Symposium in Copenhagen, and KFC.

As the neighborhood women pick at Wey's Nigerian version at Westwood Baptist, they talk about their homes, the years in them calculated by recalling the ages of children, grandchildren, and great-grandchildren. They talk about the phone calls, the unannounced doorbell rings, the literal stacks of letters and postcards they receive every week, all from real estate speculators offering to buy their houses. And then, if they're uninterested in selling, the sudden wild increases in property taxes and the mysterious code violations designed to encourage cutting bait and getting out of the neighborhood. It's easy for white people to think of gentrification debates as being about aesthetic encroachment and individual decision-making, and so to be alternately puzzled in response ("Who doesn't like nice things?") and defensive ("Who are we to blow against the wind?"). This was gentrification experienced as policy, as conspiracy, as existential threat.

Elois Freeman, a 60-something minister at Westwood Baptist who sits at the center of the table wearing a jean jacket and purple earrings, does not mince words: "I think it's a form of cultural genocide," she says.

Wey sits even more quietly than usual during this dinner, allowing the residents to speak and the potential allies present to offer practical advice: contact local city-council members, organize a community board, keep on meeting like this. There's a white lawyer there who tells the story of successfully fighting a development project in his own, far more tony neighborhood. "So you'll be able to offer these people advice?" Wey asks. Sure, says the lawyer.

"Pro bono," Wey adds, not a question.

The next morning, I meet Wey at a soccer game he's found on a field at Vanderbilt University. Soccer is one of Wey's mental escapes and a connection to the country that still feels most like home. There are times when his homesickness is palpable; he has not seen his mother in ten years.

We have lunch at Slim & Husky's, a wildly popular Black-owned pizza business that opened in 2017, not far from Westwood Baptist. I ask about the swerve the night had taken away from the high concept of Hot Chicken Shit.

"It's always good when you change your expectations to meet reality," he says. "I had an audacious goal, and it failed." In this case, "reality" had been a practical problem to solve: people who needed help staying in their homes. And the approach bears fruit: an attendee at the third Hot Chicken Shit dinner ends up donating $100,000 to the cause. Not enough to buy any houses, but plenty to start a process of neighborhood organization and education. And not bad in exchange for a plate of chicken and some honest conversation.

For a moment, at Slim & Husky's, I have the disconcerting image of Wey going straight. After all, he's now being asked to speak at Columbia University and with United Nations officials. He applied (though it was hard to say how seriously) for the vacant position of restaurant critic at the *San Francisco Chronicle*. He recently received a book contract from MCD, an imprint of Farrar, Straus & Giroux. Maybe his future was one of quiet, earnest community activism in rooms like the one at Westwood Baptist, with its folding tables and buzzing lights and vital, very local dreams. Then Wey starts telling me about the idea for his next set of dinners: Marry an Immigrant. See, the menu would be all aphrodisiacs, and attendees would be paired on blind dates with undocumented immigrants. At the end, they'd all get married.

"It's illegal, but of course it's very legal because that's how people get married these days," Wey said. "It's through the internet. It's through matchmaking services. It happens on *The Bachelor.*" He considered it happily, this absurd, crazy, dangerous idea. We laughed.

The dinners, redubbed Marriage Trumps All, began taking place in Pittsburgh in early February.

But before that, on January 7, the morning after Epiphany, Wey dressed in a dark three-piece suit and, with Nelson, made his way to the 18th floor of a building on Poydras Street, where US Customs and Immigration Services has its New Orleans office. There, after a brief interview under oath, watched over by a scowling portrait of Donald Trump, in the midst of a federal-government shutdown predicated on keeping immigrants out of the United States, in the heart of a city that was once the largest market for African bodies in North America, Tunde Wey was granted the status of legal resident.

Briefly overcome by this minor miracle, I texted: "Tell me why this story's ending isn't now a warm, fuzzy message about how, despite it all, America still works."

Immediately the three dots of a return message being composed appeared, and I smiled; Wey isn't the only one who knows how to provoke. The dots stayed for a long time, and I readied myself for the screed about to arrive. But when the message came, it was just one line:

"'Cus you know better."

MEGHAN McCARRON

Whatever Happened to Portland?

FROM *Eater*

AT FIRST GLANCE, Ned Ludd, a restaurant open since 2008 in Portland, Oregon, seems like a museum of farm-to-table clichés. Antique shelves display old-timey jugs and glassware above panels of raw wood. On the spring 2019 menu is an illustration of a chicken perched on an ax *and* a Wendell Berry quote. The name, "Ned Ludd," sounds like a frontier hero, and the folksiness continues when the restaurant bills itself as an "American craft kitchen." That phrase once had meaning; now even the burgers at McDonald's are Signature Crafted. The phrases "locally sourced" and "house-made," meant to suggest honesty, instead invite suspicion, and not just because corporations have co-opted them. House-made ketchup has been one long propaganda campaign for Heinz.

But Ned Ludd isn't a museum of clichés—it's an original. It just happens to be a long-lived restaurant in the city that popularized the entire rustic American-craft-kitchen thing. Ned Ludd's style has a depth, specificity, and self-awareness lacking in so many of its imitators. The decor spirals out into a deranged backwoods maximalism, with antique chandeliers hanging like bats and wooden barrels lurking in the rafters. Ned Ludd himself isn't a frontier cliché—he's the semimythic English hero who smashed looms in a fit of rage, the namesake of the Luddites. There's a mural of him on the wall, inviting you to smash some machines, too.

The restaurant's commitment to cooking only with its brick fireplace suggests what Ned Ludd would like to do to, say, a sous vide cooker, or a fast-food heat lamp. And the cooking is persuasive. A dish of wood-fired asparagus, draped in thin lardo and speckled with mustard seeds, makes good on the farm-to-table promise of evoking a specific season in a specific place, green and astringent as a cold spring morning, with a fattiness that evokes the luxury of sunshine after endless gray. This was a dish that could only be had on a spring evening in a city that taught us first to love and then to hate phrases like "American craft kitchen."

Not so long ago, Portland was the food world's obsession, celebrated as the incubator for the next wave of American cooking, and the template for so much of what was considered Good and Honest in urban hipster culture. Then the other side of the story hit the national consciousness: Many of these craft kitchens were in radically gentrified neighborhoods, and people of color were scarce in these lovingly designed dining rooms splashed across magazines. Craft was a rebellion for the few. All those antlers on the wall and third-wave coffee shops and chickens with names seemed not just goofy, but shameful.

But were the antlers and chickens ever what defined Portland? Or did they only embody the utopia, or dystopia, in the national imagination—the Portlandia, if you will? Even a classic example of the craft-kitchen form like Ned Ludd has a wry sense of humor about the whole enterprise. And so many restaurants in Portland don't fit the Portlandia mold at all—and don't want to.

On a recent visit, a great deal about Portland's food culture, arguably the most overcovered in America, surprised me: the stunning Vietnamese restaurants; the density of taquerias and taco trucks; the *other* Thai restaurant empire, built by Bangkok-born chef Earl Ninsom; historic businesses like the century-old Ota Tofu factory; the city's Support Black-Owned Restaurants Week; the newly arrived elite Japanese ramen. Portland is still one of the most important food cities in America, and not just because so many of the restaurants are very good (which they are). It's also the place where conversations about food, equity, and who 21st-century cities are for are happening most urgently.

In the late aughts and early 2010s Portland emerged as the coolest place to eat in America. It was a land of lamb-brain meat pies, old-world butchery, hypercontextualized Thai food, freshly roasted coffee, and microbrewed beer. The tattooed chefs worshiped foie gras and bragged about their mushroom guy, cut their teeth in underground pop-ups, or left the supposed centers of American dining to cook how they actually wanted to cook. Tiny, cramped food carts with punny names became can't-miss destinations for everything from schnitzelwiches to *khao man gai,* and were avenues to business ownership for immigrants and others without startup capital. The pickles were always, always made in-house.

The 19th-century Americana and DIY energy that became associated with Brooklyn dining were arguably transplanted from Portland. At Le Pigeon, one of the defining restaurants of mid-aughts Portland, bucking tradition remains pleasingly de rigeuer and unapologetically deranged. Lobster-stuffed fried chicken, a recent dish that could have merely been a dare, instead crams the luxury of lobster bisque inside of a fried hunk of chicken breast, the richness cut just enough by bright spring peas and slaw. The logic of the lobster fried chicken is a dogged quest to overload all pleasure centers in the weirdest possible way. Eating it makes you want to die, but happily.

This vision of craft-culture hedonism now feels overly familiar, even absurd. Some of the reason is because Portland was *too* successful in remaking American cooking in its image, while still commanding tons of attention for itself. But I'd argue the playfulness rings empty these days in part because there was never a reckoning over how obsessing over restaurants run by white Gen X and millennial men left out a lot of folks, especially in a city whose hipster wonderland was built on an ugly history. In Gizmodo in 2015, Matt Novak wrote a lengthy rundown of Oregon and Portland's explicitly racist policies and history, horrible end-to-end but also striking because, as historian and educator Walidah Imarisha said to Novak, "Oregon was bold enough to write it down." Oregon's state constitution, ratified in 1857 and going into effect in 1859, explicitly excluded Black residents from owning property, making contracts, and other legal rights. These restrictions were de facto policy across much of the United States, but this was the only state where it was de jure. Nonwhite residents arrived anyway, and faced harassment and violence. In Portland, this included a Klan infestation in the 1920s, a notoriously racist police force in the mid-20th century, and systemic and pernicious real estate discrimination into the present day.

In 2016 Alana Semuels wrote a widely shared *Atlantic* feature that, in its discussion of Oregon and Portland's white-utopia his-

tory, focused on the gentrification of the historically Black Portland neighborhood Albina, which, after being strafed by interstate
construction and urban renewal, lost nearly all of its Black-owned
businesses and many of its Black residents as emblems of white
hipsterdom took over. The election of Donald Trump only served
to worsen the tensions in the city, as white supremacists recruited
and rallied, and a man screaming anti-Muslim slurs on Portland's
light rail stabbed three men who tried to stop him.

These facts, and the virality of some of the pieces covering
them, complicated but did not decrease the national fascination
with Portland. And then there's the TV show. A satire of the city's
twee, hipster elite, *Portlandia* premiered in 2011, and became the
darling of twee, hipster elite across the country. In the food world,
sketches like "Dream of the 1890s" and "Colin the Chicken"
pointed out the absurdity of trends earnestly blanketing American cities where there were both creative people and people with
money (or both). But these sketches also legitimized a niche, neu-
rotic, expensive cuisine as the dominant mode of eating in America, and what it meant to eat in Portland.

Now, it's hard to actually visit Portland; you keep ending up in
Portlandia. It's a scrim, an augmented reality overlaying the city,
especially for someone on a visit, seeking to find what they already
think they know. It's both simple and challenging to escape.

Rose VL is located in a little strip mall set back from busy Pow-
ell Boulevard, alongside a dress shop and a realtor. On the glass
front windows, stuck-on letters promise METICULOUS SOUPS. It's
the second restaurant by Ha Christina Luu and William Vuong,
specializing in a small, rotating number of regional Vietnamese
soups, two of which are made daily from scratch.

Playground purple-and-yellow walls are decorated with soft-fo-
cus glamour shots of Vietnamese coffee service, a portrait of
Vuong in his US military uniform, a massive family portrait, and
two framed James Beard semifinalist awards, for Luu individually
and jointly with her son Peter Vuong for their smaller shop, Ha
VL, which has been open since 2006. (Luu and William Vuong
left Vietnam separately from their children after the end of the
Vietnam War; Vuong, who worked for the American embassy in
Saigon, spent 10 years in prison in Vietnam after American com-

bat troops withdrew.) Below the massive counter, decorated with overflowing vases of flowers and trained, potted bamboo, hangs the short daily menu—on Friday it consisted of shrimp cake *(bún riêu)*, shredded chicken *(bún thang)*, and fermented fish *(bún mam)* noodle soups, plus salad rolls and a smattering of drinks, including the renowned Vietnamese coffee.

Is there a more perfect breakfast than noodle soup and strong, sweet coffee? The powerful, garlic-infused chicken noodle soup at Rose VL, served with thin-sliced omelet, nourished, while the bitter and rich made-to-order Vietnamese coffee revived. *Oregonian* critic Michael Russell opened his 2017 review by noting that diners always risk FOMO—order one soup and envy the one your companion got. My editor's shrimp-cake soup, reddened by tomato and mildly funky, made me regret my choice. She got another order to go, which was, yes, meticulously packed with noodles, fragile condiments, and broth in separate packages.

Rose VL has a typical Portland story, about culinary ambition in scrappy circumstances, captured in an extensive 2019 profile in the *Oregonian*. When they opened their first restaurant, Ha VL, Luu and Vuong took a risk in serving just two daily soups made entirely from scratch by Luu, who is the chef. The rotating selection inspired at least one fan blog (now defunct) to track the options. After turning Ha VL over to Peter, who shops his way across Portland's Asian markets daily for the best ingredients, Luu and Vuong came out of retirement to open their second restaurant, where they introduced their take on *cao lau,* a signature noodle dish from the port city Hoi An, which Vuong and Luu fell in love with while visiting Vietnam in 2014. Now, they are in the process of building a family-run empire.

Ha VL and Rose VL are institutions in Portland. Local critic Karen Brooks praised their artisanal approach in a 2008 review. Pok Pok's Andy Ricker is such a megafan he broke the news about their second restaurant. Rose VL is a standby on the Portland Eater 38, and many locals suggested I go there for great soups—but no one urged me to go because it's one of the best restaurants in Portland, period. Rose VL epitomizes the creativity and rigorous focus on quality that defines the best of the city. Why doesn't it have the profile of, say, the nationally recognized Kachka? Or Nong's Khao Man Gai, famously the first place you should go when you land in Portland, which serves an equally focused menu? Is it too far out from the city center? Is Luu a chef too disconnected from the more powerful nodes of the city's kitchens? (Early press about Nong Poonsukwattana emphasized that she was a Ricker protégé.)

When recommending Ha VL or Rose VL to me, a few folks also insisted they couldn't possibly be as good as the Vietnamese restaurants in Los Angeles. But it's only recently that outsiders have considered Los Angeles a Vietnamese-food destination—and without the work of the late Jonathan Gold, it's possible the narrative of vapid Hollywood power dining might still reign supreme. LA's success as a great restaurant city is tied directly to expanding ideas about what makes a great restaurant. The James Beard nominations for the non-Portlandia but extremely Portland chefs of Ha VL suggest that process might be underway in Portland, too. And not just by accident—the dedicated work of local writers and activists in town have set the stage for a new kind of national reckoning over what American food is.

When I asked people in Portland about a defining food moment from the past few years, a number answered with something that surprised me: Burritogate. The controversy, which boiled over into the national media in 2017, comes down to this: Two women from Portland took a road trip to Puerto Nuevo, a beach town just south of Tijuana known for its (megatouristy) Lobster Village, where they were smitten with the handmade tortillas served alongside their lobsters. Back in Portland, they opened a weekend burrito pop-up called Kooks *inside* a taco truck, and told *Willamette Week* that "[the women cooking] wouldn't tell us too much about technique, but we were peeking into the windows of every kitchen, totally fascinated by how easy they made it look."

In other words, two non-Mexican women framed their restaurant as inspired by a brief trip to the tourist zone of another country, where they attempted to pick up culinary techniques without permission, or at least not much of an attempt to determine if they had permission. Then, they got coverage in a local paper for making such wonderful tortillas. There's a ton of murky issues around white chefs, with cultural and often monetary capital, cooking food from cultures not their own. But rarely do these chefs describe so specifically where their ideas came from, and where they failed to connect.

Immediately, the story received pushback online, and other publications picked it up as an example of Portland's careless whiteness run amok—or its tedious wokeness putting two women out of business, since the Kooks owners closed up shop in the face of what they claimed were death threats. In *Bitch*, M. L. Moreno wrote about the massive disconnect between how Mexican food cooked by Mexican people is often dismissed in America, and how projects like Kooks are celebrated. Writing for the *OC Weekly*, Gustavo Arellano argued that appropriating Mexican food wasn't worth the amount of ire it had generated online, because Mexicans did so intraculturally all the time—though he also noted that closing up shop wasn't the right response. He writes, "The *gabachas* knew exactly what they were doing, so [why] didn't they stand by it? Real gumption there, *pendejas*."

From the outside, the story grew so distorted it was difficult to parse, but within Portland, it was a key part of a larger conversation that had been put off for too long, about who was benefiting from the food boom, and who was being left out. Both *Willamette Week* and the *Oregonian* published chefs' roundtables on the subject, which allowed a rare depth of conversation about race in the local restaurant scene. If the original online controversy had become distorted by virality, it also seems to have sparked a larger and more careful reckoning in Portland.

Even before Burritogate, these conversations about food and race in Portland were happening on the podcast *Racist Sandwich*, cofounded by writers Soleil Ho and Zahir Janmohamed. In the beginning, the podcast focused on Portland chefs and food-world people of color, and quickly rose to national prominence. In an interview, Janmohamed, who lived in Portland from 2015 to 2017, told me that the podcast was always intended to address previously underexamined tensions in Portland. One of the things that struck him was how the largely white city had a real enthusiasm for food from other cultures, unlike other small cities he'd lived in. But that eagerness did not always translate to welcoming the actual people. "There was a really healthy appetite for Japanese food or Mexican food, but maybe not so much for Mexican residents," Janmohamed said. "Somalis were having trouble finding housing, but then a Somali pop-up dinner would sell out immediately—and that to me was fascinating."

The podcast started after Janmohamed and Ho met in a group

for Portland creatives of color, which was formed to offer support
to people who had arrived in Portland to experience the coolness
they'd heard so much about, but encountered a sense of alien-
ation instead.

Ho, who is now the restaurant critic for the *San Francisco Chronicle,* lived in Portland in 2015 and 2016 and remembers moving
there with a sense of excitement. "People were free to do whatever
the hell they wanted, that was my perception," she said in an interview. But her time working in kitchens there revealed "a lot of
layers and a lot of hierarchies—boys' club type relationships. It
was very homogenous, even if it was serving food that was diverse.
There were a lot of people with restaurants that were interesting,
and they were pushed out to the margins."

Racist Sandwich focused on who was being left out of Portland's
story. Their early guests included Bertony Faustin, the first Black
winemaker in the region, Han Ly Hwang of the food truck Kim
Jong Grillin', and Abel Hernandez and Jaime Soltero Jr. of local
Mexican restaurant Tamale Boy. The show's audience grew rapidly
in part because the questions Ho and Janmohamed were tackling
were even more vital to the American food world than any new
techniques or aesthetics chefs in Portland had popularized before.
"It's one of the big questions of the day: What are you going to
do about your home?" Ho says. "How do you make a new home
without displacing other people, and is this even a question of individual action?"

Celeste Noche, a Portland resident who moved there in 2014
and who founded the photo series Portland in Color, thinks about
the problems of who is and isn't included in the story of Portland
partly in aesthetic terms. She says the rustic, beautiful design Portland is known for also has the effect of keeping visitors away from
the less-tricked-out dining rooms across town. "People who have
social media followings don't want to go to more mom-and-pop
[places]."

Portland locals are designing better and more equitable ways
forward as the city tries to weather the dual, entwined challenges
of rising real estate values and shakier restaurant fortunes. The
boldest and most comprehensive vision is championed by Rukai-
yah Adams, the chief investment officer of the Meyer Memorial
Trust and a fourth-generation Black Portlander. She's the chair of

the Albina Vision Trust, a group that has put forward an ambitious proposal for redeveloping the Rose Quarter, a historically Black neighborhood wiped out by urban renewal. The trust seeks to create a community that is accessible to people of all income levels, down to the businesses that would exist there. "We want affordable living," Adams told the *Portland Business Review,* "and by affordable we mean not just a few mandated units of housing in a community where people who live in those units can't afford to eat or get their hair cut in their own neighborhood." A *Portland Monthly* feature on the predevelopment process notes that, "when a sketch of a riverside beer garden seemed too hipster, the rendering became a teeming family-friendly park under a bosk of trees."

The Portland Mercado is another business fighting back against the forces of displacement. It was created by community members and stakeholders to serve as a hub for Latino culture in the city. With ample shade for outdoor dining, carts serving regional cuisines from Puerto Rico, Colombia, Venezuela, and more park outside the market. At Tierra del Sol, a Oaxacan food truck located at the Mercado, an artisanal approach is evident even in a seemingly simple dish like a *tetela,* a folded masa pocket stuffed with beans. Owner Amalia Sierra makes the blue corn masa and tortillas from a family recipe, and the beans are cooked from scratch to a thick, pleasingly spicy paste. Sierra's moles and *tlayudas* are renowned in Portland, all of them cooked with decades of experience and practice, as she told Cristina Baez for *Eater PDX.*

Ho, Janmohamed, and Noche all agree that supporting restaurants and businesses owned by people of color in Portland is vital. *Racist Sandwich*'s map of POC-owned restaurants and food businesses is robust and compelling—an entirely different view of essential dining in the city. Danny Chau's James Beard Award–nominated food diary in the Ringer does similar work for a national audience. And an awareness of the city's ugly history around race will not, on its own, repair the harm: in 2016 some Black community leaders expressed concern that all this obsession over gentrification was erasing the Black businesses that were still there.

Janmohamed, who is currently a fiction MFA student at the University of Michigan, says *Racist Sandwich* could only have happened in Portland, fueled by the city's DIY culture. "In writing, you talk about negative capability. You can love and hate a thing at the

same time," he says. "I love Portland. I wish there were more struc-
tural changes to help people of color, not just attitude shifts. I
can't wait to see what Portland is like in twenty years."

That next Portland might look like Stoopid Burger, a food truck
darling gone brick-and-mortar, and one of the city's most prominent Black-owned restaurants. Co-owners John Hunt and Danny
Moore, both Portland natives, got their start with a food cart that
went on to win the people's choice for best burger from the *Oregonian*. In an interview, Moore says he started working in restaurants
at the age of nine, when he helped out at Nelson's Barbecue, a
local restaurant owned by a family friend. Later, he split his time
between culinary school and local kitchens; he and Hunt hatched
a plan to open their own food truck during a brief stint at a Buffalo Wild Wings. "We're the Voodoo Doughnut of burgers," Moore
says, referencing the hole-in-the-wall doughnut shop that's since
become a national chain.

The restaurant's namesake, the Stoopid Burger, is topped with
ham, bacon, a hot link, egg, and cheese. Moore says that burger,
minus their signature Stoopid sauce, is a Portland classic, once
available at restaurants like Cleo's, Mr. Burger, and other neighborhood staples that are now all gone. "Keeping the legacy alive
means a lot," Moore says. "We're both Portland natives, born in
Portland and raised in Portland, all of our families are from Portland. Our role is very significant in our community because there's
not a lot of Black-owned restaurants as dominant as Stoopid
Burger. It means a lot for our younger generation looking up to
us to know that there's more than just white-owned businesses that
can be successful."

On a sunny weekday lunch, the restaurant's facade was open to
the nice weather, overlooking a shared patio space in one fashionable restaurant block. Every burger seeks to outdo the last—the Ig-
norant Burger, a social media darling, is a towering three-story pile
of meat, including steak. You can order a Boring Burger, if you can
stand to be so timid. I went with the Wicked Burger, topped with
bacon, cheese, pickles, pineapple habanero salsa, and peanut butter. Like the lobster fried chicken at Le Pigeon, it could have just
been a weird concept with no pleasure beyond its weirdness. And
like the lobster fried chicken at Le Pigeon, it instead overloaded
so many inputs at once, the only solution was to take another bite.

The tart pickles, fatty bacon, hot chutney, and sticky-sweet peanut butter crunch was just crazy enough to be genius.

Portland's commitment to a daring, perfectionist hedonism is still the city's strongest culinary unifier. At Hat Yai, the casual southern-Thai restaurant from local empire-builder Ninsom, fried chicken comes as a set with curry and roti, and its thin, spiced crust shatters over meat seasoned to the bone. At the newly opened Yonder, chef Maya Lovelace's counter-service ode to her North Carolina childhood, the spicy, tender fried catfish demanded not just enjoyment but gluttony. Dinner at Naomi Pomeroy's Beast on Tuesday nights is a throwback four-course menu meant to evoke its supper club origins, serving utterly of-the-moment morel and asparagus pastas and a hunter's chicken made with last summer's preserved tomatoes. The 19-course tasting menu at Erizo, run by *Eater* Young Gun Jacob Harth, ends with a massive halibut collar and a raft of Parker House rolls. It's sort of useless to consider whether any of these meals are Honest, but you can't deny they are Good.

About that Wendell Berry quote on the Ned Ludd menu: Beneath the chicken on an ax, it reads, "A significant part of the pleasure of eating is on one's own accurate consciousness of the lives and the world from which the food comes." Ten years ago, that meant knowing the chicken's name and the chef's nickname for his mushroom guy. Now dining culture is moving (or being dragged) to the fuller vision: the farmworkers, the bussers, and the community that's been there for decades—who's in the dining room and who isn't. We have a more accurate consciousness. Now, it's time to do what the best part of craft culture invites us to do: turn off the simulation, and enjoy what's really there.

When Jacques Pépin Made All the World an Omelet

FROM *Taste*

WITH EIGHT EGGS, a ramekin of Land O'Lakes butter, a pinch of chopped chives, and a life's worth of experience among the pots and pans, Jacques Pépin walked into the KQED studio in San Francisco and changed the course of eggs in the United States of America forever. At just under six minutes, Pépin's now-famous omelet segment, recorded in the spring of 1995, is perhaps the single greatest cooking sequence ever to be captured on film. The man made two omelets, and American chefs, food writers, and dedicated home cooks have been inspired for the nearly quarter century since.

The 5:52 segment opens with Pépin walking toward the counter. Hair like Rock Hudson's, blue denim Levi's shirt with the sleeves rolled up under a forest-green apron, Pépin is already talking to the camera, as if we caught him midconversation. "If I had to judge how good technically a chef is, I probably would ask him to do an omelet," he says, with a Lyonnaise accent that is at once authoritative and approachable. As he's saying this, he approaches the counter and unconsciously starts doing the things a chef does with his hands at his station: a cataloging of the physical objects before him that's half evaluation and half confirmation of their existence.

He picks up then puts down the fork and the glass bowl, the only two items on the cutting board. He moves the pan—a wide, heavy-bottomed nonstick skillet—onto the front burner of his range, all the while talking to you about omelets, like both you and they were old friends. "I'm going to show you two different types of omelets," he begins, breaking four eggs into a glass bowl with metronymic regularity, "a kind of country French omelet, which is basically the way we do it in America, and then a classic French omelet. One is not better than the other; it's just a different technique, a different taste, a different look that you have in it."

Of course, I don't have to go on about the video. You've seen it. Millions have seen it. Today, you can't get two whisks into making an omelet before your mind Pavlovianly turns to Pépin, his Gallic vowels, his informal perfection, the benign violence of his fork in yolk as he whisks with vigor. But I do wonder what it is about this segment, one of over 105 filmed during an enormously productive two-day period in the spring of '95, that continues to echo through larders of our time? Was it just another day in the studio for Pépin, or was it his Dylan '66 or Simone at Montreux or, I don't know, Cheap Trick at Budokan?

Certainly it was nothing special for those in the studio. Peter L. Stein, the producer of Pépin's show on KQED, *Today's Gourmet*, admits, "You have to remember, by the time we made what would become the technique series, we'd already shot three twenty-six-part seasons with Jacques in which he demonstrated everything phenomenally, flawlessly, with charm. We had, frankly, gotten a little bit inured." Tina Salter, at the time the culinary producer, recalls that Pépin was just being Pépin. "He'll replicate the same thing over and over again," she says. "Doesn't matter if it's in a fancy kitchen, a studio, or a shopping mall."

The omelet segment itself was drawn from what was initially a public-television pledge-drive special. Pépin had had the idea that instead of a standard recipe-driven show, he'd focus simply on technique. (His books, *La Technique* and *La Methode*, had established the man as a master technician.) How to make an omelet was, for instance, preceded by tips for reconstituting broken mayonnaise and followed by vegetable decorations for pâtés and terrines. These were skills, Pépin told me recently, that had been engraved into his bones like culinary scrimshaw from his years as an apprentice. "It is part of what I do," he said, "part of who I am. You repeat a technique, then you repeat it and repeat it until it becomes part of you."

The segment itself is strikingly straightforward. Like each of the other 104 skills, it takes place in a spartan studio. This was no faux Connecticut kitchen, with pothos plants and chicken-shaped pottery in the background. "This was a reference work," explains Stein, "so I wanted the set to be spare, clean, and abstract." A few standing set pieces, sort of flattened columns, occupy the background. They are silk-screened with illustrations of kitchen ephemera (a clove of garlic, a knife, a rolling pin) that the set designer, Ron Haake, had modeled after Pépin's own illustrations. There is no fancy camera work, just the three cameras rolling simultaneously, shooting to videotape, with few cuts—and the few that occur are purely functional. It's almost *Russian Ark*–ian, avant-garde without trying to be.

"It was mostly continuous," says Salter, "a lesson in its entirety." Pépin's language, though fluent, is plain, bordering on folksy. I counted only one simile, no metaphors, and a remarkable dearth of adjectives. It was all improvised, Pépin tells me. ("No, are you kidding?" he says when I ask. "There was never a script.") And yet it's a thing of flawless beauty to watch him narrate turning four eggs into two omelets.

And at the end, when he slices open the classic omelet to reveal quivering curds—"curd" in his accent, always singular—and a nice jazz piano riff comes in (the work of a local Bay Area pianist named Mike Greensill), one is moved in a way omelets rarely can. One is emotional. Why? Because as it turns out, Jacques Pépin isn't teaching us how to make an omelet. He is giving us a lesson in epistemological certainty. This is what it is to know something so profoundly that the knowledge flows from you effortlessly, like water.

The year 1995 was, for me and many Americans my age, a complicated and confusing time. It was the year I turned 14, the year I first kissed a girl, a year I shrouded my spindly legs in JNCO jeans and my avian torso in Alien Workshop, the year I didn't learn how to heelflip, and the year I lied about it. Was it the year of Crystal Pepsi or the year of Orbitz? I can't remember. It was the year Doritos introduced a new chip shape. It was the year we all danced to Ini Kamoze's "Here Comes the Hotstepper" without knowing at all what it was about.

And then, all of a sudden, there's a French guy on television, talking to me as if we'd already been talking for years now, and in his hands (muscular, knobby) is a pan, a beautiful pan, he says, because it "doesn't have any corners, you see it has a beautiful sway.

It is a nonstick pan, so it's ideal. It's an omelet pan, actually." And he speaks in a direct way, with a sort of plaintive singsong. But he also speaks with the authority of someone who knows so much he needn't think, about a topic both quotidian and mystical, and the *bruit* of the '90s subsides and it's just you and Jacques and a thin layer of quickly-cooking egg curd.

As demonstrated by Pépin, the perfect omelet is the result not of exalted ingredients—the eggs, says Salter, were from a supermarket aisle—but rather of the alchemy of heat and technique. In this segment, Pépin presents two omelets: a country-style French omelet and a classic French omelet. The country-style omelet—the omelet Pépin tells me today his mother made and his daughter Claudine tells me he made—is earthier, ruder, more grounded. It is browned like the earth, gutsy and rough. It is an omelet with its hands dirty and edges browned. This is the omelet of the 24-hour diner, the omelet served by old ladies with Parliament voices in black vests with tangerine eye shadow who call you "honey." This is the omelet that accompanies bottomless coffee, endless despair, and hard-fought joy.

The classic French omelet, on the other hand, doesn't worry about the world's suffering. Perfect, pristine, coddled. The curds, still creamy, are constantly agitated, and the entire thing quickly turns in on itself. Pépin, as he grasps the skillet handle with an inverted grip, turns it over onto the plate where it quivers like a dauphin prince at court for the very first time: the refined Apollo to the ruddy Dionysus.

Though there is considerable technique deployed in both—not the least of which is loosening the curd from the pan with nothing but a skillfully deployed fork and then simply knocking the pan against the counter until, like a slow-motion wave, the edge of the omelet rises and falls back on itself—but there can be no argument that the classic French omelet is the loftier of the two.

Watching and rewatching the segment, I couldn't put my finger on what, exactly, makes it so striking. Sure, the execution of a task at once difficult and simple is enormously satisfying. But it's not just the technique. It's the visceral pleasure felt when the form of a thing and the content of it are perfectly aligned. See, the secret of an omelet is skillful action without fuss.

There are no tricks to the omelet. No shortcuts or hacks. And

the secret to teaching the secret of an omelet is the same skillful action, an absence of neuroses and flimflam—and this is what
Pépin nails. Plainspoken yet brilliant, humble yet exalted, Pépin *is*
the omelet he makes. So there's that.

But let us not forget that Pépin didn't make just one omelet. He
made two: a country-style omelet with browned edges and tough
curds that you might find in a Howard Johnson's or a Lyonnaise
farmhouse and a classic-style omelet, creamy and ethereal, that
you'd find at a place like Le Pavillon or at the palace kitchen of
Charles de Gaulle.

And the thing was that Pépin, alone among men, had been inside all of these. And what he had to say about them was equani-
mous. He had been to the mountaintop and in the valley, too, and
his ultimate conclusion was this: "One is not really necessarily better than the other," he says. "It's a different technique, a different
taste." So here, on the range, embodied by two differing omelets,
is the triumph of Aeschylus and Sophocles: the harmony between
the Dionysian and Apollonian.

If Helen's was the face that launched a thousand ships, Pépin's
was the face that folded a million omelets, and this was the moment he went from PBS presence to cultural touchstone. This
special, which was eventually released as part of a five-tape VHS
box set in 1995 with the name *Jacques Pépin's Cooking Techniques*,
and, with the addition of *Jacques Pépin's Dessert Techniques*, as part
of a 13-part series in 1997, established Pépin as a culinary heavy-
weight. These two days in San Francisco began a trajectory that
would eventually include *Julia and Jacques Cooking at Home*. But the
long term goes further: the segment proves that home cooking
could be transformative, and inspired thousands of citizens to take
up forks and pans and break eggs.

Jim Oseland, long before he became the editor in chief of
Saveur, recalls being in the thrall of Pépin. "I used to watch this
show after coming home from a hard day's work being a copy editor in women's fashion magazines, when I just needed to dream."
Ignacio Mattos, who serves his own French classic omelet at Estela
(albeit with sea urchin), remembers, "Watching JP making omelets felt almost as good as eating them. So bare and compelling."
The memory is still so salient in the mind of Gavin Kaysen that in
2011, 15 years after it first aired, his first thought upon learning

Pépin was in Café Boulud was "Thank God we took the omelet off the menu!"

As for me and the millions of others who have watched Jacques Pépin make an omelet, of all that happened in the '90s, it is the well to which we return over and over again and which seems just as fresh today as it did 25 years ago. There are no shortcuts. There are no hacks. There is just hard work and life experience and two different kinds of omelets, neither one of which is better than the other, just as long as they're well made.

Where'd You Go, Rocco DiSpirito?

FROM *Food & Wine*

ROCCO DISPIRITO BROKE up my relationship. To be fair, it was on the rocks already, but that lunch at Union Pacific in the summer of 2004 opened the cracks even wider. I spent the subway ride home rhapsodizing about chicken salad with daikon and champagne vinaigrette and sautéed skate with lime pickle, Swiss chard, and brown butter to the increasing annoyance of the man I was dating. He fancied himself a lover of food, had worked in a restaurant kitchen for a time, and seemed content at the table, but apparently he'd had all he could swallow from me. "Why does everything have to be 'the best' with you? You always have to look for the most amaaaazing dish ever. Can't you just settle for a meal or anything else that's just fine?"

Apparently, none of us could. My boyfriend and I ended things a few weeks later, as the then-37-year-old DiSpirito was very publicly getting the boot from his namesake restaurant on 22nd Street (made infamous as *The Restaurant* in the early days of reality TV) and abdicating his post as executive chef of Union Pacific—which he'd held since the restaurant opened in 1997. That was where he'd once earned three stars from Ruth Reichl (as well as the respect and envy of his fellow chefs), and been named a 1999 *Food & Wine* Best New Chef. According to the *New York Times*, DiSpirito released a statement saying in part, "I have made a decision to take a break from the day-to-day operations of a restaurant to focus on other opportunities outside the restaurant world."

Those "opportunities" swiftly eroded his once-solid standing in the food world. Both his peers and his former customers could not reconcile the image of their pretty, naughty wunderkind as a pitchman for mass-market pasta and pet food, hawking pots on QVC, or hustling in sequins on *Dancing with the Stars*. Unearth any tabloid, food publication, or gossip site from the late '90s to the early '00s, and the ire is evident. Even though gossip items—and there were mountains of them—tipped heavily toward breathless coverage of his dating life (one particularly prying reporter grilled him on if he'd ever had sex in his restaurants' kitchens), he had the benediction of his peers so long as he was still cemented in a restaurant kitchen. When he left, they unleashed their fury, painting him as a fame chaser, a megalomaniac, a wasted talent. Anthony Bourdain famously created a Golden Clog Award, called the Rocco Award, for worst career move by a talented chef. (DiSpirito gamely showed up in person to present it.)

For the past 15 years, an image of him had been fixed in my head, swaggering across Page Six, babe du jour in tow, or smirking from the cover of an early-aughts food mag inexplicably cradling a 60-pound tilefish, or being named one of *People*'s Sexiest Men Alive, but never in a restaurant kitchen.

And then out of nowhere, he was back, talking through the evening's specials at the Standard Grill in New York City where, improbably and joyfully, he was once again an executive chef after a nearly decade-and-a-half absence. Until, suddenly, he wasn't again. This week, the news broke that Rocco and the Standard have parted ways, and once again, he's a chef without a restaurant kitchen.

But this time, he hasn't disappeared. This time, when his fans ask, "Where'd you go, Rocco DiSpirito?" there is an answer. It begins with where he went the last time he stepped away from restaurants, 15 years ago.

The glitz and swagger that made DiSpirito a media and dining room darling did not come naturally, I learned one morning while he and I hunkered in a banquette at the Standard Grill a few months ago. As his team prepped for service—he'd join them on the line later, alongside his former Union Pacific colleague Daniel Parilla (known more commonly by a single name: Chino) —the now-52-year-old chef quietly laughed when I marveled at the seeming ease he'd displayed with diners both back in the day, and maybe a bit more cautiously now. Starting in second grade, he'd been pulled out of class to work with a therapist, and by the time he opened Union Pacific, his social anxiety was so paralyzing that he worked with an acting coach for several months to script and rehearse interactions with his guests.

"You would think going out and saying 'Hello, how was your food? I'm Rocco' would be so easy, but not for freaks like me," he said. "I was always insecure, paranoid, and terrified that everyone hated everything. I am basically mostly still that guy, twenty years of therapy later."

While the nightly floor show didn't come naturally then or now, it did become routine for DiSpirito and increasing numbers of his peers. No matter the beauty of the dining room or sublimity of the food, it was a knife fight to get customers through the door in the late '90s. He and his partners knew that—and it didn't hurt that he was easy on the eyes. So even if it was tough on his psyche, he stepped out of the kitchen and onto the stage.

There was a tension—one he's trying to reconcile to this day. "How do you balance being the thing and promoting the thing that you are trying to be? You have to market more than master. In our industry, that tension is the source of many, many problems and Xanax prescriptions."

Still, he made a fragile peace with that part of it, even convinced himself that he was having fun with it for a while, maybe got lost in it. And then that was all he had. With the closure of his restaurants (he actually made money from the sale of Union Pacific, a rare thing in the industry) and the end of his TV show in 2004, DiSpirito no longer had the safe backstage of a kitchen to retreat to when the spotlight started to burn.

He couldn't quite remember when it all began to break down. There was a kick-in-the-gut "you're going to die young" talk from his doctor that spurred him to train for triathlons, overhaul the way he was eating and cooking, and get into the best shape of his life. Then his mother, Nicolina, who shared the screen with him on *The Restaurant,* suffered a near-fatal heart attack in 2005.

"I watched her die in the emergency room, and they asked me to sign a proxy. My mom goes from making three thousand meatballs a day to incapacitated in a rehab center, needing twenty-four-hour care." DiSpirito slowly realized that the caregiver was going to have to be him. Not solely—there were home health care workers. But as anyone who's had a loved one slip into a long-term decline knows painfully well, the logistics, finances, physical-ity, and unrelenting worry can threaten to drown you alongside them—no matter how fiercely you love them or what resources you have. Family can be complicated at the best of times, but add illness, grief, and finances into the cauldron, and it can roil into a toxic brew. Sprinkle some celebrity into the mix, and suddenly everyone gets to have an opinion. DiSpirito's was this: keep moving. He relocated Nicolina from above the restaurant to a home next door to his so he could easily visit, take her to appointments, make sure the home health aides were present, and hold on to his other sources of income.

"I wasn't able to even think about a restaurant anymore . . . that was not even remotely possible," DiSpirito told me. "That's probably where the reputation of me as a person who loves the limelight versus the kitchen got solidified." And yes, despite his better judgment, he read the press, and yes, of course it hurt, and deeply, especially because he still very much thought of himself as a chef. "That's what I am. I'll never be anything but. I felt that the research I was doing with the books and eventually developing this home-delivery service, I thought it was still cooking all the time. But I guess if it's not in a restaurant, it doesn't count."

DiSpirito wrote cookbooks, headlined food festivals, developed food products, did consulting work, hosted a now-notorious book signing at an event for a cat-food brand ("I didn't put all my heart and soul into it because it wasn't required. I just took the money, right? I've done two of those things and eight thousand of the other things," he sighed), went on *Dancing with the Stars*—his mother's favorite program—and did plenty of other TV. He kept up his Ironman training until he couldn't.

"I thought, This is the absolute best thing I could be doing with my life. She deserves to have a dignified and comfortable end of life. We were so close and she's done so much for me, that this is absolutely the right thing to do. I didn't really think about what the costs were, what the trade-offs were." Her final days in 2013 were "inhumane," Dispirito said. "You have to go through this rigmarole, this sort of fake process of taking painkillers and then upping it to morphine. We're more humane with pets than we are with human beings."

He made sure that his mother's final hours played out as she'd requested, with family all around and Perry Como crooning in the background—a dignified end to nearly a decade of pain for Nicolina, and the start of some very public familial legal struggles for DiSpirito. Read about them if you care to; it's not hard to find.

What you won't see in those newspaper and magazine archives are images of Rocco DiSpirito in a wheelchair, immobile in his home, or in physical therapy while he learned to walk again. In the course of his mother's illness, as often happens to caretakers, DiSpirito neglected his own needs. He'd suffered from back issues his whole life—surely exacerbated by the physical toll all chefs accept as part of the job—and couldn't find time for his own doctor's appointments. Two years after Nicolina's death, his bill came due.

"I was especially fond of the chiropractor I was referred to because when I first met him, he said, 'I'm going to make sure you never need surgery.' And unfortunately I did need surgery because I didn't listen to him." The emergency diskectomy—a kind of spinal surgery—for his acute sciatica was something DiSpirito had dreaded for his entire adult life, and it left him as an invalid for a time.

Weeks of being unable to move at all were compounded by an inability to ask for help, he admitted. "I'm not great at it. I crave it immensely. I want people to recognize that I need help and reach out and do things, but it's impossible to ask for. But when someone does it genuinely, thoughtfully, and kindly, with all their heart, it's a wonderful feeling. And then I can accept it."

He was barely able to get in and out of a wheelchair, but that's not how he wanted the public or his peers to regard him. So like he had so many times before, he put on a grand show for the public while his mind and body cried out for respite.

In typical Rocco DiSpirito fashion, he agreed to participate in an event in Florida while still unable to walk. A fellow chef pushed him around in a wheelchair, and his fans, not knowing the severity of the situation, found the whole thing hilarious—delighted that he'd shown up, unaware of what it cost him to be there. He looked back on it while we talked, shaking his head: "A normal person would just say, 'I have to cancel. Sorry.' That didn't even occur to me.'" He'd made a commitment, and he was sticking with it, no matter how painful it was. To his mind, that's what chefs do. And that's who and what he is to his core. He had to get back in the kitchen.

DiSpirito promised himself that this time, it was going to be on his own terms, serving the kind of health-focused food that had pulled him back from the brink and that he'd been writing about in books like *Rocco's Healthy & Delicious: More Than 200 (Mostly) Plant-Based Recipes for Everyday Life* and *Cook Your Butt Off!: Lose Up to a Pound a Day with Fat-Burning Foods and Gluten-Free Recipes.* "All the things I write about in my books, I have been just hungry to show people—that you can eat an indulgent meal and still eat a healthy meal," DiSpirito said. "I've been pitching it to restaurateurs and food companies and fast casual concepts. I started doing that in 2006, and of course back then, no one thought it made sense."

Over a decade later, Stephen Brandman did. The Journal Hotels co-owner and CEO sought out DiSpirito, offering an opportunity to revamp the Standard, High Line's flagship, celeb-magnet restaurant with a more plant-based menu—but once again, his presence in the dining room was going to be a key ingredient. He had to make his peace with that, even if it still makes him nervous to this day. "It was very clear after twenty-four hours, this would not be something you could phone in," DiSpirito realized. "I thought, It's a hotel, there's a massive culinary team. They've got an executive chef and chef de cuisine and pastry chef; it's not going to be like a normal restaurant opening. I'm going to have all this support. It turns out it's just like a normal restaurant opening." He quietly stepped back to the stove at the Standard Grill in May 2018 and, before departing this week, spent most of his waking hours there.

Those long hours are a different proposition in your 50s than it is in your 20s or 30s, and DiSpirito knew that down to his often-aching bones. When he bent down to get the truffles out of the lowboy, getting up was hard again, and he was still dealing with the last vestiges of the drop foot. Restaurant work is physically and emotionally taxing, and many nights he just wanted to get home and sink onto the couch with his dogs, Captain and Lenny. But he was still strong, he said, and full of the passion that had always driven him.

It comes through in the food, I told him. The scallop and uni in mustard oil and tomato water sent me rocketing back to that lunch at Union Pacific a decade and a half before, and then a cleverly sharp beet tartare snapped me back to the present. I genuinely teared up at an ingenious dairy-free creamed Swiss chard —a dish I'd assumed would be off the menu for me forever, due to my deeply annoying gut-based dietary restrictions. I ate with abandon because I knew DiSpirito had done everything he could to make sure it was as safe as it was sensually glorious, and I settled in against my husband's shoulder in the cab on the way home, thoroughly contented. He'd never gotten to eat at Union Pacific, and I was giddy that I'd gotten to share Rocco's food with him. "Wasn't that just the best?" I asked him, and he wholeheartedly agreed.

When DiSpirito parted ways with the Standard Grill this week, just a few months after that transcendent meal (which I found out via a news story minutes before the plane I was on took off), this time I knew he hadn't disappeared. Because this time, when I landed, there was a text from him apologizing for not telling me sooner, saying he hoped we could talk.

Contracts exist for various reasons, including making paths by which both parties may exit gracefully. But DiSpirito isn't walking away from the industry. Not this time. The past year behind a restaurant stove reignited something inside him, and he knows more than ever that he cannot live without it.

He's tired, having worked 179 days out of the past 180, and he may need a moment to figure out where he's going next—but there is definitely a next. I know it will be worth the wait.

Easy, Peasy, Japanese-y:
Benihana and the Question
of Cultural Appropriation

FROM *Serious Eats*

I LOVE BENIHANA.

It isn't the food that does it for me; it isn't the USDA Choice steak and certainly not the chicken, although I'll admit I'm a sucker for shrimp of any kind, for Benihana's bad dipping sauces, for the mushrooms that are invariably over- and undercooked at the same time. It isn't even the exuberant faux friendliness of the service, even if I get a little thrill of excitement whenever the entire floor staff gathers round to sing happy birthday to a table twice, once in English and another in perfunctory if adequate Japanese.

Even though I'll happily eat a plate of food cut into scat-sized bits or clap along with the staff and their birthday song, and will even, if the spirit calls to me—and it has, frequently—pipe up in Japanese when the time comes, what I love about Benihana is more intangible than the food served or the ambience or the reasonable-for-Manhattan drink prices and specials.

It isn't even the outright wackiness—the flying shrimp tails or the onion volcano or the egg juggling or any of the other cooking acrobatics.

No, it's the bare, brutal honesty of the whole experience. I don't just mean the upselling is as clear as the bland onion soup served with your meal. It's that every restaurant does what Benihana does but more sneakily and less efficiently; it's that Benihana murdered the preciousness of the "chef's table" and cooked it up along with shrimp long before the "chef's table" ever existed; it's that Benihana understands most people don't go out just to eat, just to drink, just for the show; it's that Benihana *knows* most people just want a good time, and it only exists to give it to them quickly—no matter how large your group, no matter how many yelling kids, no matter how many drinks you've had or ordered, you're in and out in less time than it takes to see a movie. *That* is why I admire the man who came up with the concept that Benihana perfected and thereby spawned a legion of copycat "hibachi" Japanese steakhouses all across the world.

Now, I don't usually sit around and think about Benihana and why it's good, although I often sit around and think about why other restaurants I go to are bad. Which is another way of saying I've never found Benihana offensive in the slightest, even though I can't really say I enjoy the food. But social media conspired against my studied complacency about examining the Benihana experience too closely. Ashley Feinberg, a reporter for *Slate*, tweeted out a photo posted by Donald Trump Jr. on his Instagram: a snap of some fried rice shaped into "I <3 U" on a griddle, over which Trump had typed, incomprehensibly, "My culture is not your fried rice 'I love you' with a beating heart sign!!! [crying laughing emoji] #culturalappropriation."

Oh no! Politics! In food! In restaurants even! And even worse I realized it was possible that all along, over the years—even as I laughed and clapped along as countless Benihana cooks scootched a stack of onions spouting steam across what might as well have been the same flattop, a flattop so long it could very well span my 35 years, and said, or yelled, or merely observed as they are obviously required to, "A choo-choo train"—I had been the unwitting accomplice in some form of awful appropriation of my culture, my culture as a half-Japanese person, yes, but more importantly, my culture as a Japanese *American*.

So I decided to go back to Benihana and see for myself.

And, of course, I was disappointed.

Not with the quality of the food, which was not good (as was expected, as was—let's just say it—preferred, the way I prefer Stove Top Stuffing's MSG-powdered garlic flavor over any other stuffing); not with the service, since every server performed Benihana's trademark enthusiastic disinterest admirably; not with the show, of course (no, never with the show).

I was disappointed to fully understand just how un-Japanese the whole Benihana experience is.

Granted, Benihana does serve sushi, but the main attraction, the stuff you order so Benihana cooks can sterilize it mercilessly in front of you, the stuff the place is known for—if it's known for its food at all, that is—isn't Japanese.

I suppose Japanese people eat chicken; they eat shrimp, steak, and lobster; they eat fried rice. But the same could be said of any number of other people—the Chinese, say, or Peruvians.

One might argue that the style of cooking is Japanese, I guess. Not the clacking of utensils, not the volcano onion, and certainly not the flying shrimp, but the bit about cooking meals in front of customers on a griddle. Misono, a restaurant that opened in 1945 in the city of Kobe, claims to have introduced to Japan the idea of cooking things on a cast-iron griddle or steel flattop, which is known in Japanese as *teppanyaki*. The restaurant was primarily popular with Americans stationed there as part of the post–World War II occupation because it sold beef steaks, a food familiar to the occupiers' palates, and—surprise!—it continues to be popular with American tourists today, presumably for the very same reason.

Of course, Misono cannot claim to have invented the griddle, which is almost as old as fire, and the idea that cooking steaks for the occupying American forces constituted the creation of a distinct style of Japanese cuisine seems absurd on its face. Also, to get a bit more technical about it, teppanyaki is not typically placed in the category of *yoshoku*, or Western-influenced Japanese food, like tempura, say, or tonkatsu. Yoshoku dates to the Meiji era, when Japan actively sought to westernize its culture after hundreds of years of self-imposed and rigorously enforced isolation, which eventually led the country to decide to conquer half the globe in the most brutal way imaginable.

All of which is to say, the style of cooking is not very Japanese to begin with.

And so, after my meal, as I walked to the subway, I was left wondering why it is that anyone, anywhere, thinks of Benihana or any of the imitation hibachi* restaurants as Japanese.

---

* A hibachi is not a flattop upon which one cooks badly. It is a kind of rustic hearth

*

Obviously, it has to do with the fact that Benihana's founder, Hiroaki "Rocky" Aoki, who died in 2008, was Japanese.

He was a "character," a person about whom people say "he was larger than life," whatever that means. And although over the course of his life he did many, many things other than run Benihana—he raced boats, he flew a hot-air balloon across an ocean, he published a soft-core porno mag, he served time for insider trading—Aoki was never an ambassador of Japanese culture, as his obituary in the *New York Times* claims.

You can see this in his biography, *Mr. Benihana: The Rocky Aoki Story* by Takahashi Miyuki, which, fittingly, is now only available as a manga. You can also see this in *Making It in America: The Life and Times of Rocky Aoki, Benihana's Pioneer,* by Jack McCallum, a bit of corporate hagiography commissioned by the company (the 1985 copyright is owned by Benihana of Tokyo, Inc.). Aoki famously told a *Times* reporter, "The minute I forgot I was Japanese, success began," and both books reinforce the idea that Aoki possessed qualities that were atypical of Japanese people—he had personality, he valued individuality—and his very un-Japaneseness is what made him successful in America.[†]

As the books have it, Aoki tried to set Benihana apart from other Japanese restaurants in the same way he sought to stand apart from his compatriots: by sheer force of personality. And so the restaurant chain offers up the odd case of a Japanese businessman who gave the American dining public what he thought they wanted—steak, chicken, shrimp; no "icky, slimy things," as McCallum quotes him—in an environment that was purposely designed to look exaggeratedly Japanese—the original Benihana's interior was outfitted to look like a *gassho zukuri,* or a farmhouse built in a traditional Japanese style—using a campy cooking performance that Aoki created from whole cloth. Benihana was successful because Aoki designed it to appeal to Americans, much as he molded his own personality, even though it looked Japanese.

---

or a charcoal grill, which is also known by the name Ariana Grande mistakenly got tattooed on her hand: *shichirin.*

† I can't help but note the McCallum book does this by leaning heavily on racial stereotypes. "Conditioned to fight through the wall of Asian reticence, Americans meeting Rocky for the first time instead find a smiling, warm open-door of a man," McCallum writes, for example.

It doesn't seem possible to accuse Aoki of appropriating his own culture, although on my most recent visit it occurred to me that the company today might still have to answer for the decor. My memories of Benihana are all stainless steel and bright lights and red and black uniforms, none of which particularly shout "Japan!" to me, but when I went back to Benihana's Manhattan flagship location, I saw, as if for the first time—maybe actually for the first time—that some tables are bracketed by little raised rock gardens in which wan bonsai trees have been imprisoned; there are lines of decorative ceramic plates along some walls; and there is one of the ugliest *maneki nekos* I have ever seen, designed by someone who apparently believed good luck could be scared into attendance.

These nods to Japanese-*ness* are all the more odd when you consider the corporate branding on the menu and its studied aversion to the word "Japanese," which only appears on the drinks menu. Although, upon consideration, that might just be a case of honest description: the only actually Japanese products on the menu are the sakes, the spirits, the soft drinks, and a small selection of beer.

It doesn't seem like Benihana needs the aura of being Japanese anymore—being Japanese is entirely ancillary to its product—and it seems like the corporation understands this, given how subdued the Japanese theme is in its branding. And yet it still holds on to a simulacrum of Japanese-ness, one that is just odd enough to provoke a trolling response from people like Donald Trump Jr., and might open up the restaurant chain to accusations of cultural appropriation, no matter how specious.

Since Benihana doesn't seem to me to actually be guilty of appropriating Japanese culture, what I find more interesting is how the chain clings to the faux-Japanese stuff, and what that says about the way Japanese culture is viewed by many American diners.

When Aoki opened the first Benihana, the Japanese and their culture were largely viewed as a punchline in the United States. The animosity displayed toward Japanese and Japanese Americans during the World War II era, best exemplified by the placement of about 120,000 Japanese Americans and Japanese immigrants in concentration camps, had given way to a view of Japan as a country that primarily made goods of substandard quality for export. In

McCallum's book, Tad Suga, a Japanese American friend of Aoki's, recalls how "it must be made in Japan" was a punchline for one of famed comedian Danny Kaye's bits. The 1985 movie *Back to the Future* has a similar gag: When Marty McFly travels back in time to 1955, Doc Brown says of some malfunctioning bit of equipment that it must've been made in Japan, to which Marty from 1985 responds with a quizzical look. The dramatic irony of the moment, of course, is that the 1985 audience, like Marty, associated Japan with technological marvels like the Sony Walkman.

Aoki's desire to stand apart from the American stereotypes of Japanese businessmen is entirely understandable, in the same way that it's understandable that he sought to differentiate his restaurant from other Japanese restaurants: the difference was the selling point. But over the decades during which Benihana became a global chain, the image of Japan evolved further, transforming from a purveyor of substandard goods to the epicenter of both state-of-the-art technology and a kind of ruthless business acumen as evinced by companies like Sony and Toyota, which seemed to be on a path to achieve global dominance. And now, even as Japan's rising star has ceded its place to China and South Korea, it still retains a positive, almost beatific glow in the American imagination.

The transformation of the popular conception of Japanese culture in this country from the World War II era to the present is entirely unique. Japan was once an enemy so menacing that the federal government believed it was necessary to imprison its emigrants in concentration camps; now it exists as a kind of benign oddity in the American mind. Today, the Japanese are widely known for their food, their cleanliness, their attention to detail, their customer service, and their comics and cartoons, which serve to reinforce the image of Japan as a pleasant, albeit weird, place populated with correspondingly weird and pleasant people—a caricature that is about two parts Marie Kondo, one part Jiro Ono, and one part Haruki Murakami.

This caricature is relentlessly reinforced by the country's admirers in the Western press. We are told by people like Noah Smith, an opinion columnist for Bloomberg, that the Japanese are just so positive or, as in a *New Yorker* article by the Tokyo-based writer and translator Matt Alt, that we Americans would do well to emulate them, despite regular news reports about the society's deeply ingrained misogyny, exploitative work culture, and the rampant xenophobia that finds its expression in its suicidally exclusionary immigration policies, which is why it's held up as an exemplar by ethnonationalists the world over. And let's not forget the jingoism evident in the pilgrimages and tributes sent by Japanese heads of state to a shrine dedicated to the few token war criminals prosecuted in the aftermath of World War II, which justifiably enrages Japan's neighbors.

All of which is to say, Japan is a complicated country with a troubled culture, but for most Americans, it's merely the source of products that they're willing to pay a premium to possess, not because they are technologically more advanced or qualitatively better, but because they have a certain aesthetic, whether it's animated cartoons, middle-brow fiction, or scented oil dispensers guaranteed to spark joy for years to come.

Nowhere is this tendency to overvalue Japanese-ness more evident than in restaurant culture, which is why it would be silly for Benihana to ditch any references to its legitimately Japanese origin, even if it doesn't need them. Japanese stuff sells, and it would be malpractice for any restaurateur not to take advantage of the fact that many Americans are more willing to spend money on "small plates" at an *"izakaya"* than on bar food at a restaurant and bar. To illustrate this point, let us turn to another global chain of restaurants that has distinctly Japanese branding but sells pretty un-Japanese stuff: David Chang's Momofuku Group.

When the group opened one of its newer restaurants, Majordomo, in Los Angeles, the fruit plate on the menu raised some eyebrows. Chang had famously criticized California restaurants for similarly stripped-down dishes, and the new dessert item seemed to be a retreat from his previous position. But what caught my eye as I read the little news item in *Eater* about the fruit plate was the following lines: "The first night the restaurant ran the fruit plate, only one sold. But then [chef de cuisine Marc] Johnson decided to freeze the grapes and make the dish look more Japanese. In its current iteration, it looks like the fruits served at the end of a *kaiseki* menu and is also reminiscent of the ceremonial fruits on display at specialty vendors. It's selling better now."

One could argue this is an example of Chang—a Korean American—and his colleagues appropriating Japanese culture, but in my view that would be wrong. Chang, like Aoki, is only giving the American dining public what it wants. And what most Americans want is the elements of Japanese culture that they like—the nice-looking things; the tender, palatable foods; the weird stuff, but nothing icky or slimy. What most Americans want isn't Japanese: what they want is Japanese-y.

It's Not Always Easy to Be Jamie Oliver

FROM *The New York Times*

JUST BEFORE LUNCH on a recent Monday, Jamie Oliver wrapped an apron around his dad bod and started mashing mint and broad beans with a mortar and pestle, which has long been his favorite kitchen tool.

That adorable mop of hair he had 20 years ago when he slid down a banister and splashed into popular food culture as the Naked Chef is cropped now. At 44, Mr. Oliver comes off more like a pleasant, world-weary high school teacher than the arrogant jokey bloke everyone wanted to hang around with back when he blew up food TV.

And are those bags under his blue eyes?

"Sorry, darling," he said as he seasoned a fillet of Dover sole. "I'm a bit tired."

The day started before 6:00 a.m. He dropped the kids at school, then made his way to the refurbished North London warehouse that serves as his headquarters. After feeding a reporter lunch, he had to meet top officials from Liverpool, Manchester, Birmingham, and London who were coming by the office to hammer out a plan to halve childhood obesity rates by 2030.

It didn't help that he and his wife, Juliette, who goes by Jools, had exhausted themselves over the weekend moving into a $7.2 million 16th-century Tudor mansion not far from his parents' pub in Essex. (They're keeping the eight-bedroom North London townhouse.)

Granted, that kind of move is a little different from asking your friends to help you muscle a mattress into a studio walk-up. Still, moving is moving, especially with five children, including a fever-ish three-year-old who spent the night "jumping around me like a rattlesnake," Mr. Oliver said.

It wasn't just a bad night's sleep, a new house, and a packed day that weighed on him. "I have probably been pushed to the edge of my capacity over the last four years," he said.

In May, the Jamie Oliver Restaurant Group went into adminis-tration, a form of bankruptcy protection. The company, accord-ing to some accounts, owed creditors nearly 83 million pounds, or about $100 million. Mr. Oliver said he tried his hardest to keep the business alive. But after closing some restaurants, injecting the equivalent of more than $15 million of his own money into the company and searching for a new investor, he gave up. In all, he shuttered or sold 25 restaurants, putting more than 1,000 people out of work.

Closing his first restaurant, the fashionable Fifteen in London, hurt the most. He had opened it in 2002 to train unemployed young people, many from difficult backgrounds, how to prepare tasting menus, make fresh pasta, and run a proper dining room.

"That was the hardest thing I've ever had to do," he said of the closing. "Just terrible. Awful."

It would be easy to see a touch of Icarus in Mr. Oliver, or to view his saga as some sort of life lesson from an overachiever. But it's too soon for deep reflection, and that's not really his strong suit.

Mr. Oliver is, by most accounts, an optimist and, by his own account, what the Brits call a grafter—someone who just puts his head down and works, whatever the circumstance. That's what has gotten him this far.

"I always graft it," he said. "I put the effort in."

Mr. Oliver learned that hustle early, growing up in the Cricketers, the pub his parents still own in the village of Clavering. "I was ducking. I was diving. I was washing cars, washing toilets," he re-called.

He was a lousy student, but he knew his way around a kitchen, so he went to culinary school. He was a sous-chef at the River Café in London when a BBC crew showed up to shoot a documentary. A smart producer saw how much the camera loved him.

The Naked Chef debuted in 1999 on BBC Two in Britain, and a year later on Food Network in the United States. The camera work was shaky, and his style kinetic. Mr. Oliver froze up when speaking directly to the camera, so producers hung just off to the side and asked him questions.

By current digital standards, the show looks like something your brother the aspirational cook might shoot on his iPhone. But back then, it felt fresh, unscripted and sexy. Mr. Oliver whipped around town on a motor scooter (which now sits in front of his headquarters) and slid down a spiral banister to let friends into his East End flat to help him cook.

He stuck his fingers into limes and lamb, and tossed every salad with his hands. He ushered a generation of young men into the kitchen, and taught them expressions like "pukka" (excellent) and "lovely jubbly" (also excellent).

Mr. Oliver secured an endorsement deal with Sainsbury's, the second-largest supermarket chain in Britain, that would last 11 years and earn him close to $12 million. He wrote a best-selling cookbook. It was a lot for someone in his early 20s.

In 2008 he opened his first Jamie's Italian restaurant with help from his mentor, the Italian chef Gennaro Contaldo. The idea was to disrupt midmarket dining. The meat had an animal-welfare pedigree. Butter was organic. Wages were decent and prices affordable.

The restaurants were packed from the get-go. He started other chains, including Barbecoa, a pair of upscale steak and barbecue restaurants, in partnership with the American chef Adam Perry Lang. At his peak, Mr. Oliver served 7.5 million meals a year and employed 4,500 people.

It's rarely one thing that brings a big enterprise down, and Mr. Oliver was battling several dragons at once. Taxes and the cost of ingredients he favored went up. So did rent, especially in fast-gentrifying neighborhoods. But he kept expanding, sometimes into neighborhoods without enough traffic.

Casual dining had become a lucrative draw for investors, and the market flooded with competitors. People started using delivery apps instead of eating out. After the United Kingdom voted to leave the European Union in 2016, the value of the pound fell.

Retail spending plummeted. Critics began to complain about his restaurants' food and service.

Things were no longer looking so pukka.

"If you're not bendy like this pasta, then you break," he said as rolled out sheets for the ravioli he was stuffing for lunch. "And that's what happened."

Friends wondered if he was spread too thin, or not paying enough attention. Others suggested he shouldn't have hired his brother-in-law, Paul Hunt, a flamboyant former stock trader, as the chief executive. (Mr. Oliver said he needed to put someone he trusted in charge.)

Or, perhaps, he simply is not as good at business as he is at cooking and campaigning to help children eat healthier.

"Probably I was too trusting, which is one of my problems and also one of my benefits," said Mr. Oliver, who estimated that he screws up about 40 percent of his business ventures.

"There's no way to sugarcoat it," he said. "I thought I could fix it, but I couldn't. I can absolutely look at myself in the mirror knowing I tried everything to the last very minute. We ran out of money. It's as simple as that."

Although he still has plenty of fans, there are, and always have been, detractors. They deride his accent as "mockney," and hold him responsible for new school-lunch rules that banished foods like Turkey Twizzlers (essentially meat curly fries). They call him a hypocrite for his $6 million deal to sell healthy-ish Oliver-branded food at Shell gas stations despite his crusade against climate change.

When his empire collapsed, the tabloids were particularly brutal.

"There is something in the British psyche that sort of quite enjoys the discomfiture of successful people," said the food writer Nigella Lawson. "You get laughed at in this country for wanting the world to be a better place."

It is hard, she said, for someone who attained so much fame so young to navigate the business world. "It's nice to have some good things said about him because he's had such a hard time lately," she said. "I have no doubt he will turn it around."

In many ways, Mr. Oliver is relieved to be out of the restaurant business. His empire is smaller now, with about 120 employees. He spends most of his day doing the things he loves: cooking, talking about cooking, producing content about cooking, and trying to make the world a healthier place to eat.

Mr. Oliver's other ventures still make plenty of money. He has sold a lifetime total of 27 million pieces of Tefal cookware, and it's easy to find his kitchen gadgets on Amazon. He recently signed a deal to become the health ambassador for Tesco, Britain's largest grocery chain.

Mr. Oliver's preternatural ability to connect with an audience has helped him make the leap to digital content while other food media stars from his litter have struggled to fit content made for television onto platforms like YouTube.

He mostly stays off Twitter—"it's not a platform that makes me a happier person"—but he crushes Instagram, where he has 7.3 million followers. His YouTube channel, Jamie Oliver's Food Tube, has 4.4 million subscribers. His average monthly social media reach is more than 30 million followers, and his global TV audience is 67 million, said Saskia Wirth, head of communications for the Jamie Oliver Group.

Matt Duckor, vice president of video programming for *Bon Appétit*, says Mr. Oliver has a natural appeal that crosses generations.

"People eighteen to thirty-four know who he is, and people over fifty know who he is. That's very rare," Mr. Duckor said. "In a way, there is this nostalgia play to it, but there is this sense that this guy is closer to the ground and closer to reality than a lot of his contemporaries."

That's one reason *Bon Appétit* focused on Mr. Oliver's Insanity Burger in a segment of its new online series, *Reverse Engineering*. Chris Morocco, an editor with exceptional tasting skills, is blindfolded and must identify a dish only through taste, touch, and smell, then try to re-create it. The 25-minute video featuring Mr. Oliver's burger has been viewed 2.3 million times.

Books, however, remain the engine of the Oliver machine: He has sold more than 45 million of them—$7.4 million worth just last year, according to Nielsen Book Research—and is the country's best-selling nonfiction author. For a time, only J. K. Rowling outsold him.

Mr. Oliver, who has dyslexia and what he says is an unusually short attention span, likes to dictate his books rather than type them. His topics swing with the times. He has veered from comfort foods to superfoods. He has produced 30-minute meals and

15-minute meals and five-ingredient meals. He has written recipes
for squash mac and cheese for a family cookbook and, in 2018,
interpreted dishes he learned from Italian *nonnas*.

His latest is *Veg: Easy & Delicious Meals for Everyone*. An edition
for the American market (retitled *Ultimate Veg*) will come out in
January.

He brushes off criticism that his books are derivative. "No one
has a copyright on five ingredients or thirty-minute meals," he said.

He can be just as riled by people who accuse him of cultural appropriation for the way he adapts recipes. He has taken flak from
Spaniards for putting chorizo in paella; from Jamaicans for spicing
microwaveable, packaged rice with ginger and jalapeños and calling it Punchy Jerk Rice; and from West Africans for using parsley
and a lemon wedge in jollof.

"I like parsley, and if I want to put it in my jollof, I will," he said.
"No one's invented nothing unless they've invented sun and rain,
and they ain't."

Dishes evolve, impacted by trade, war, famine, and a hundred
other forces, he said. "You've got the Brits getting passionate about
fish-and-chips right now, then they get really upset when you say,
'You know it's a Portuguese Jewish dish in the first place,'" he said.
"If you want to get back to really original British cooking, it's this-
tle and cabbage."

Through all the turmoil, his marriage has stayed solid, he said.
The couple plan to renew their vows on their 20th anniversary
next June. Mr. Oliver still wears the necklace Jools gave him early
in their relationship that reads I LOVE YOU ALWAYS, and he writes
her love notes on paper towels.

She is pushing for a sixth child, although he's not so sure. Not
that he doesn't love being a father. He calls himself "an exceptional under-eleven-year-old dad" but perhaps only an "above average teenager dad."

"Apparently, I'm a bit barky," he said.

"I didn't know how it felt to get achievement in education, but I
knew how it felt to have tired feet and blistered hands from working," he added. "So this means I am completely unprepared for
two teenage girls that do care about learning and who do try at
school."

His oldest, Poppy, will be the first Oliver to attend college. "This," he said, "is a big moment for us."

And then there is the mission. Next to his family, doing his part to fix the food system matters to him the most. His list of campaigns, which he has waged with television shows and documentaries and all manner of political pressure, is long. Among them are improving school food, bettering conditions for chickens, reducing food waste, helping to pass a tax on sugary drinks, and his latest, curtailing ads for fatty, sugary foods aimed at children.

His Ministry of Food, an eight-week community cooking course now in its 11th year, has trained nearly 100,000 people to prepare healthier food. His new North Star is the 2030 Project, an effort to coordinate health and governmental organizations in a campaign to halve childhood obesity by 2030, and it's hard for him to stop talking about it.

That's why the gaggle of government officials who shuffled by the test kitchen an hour earlier were still waiting for him to finish up lunch. He waved off his communications director, who had been gently trying to cut him off. He had a few last points to make.

"If I'm being reflective, I've had the best and the worst of it," he said. "I've learned a lot. I smell differently now. I see differently now. It doesn't mean I'm cynical. I still feel I have twenty years of good work ahead of me, but I don't have an appetite to sort of see my name all over the globe in restaurants."

He just wants people to be able to eat better, no matter what their economic situation. And who better to take on such an impossible task?

"You don't want someone who's had success after success after success," he said. "You want someone like me."

New Coke Didn't Fail.
It Was Murdered.

FROM *Mother Jones*

IN LATE MAY, Coca-Cola announced it would produce 50,000 cans of New Coke as part of a promotional campaign linked to the third season of Netflix's *Stranger Things*, which takes place in 1985, the same year the fizzy reboot made its short-lived debut. The new drink makes repeated cameos throughout the latest run, leading to a brief discussion of its qualities during an otherwise tense scene in episode 7.

"It's delicious," Lucas says, taking a long slurp. Five other kids stare at him in horror.

This is a fair representation of the prevailing literature on New Coke. For more than three decades, New Coke has been held up as the bad idea by which all other bad ideas are measured. Do a quick Google search for "the worst idea since New Coke" and you'll find an encyclopedia of face-palms. *Handmaid's Tale*–themed pinot noir. Mint-chocolate toothpaste. *Indiana Jones and the Kingdom of the Crystal Skull*. No one seems to dispute its shortcomings, least of all the people who ushered New Coke into the world. On the 10th anniversary of the drink's introduction, the company's CEO, Roberto Goizueta, told employees, sounding more than a bit like Churchill after Dunkirk, that what happened was "a blunder and a disaster, and it will forever be." People speak with less moral clarity about war crimes.

The popular version goes like this: In the early 1980s, not content with producing the world's most recognizable beverage, greedy executives tweaked the recipe for the first time in 94 years.

They redesigned the can, launched a massive marketing blitz, and promised a better taste. But Americans wouldn't stand for it. In the face of a nationwide backlash, the company brought back the old formula—now dubbed Coke Classic—after two months. The story of New Coke is eternal. It's a parable of hubris.

It's also a lie.

Far from the dud it's been made out to be, New Coke was actually delicious—or at least, most people who tried it thought so. Some of its harshest critics couldn't even taste a difference. It was done in by a complicated web of interests, a mixture of cranks and opportunists—a sugar-starved mob of pitchfork-clutching Andy Rooneys, powered by the thrill of rebellion and an aggrieved sense of dispossession. At its most fundamental level, the backlash wasn't about New Coke at all. It was a revolt against the idea of change. That story should sound familiar. We're still living it.

There's one big thing you have to understand about the New Coke rollout: If people actually *liked* old Coke as much as they later claimed, the new version never would have existed. But in the early 1980s the company's fortunes were sagging. Soft drink sales were down across the board, but Coke was losing ground to the smoother, sweeter Pepsi. Coke was still doing well in places with a captive market, like restaurants or concessionaires, but at stores —where consumers had a choice—sales were dropping in a way that Pepsi's weren't.

Coca-Cola had been slow to adapt to changing preferences in the past. Diet Pepsi premiered in 1964, but it was another 18 years before Diet Coke debuted. In the meantime, the company offered sugar-free Tab, which carried a warning label informing drinkers that it was linked to bladder cancer in rats. Drink up! The journalist Bartow Elmore's *Citizen Coke* speculates that the Reagan administration's escalating drug war may have added a level of urgency to the company's long-range planning by threatening Peruvian coca production.

So when researchers in Atlanta, in the process of belatedly developing Diet Coke in 1980, stumbled on a new formula, Goizueta and his fellow execs decided to study it. By late 1984, they'd decided to move ahead with a switch, and formed a small team to war-game the launch. They named their plan Project Kansas (an earlier iteration was dubbed Tampa) and drew inspiration from

Dwight D. Eisenhower's plans for the invasion of Normandy. That
sounds made-up but it's not. The Project Kansas documents are
displayed behind a glass case at the World of Coca-Cola museum
in Atlanta. Here's a sample:

> In its size, scope and boldness, it is not unlike the Allied invasion of
> Europe in 1944. This is not just another product improvement, not just
> a repositioning or new product introduction. Kansas, quite simply, can
> not, must not fail.
>
> As in the planning of a major military operation, it is necessary to
> understand the risks clearly, to plan contingencies, to build in the mo-
> bility to deal with those risks as they arise to confront the operation at
> various stages. In a meeting of the Core Strategy Group in Fort Lauder-
> dale earlier this month, we took a look at the lessons to be learned from
> the 1944 Allied invasion, "Operation Overlord."
>
> The invasion led to a total Allied victory in less than a year. It was
> a broad strategic thrust that marshalled the ultimate resources of the
> allies to totally upset the strategic balance then existing. Its success
> changed the character of the war. If it had failed, the course of the war,
> if not its eventual outcome, would have been drastically altered.
>
> It was a bold, decisive gamble; so bold and risky a roll of the dice that
> Winston Churchill persisted for two years in attempting to delay and
> divert the plan.

I mean, these are just insane things to say about a soft drink
—Eisenhower, D-Day, things of that nature. But the point is, they
didn't just wake up one day and decide to change the formula.
They obsessed over every detail, in mortal fear of failure, until everything was in order. In the document on display at World of Coca-
Cola, someone has gone and underlined Churchill's name by
hand, as if to say, *Remember this, this is important, it will be on the test.*
So why did they lose to the Germans?
At first, the mission showed promise. After months of secrecy
—including fake leaks to throw reporters off—Coke announced
its plans at Lincoln Center in New York City in late April 1985.
The company had spent years testing the product, and the results
to them seemed overwhelming. The new soda consistently beat
out the old version across the country—even in Coca-Cola's ances-
tral base, the South, where New Coke held a narrow 52–48 edge.
When southern testers were told the identities of the two samples,
the popularity of New Coke jumped nine points. One bottler be-

lieved so strongly in the product that he threatened to sue the
company if New Coke *wasn't* released.

For the first few weeks, things were going well. New Coke won
newspaper taste tests in Rochester, New York, and in Anniston, Alabama. Baseball fans in San Francisco liked it. Sales were up in
Miami and Detroit. The *London Observer*'s panel of children preferred the new stuff to the old stuff, too. The company's weekly
telephone surveys of 900 consumers consistently indicated high
favorability. Even people who preferred the old soda seemed okay
with the switch. New Coke was good! At worst, New Coke was *fine*.

"Change," a triumphant Coke executive declared, "is something
the American people identify with."

A beverage's broad popularity, though, is not a very interesting
story. Dissent makes a good story. People expressing strongly held
and borderline pathological opinions about soft drinks makes a
good story. And it didn't take long for reporters to start finding
them.

In Wisconsin, the *Wausau Daily Herald* reported on the trials of a
man named Andy Gribble. "So much of my life is changing outside
of my control," he told the paper. "Now Coke, the one thing left
from my childhood, has been changed." He was 19.

In San Antonio, the *Atlanta Journal-Constitution* (and the *Chicago
Tribune*, and the *New York Times*) found a man named Dan Lauck
who brought his own coolers full of soda with him to restaurants
and drank five cases of old Coke a week—6.5-ounce glass bottles
only, never cans. Lauck called New Coke's debut "the blackest day
of my life."

"From now on my life will be divided into BC and AC—before
the change in Coke and after the change," he told the *AJC*. "I hon-
estly don't know what I'm going to do."

In Seattle, a real estate speculator named Gay Mullins formed
a group called Old Cola Drinkers of America and set up a hotline
where people could call to voice their complaints.

"They have taken away my freedom of choice," he told *People*.
"It's un-American!"

Former Coke CEO Neville Isdell writes in his memoir, *Inside
Coca-Cola*, "You could feel the tension at headquarters, which was
fielding similar complaints, even from bottlers who said they were
ostracized at their hometown country clubs." And since when

has a country club discriminated against something for no good reason!

In some other context, these people would have been politely brushed aside, or at least some gentle soul might have introduced them to seltzer. But if, for a brief window in 1985, your sense of self was inextricably linked to soda consumption, if you were the kind of belligerent oddball who would tell someone at an airport, "You've ruined my life," because his luggage bore the emblem of the soda company that had betrayed you—this actually happened to Isdell—newspapers treated you like the Oracle of Delphi.

It's not hard to see in retrospect why people began to pile on. It's *fun* to be cranky about stupid things. It's almost the entire point of Twitter. But there was something else going on here. The critiques often weren't really about soda at all.

Thomas Oliver's 1986 book, *The Real Coke, The Real Story,* which is the definitive look at this saga, saw a strain of southern reactionary politics in the backlash. "To them it was an extension of the Civil War," he argues. "Here was Coca-Cola, a southern company, laying down its arms in deference to its Yankee counterpart." Oliver means Pepsi, headquartered in Purchase, New York. He continues, "Coke, the quintessential southern drink, was changing its image and content to conform with the rivals in the North."

That's a little overwrought, but read the clippings and you realize he's getting at something. "Changing Coca-Cola is an intrusion on tradition, and a lot of southerners won't like it, regardless of how it tastes," a University of Mississippi professor told the *Chicago Tribune* in 1985. "Why'd they announce it in New York?" wondered an Alabaman in the same story. It was another act of northern aggression—a war between the tastes.

Early on in the saga, the *Journal-Constitution* conducted its own taste test at the Varsity, a venerable Atlanta drive-in, and reported that 45 of the 72 participants preferred the old stuff. Turns out people at the nostalgia factory love nostalgia! A quote from the restaurant's co-owner sticks out because we've heard it before: "Why didn't they test anybody here?"

These were the forgotten people, or so they wanted you to believe. They were sick of other people defining the pace and texture of change. In that respect, Coca-Cola was grappling with a monster of its own making, because it had spent tens of millions of dollars wrapping the corporation's identity around this particular kind of small-*c* conservatism—an idyll of small towns and wholesome values, where all the women are strong, all the men are good-looking, and all the kids have high blood sugar. In the early 1980s it had rejected a proposal to make Michael Jackson a Coke pitchman, because, Oliver reported, he didn't fit the company's "All-American" image. He went to Pepsi instead.

You don't have to listen to me speculate about what the New Coke backlash was really about, because the critics often came out and told you.

A New Jersey newspaper lamented that Coke was "catering to pantywaists" by abandoning its "macho" bite.

"Creeping yuppification, that's what it is," wrote syndicated columnist Mark Russell, echoing a common generational refrain. "Have a sweeter Coca-Cola with your green pasta, top it off with a frozen tofu cone, then put on a video and do your aerobics to a modem of synthesized quadri-sound."

One Alabama newspaper columnist hinted at a foreign, possibly Communist, influence behind the whole project:

> I've had an uneasy feeling about Coca-Cola ever since a fellow by the name of Roberto Goizueta was named chairman and chief executive officer of the Coca-Cola Company of Atlanta, Ga., US of A.
>
> Roberto Goizueta, if memory serves me correctly, is from Havana, Cuba.
>
> Imagine that . . .

At least some things hadn't changed. Andy Rooney, the professionally cranky *60 Minutes* personality, panned the new drink before he even tried it. "I've been very upset with the Coke people ever since they decided to phase out that great little green, hourglass-shaped bottle," he wrote. Yeah, Andy, we know.

All wayward causes have their false prophets. The Stephen the Shepherd Boy of the New Coke backlash was Mullins, the Seattle retiree who told reporters he'd been preparing to move to Costa Rica before Coke forced him to stay at home and live out his *Red Dawn* fantasy.

"The Declaration of Independence and the Revolutionary War occurred because of taxation without representation; there was no freedom of choice," he explained. "We went to war [in Europe] to help England, because another country was impinging on their freedom of choice. I feel that this is a battle of that magnitude."

If you're keeping score here, both camps have now compared their struggle to D-Day. But the statement is clarifying as to the nature of the fight. Mullins's major gripe wasn't about taste; it was about, as he put it, "the very fabric of America."

Run out of a rented office in a downtown hotel, Old Cola Drinkers of America boasted of having 100,000 members. For $10, supporters could purchase "war kits" that included anti–New Coke bumper stickers. Mullins was a ubiquitous figure in the press, though estimates of how much of his own money he poured into the venture seemed to keep rising—it was $40,000, then it was $80,000, then it was $100,000.

Whatever the actual figure was, the Old Cola Drinkers were loud. They held protests, set up local chapters, and flooded Coca-Cola's own hotline with complaints. Mullins and his followers filed a class action lawsuit to try to force Coke to abandon its new formula. It didn't go anywhere, but that wasn't really the point. The company had no good response to what Mullins's guerrilla army was doing, and once Coke understood *why,* the war was over.

"We could have introduced the elixir of the gods" as New Coke, one executive said later, "and it wouldn't have made any difference."

Two months after New Coke launched, the company formally surrendered to Mullins. After announcing plans to bring back the old version, they added that they were sending the very first case to Mullins—this one guy in Seattle—via special delivery from Atlanta to a bottling facility in Washington State. The next day, newspapers across the country splashed Mullins on their front pages. He's still wearing his anti-Coke T-shirt, baptized in the liquid from the bottles he'd stockpiled.

Americans, he said, had reclaimed "our heritage."

Coca-Cola dubbed the product it reintroduced in July 1985 Coke Classic, but it wasn't quite the recipe everyone at the Varsity was drinking in the '40s. That version was made with cane sugar. Coke Classic—the new old Coke, or was it the old New Coke?—was made with high-fructose corn syrup instead. Eager to press the advantage won by Mullins and his pals, the sugar industry launched a new campaign arguing that the new old Coke was still not "the real thing." And that was how America would come to learn something significant about the man whose rebellion, more than anything else, brought down a soda giant: he didn't even *like* Coke.

After the dousing ceremony, Mullins hardly took a break. At the end of July, he held a press conference to announce his next crusade. He would not rest until Coke was once more made with real sugar. Coke Classic had made him sick, he reported. He felt ill after drinking only two rum and Cokes.

A few days later, a group of sugar-industry reps from Hawaii, where the product was still made with sugar, invited reporters to watch them ship an eight-pack of old Coca-Cola to Mullins—bottles, of course—to encourage him to keep up his attack. "We wish you well in your crusade," they said. "One man has made a difference."

Within a few weeks—August 15—the Sugar Association, the Washington, DC–based lobbying shop for the beet- and cane-sugar industry, took out full-page ads in national newspapers echoing Mullins's complaints:

> The "Old Cola Drinkers of America" is an organization that monitors consumer responses to soft drinks and other products. At a July 31 press conference, they turned their noses up at "Classic Coke" because it is sweetened with a cheaper sweetener—corn syrup—instead of sugar.
>
> "It is not the original formula; it is not the Coke of my youth," OCDA leader, Gay Mullins said at the time.
>
> They were right. For 94 years Coca-Cola was in fact "The Real Thing" —a classic sweetened with real sugar—an unvarying taste standard known and trusted the world over. But five years ago, Coca-Cola quietly began to change its formula.

But wait a second. What was that last part? Coca-Cola had actually changed its formula *five years earlier?*

The real story slowly emerged. The *Detroit Free Press* put two and two together and asked Mullins why he had not previously mentioned, during his two-month campaign to bring back old Coke, that the stuff made him physically ill. Mullins said he thought at first the problem was with his own body, but he'd since come to understand that it was actually the beverage. He also blamed the switch for his inability to taste the difference between New Coke and regular Coke in a nationally televised taste test: drinking Coke had killed his taste buds.

When Oliver, the author of *The Real Coke, The Real Story*, started digging around, the rest of Mullins's story started to unravel. Old Cola Drinkers of America didn't start off as a populist campaign. It was a hustle, plain and simple. Its founder hoped to sow conflict and cash in on it by getting either Coca-Cola or Pepsi to buy him out. It was an astroturf operation—or at least it would have been if either company had ponied up. After Coke Classic was reintroduced, Mullins even asked Coca-Cola to pay him $200,000 for an endorsement. (The company declined.)

His pivot to high-fructose agitation wasn't exactly disinterested either. Mullins hoped that by joining the pile-on, he might entice the trade association to cut him in on some profits.

"We were interested in being supported by the Sugar Association," he admitted to Oliver.

When the money he was hoping would come in from Big Sugar never materialized, he canceled a planned protest in Atlanta. The organization's anti-Coke activism slowly faded. Membership in the group fell by 90 percent after New Coke was killed off, and the sugar-versus-corn fight would be fought in the suites, not the streets. But Mullins made one last run of headlines before he and his group faded from view.

"Coke isn't it anymore, not for Gay Mullins," the *Rochester Democrat and Chronicle* reported.

"He's hooked on Jolt Cola."

There's a whole body of research related to taste testing that later writers have used to try to explain away the New Coke fiasco. Malcolm Gladwell, who wrote about New Coke in his book *Blink*, points to studies showing that taste tests have a bias toward sweeter beverages. This helps explain why Pepsi (generally considered sweeter) based its whole ad campaign around taste tests, and why the New Coke tests led the company astray. People liked the first sip more, but maybe not the last hundred. This is a comforting explanation: *It was actually a bad soda and here's the science that proves it.* By playing the first-sip game, Coca-Cola was essentially conceding the point to its opponent. As one Pepsi ad put it, "The other guy blinked."

But many people really do prefer Pepsi, even after that all-important first taste. And the post-rollout company surveys of people who had finished their cans found a favorability for New Coke that matched the first-sip test. Maybe the sweet drink winning the sweet-drink contest doesn't need too many caveats. Soft drink trends have also proven Coke right about a willingness to adapt to new tastes: a majority of Coke sales today are non-Classic products, such as Diet and Coke Zero. Interestingly, people who have sampled New Coke in recent weeks, at places like *BuzzFeed* and *Food & Wine,* have given the beverage high marks because it reminds them of Diet Coke—it tasted weird then; it tastes like what's normal *now.*

Coke executives, in their D-Day planning, always expected a small but vocal faction of Never Cokers. What they miscalculated was the effect that those people would have on neutrals. Nine out of ten Coke drinkers might have no problem with the change if you asked them individually. But put them in a room, and then put Andy Rooney in that room, and suddenly four of them are banging their fists on the table and talking about glass bottles. That's how social influence works. It's how containable brush fires become a blowup.

And Coke certainly didn't count on the backlash linking up with larger currents of grievance in American life. Listen again to the words people used to describe how they felt—"heritage," "freedom," "tradition," "American," "Yuppies," "tofu," "New York," "green pasta." (Green pasta?)

This is how people talk when they're channeling their resentment at something big into anger at something small. They invoke tradition when someone proposes a new taste, or when the tastes of some different audience or some new generation are appealed to. The dynamic is at the heart of basically every American culture-war battle. The language can't help but reveal its origins: a sense of dispossession on the part of people who possess plenty. Unhappy that the modern world no longer fully indexes itself to their preferences, they express their frustration in a way that only a largely unthreatened group would have the time for.

"Change is something the American people identify with," the Coke executive boasted. But not everyone. Change was that nagging itch some people just couldn't scratch. They were upset about the "Pepsi Generation," not because of the Pepsi but because of the generation, and the changing of the guard it suggested. The nature of grievance politics is that no one else ever gets to drive.

We know this story. It's familiar. This is country music rebelling against Elvis or Lil Nas X. It is people cutting the logos off their socks. It is Ted Cruz announcing Tuesday that he would boycott Nike for discontinuing a shoe he'd never bought. (There's always a grift; it wouldn't be true grievance politics without one.) It is protesting your alma mater because it replaced its racist mascot with a bear. It is every weird op-ed you've read about participation trophies or backpacks. It is the undercurrent of every cover story ever written about kids these days.

Frankly, I prefer the soda people to the rest of them. Not the Lost Causers, of course. I'm thinking of Mullins and his crew. There's some value in bringing a corporate giant to heel, just to know we still can. Even if it was because a guy in Washington State wanted to make a quick buck. Maybe *especially* because a guy in Washington State wanted to make a quick buck. You can't let the suits get too comfortable. Every now and then they have to see the flames in the whites of your eyes.

But anyway, it's all a little late to be having this conversation. After all, soda's dead now. Didn't you hear? Millennials killed it.

Wet 'n Wild

FROM *Topic*

BRYAN PULLEN WANTS to show me his toilet. He leads me through the Summit Spring bottling facility in Harrison, Maine, past the floor-to-ceiling shelves packed with cases of bottled water, past the clipboards on the wall and the cleaning supplies propped up in a crowded corner, and into the small employee restroom. He approaches the tank, wraps two meaty hands around the lid, lifts, and tells me to take a look. "I know your toilet looks nothing like that," he says.

He's right: the tank, like the bowl—which has been cleaned, Pullen assures me—is bright white and filled with clear water. There is no residue ringing the sides, no rust stains or mineral deposits. Pullen tells me that the toilet is 15 years old. That's the point of this little exercise: he wants to emphasize how clean the water is here, and how much better it is than my water at home.

I live just an hour away, in a wooded, rural part of inland Maine that doesn't look terribly different from Harrison. Like 40 percent of Mainers, I drink private, and unregulated, well water, but many people in the state get their water from springs, which are plentiful throughout the region. Pullen insists that *his* spring, located in the northern Appalachian Mountains, is different from the roadside springs that service campers, and from the big, borehole-encouraged springs that help line the coffers of Nestlé, which owns the nearby Poland Spring bottling facility. The proof, he says, can not only be seen in a toilet, but felt in the mouth.

Pullen and his business partner, Seth Pruzansky, bottle Summit Spring water and sell it under the brand name Tourmaline Spring.

Their product is known as "raw water"; unlike my well water, which is basically just groundwater from rain and snowmelt that has been pumped up through the soil and into plastic pipes and iron pipes, Summit Spring water flows freely without any mechanical assistance. Unlike municipal water, raw water isn't filtered, and it hasn't been treated with chlorine or fluoride—processes that are required by the government for the municipal water consumed by an estimated 86 percent of Americans. Summit Spring water bubbles up through the earth into a stainless steel enclosure, before flowing along stainless steel pipes and directly into plastic bottles, all emblazoned with either the Tourmaline Spring logo (for untreated or raw water) or the Summit Spring trademark (for water that has been filtered to remove iron, bacteria, sulfides, and manganese). Their water, Pullen insists, is very special.

Ancient Greeks believed that springs were the home of water nymphs, daughters of Zeus and Pan, and that to worship these springs was to honor the highest gods. When passing by a rural spring, it was traditional to leave an offering—a piece of meat, a bit of fruit, a coin. Early Christians linked springs to the worship of the Virgin Mary. Paleolithic people living in what is now the United Kingdom built altars around springs, and tourists still travel to visit springs known as Clootie wells in Ireland and Scotland.

The earliest written record of Summit Spring comes from 1792, but the spring didn't become known for its healing properties until the 1860s, when the land was sold to a wealthy farmer named Francis H. Whitman. According to a 1908 history of the region, Whitman—who was in poor health—became convinced that his spring water "possessed valuable medicinal qualities," and had it analyzed by chemists who determined that his water was "equal in value to any of the various mineral waters that were then on the market." In 1875 Whitman began to offer his water to a thirsty public, shipping 35-gallon, water-filled wooden barrels down the narrow-gage railway from Norway, Maine (population: around 2,000), to New York City, where it sold for 40 cents per gallon —equivalent to over $100 per gallon today. At the time, Whitman's water was more expensive than alcohol, more precious than coffee.

Pullen, 60, has sunk millions of dollars and years of his life into his business. He purchased the spring from a retired schoolteacher in 2004 for $2.5 million. In order to purchase the property, he had to sign an agreement stating that he wouldn't sell the spring to Nestlé or any other beverage giant for at least 15 years —a promise he says he has no trouble keeping.

He had spent most of his adult life up to that point working as a pilot for American Airlines, an experience that taught him how different tap water could taste in different parts of the country. "When I left Maine for the first time, I wanted to vomit," he remembers. "I was like, Really, New Jersey? I can't drink this water." Pullen was used to softer water, water that had been naturally filtered through the earth rather than treated at a plant. So he began bringing bottles of Maine water with him everywhere he traveled. (He still does: when he travels to California to speak on daytime TV, he packs gallons of Summit Spring water—"as much as I can," he says.)

In December 2017 the *New York Times* ran a piece on the raw-water fad that was supposedly taking over Silicon Valley. Some of raw water's fans believe it has more probiotics than municipal water, while others drink it to avoid additives such as chlorine and fluoride or possible contaminants, including birth control hormones or other soluble medications. Tourmaline Spring was mentioned briefly in the *Times* piece, and Pullen and Pruzansky became the subjects of online ridicule. The company's inbox quickly filled with expressions of mockery, accusations of elitism, and death threats. (The consumption of untreated water is a controversial subject, as it has the potential to contain bacteria or pesticides. For what it's worth, Pullen says he has spent thousands of dollars over the years getting his water tested and retested to ensure that no bacterial or chemical contaminants are seeping in. In the spring's 150-year history as a bottled-water supplier, he claims that there hasn't been a single complaint about the water.)

After the tour, I sat at home with a bottle of Tourmaline Spring, ready to sip it slowly and really consider the flavor. I poured some into a glass and regarded it as one would a wine—sniffing it, swirling it in my mouth, chewing it. It might have just been my imagination, but I think I detected a slightly different mouthfeel than that of regular tap or bottled water. It did seem softer somehow —very smooth and wet. What I really wanted was to wash my hair with it. It would give me summer hair, I imagined, like lake water. Shiny, soft. I finished the glass and went about my day, feeling more or less the same, a bit more hydrated than before.

*

Poland Spring bottled water is perhaps the state's best-known export. The company's campus is located in the town of Poland, Maine, less than an hour's drive from Summit Spring, which in Maine means it's just down the road. What started as a small, family-run business is now part of the Swiss conglomerate Nestlé, the largest food and beverage company on earth. If you drink bottled water, you've probably tried a Nestlé brand. It owns the largest share of the global bottled-water market (11 percent) and sells 51 different brands, including Nestlé Pure Life, San Pellegrino, Perrier, Deer Park, Ozarka, and others. Henri Nestlé, a German-born Swiss candymaker, started bottling water back in 1843. In 2016 sales of bottled water outpaced soda sales in the United States for the first time in history.

Nestlé has come under repeated fire for its predatory practices. In the 1970s and '80s doctors around the globe advised the public to boycott the company's infant formula in response to an aggressive marketing campaign by Nestlé that advised women in third world countries to give up breastfeeding in favor of buying formula and mixing it with local water, which was often untreated and unsafe. In 2017 *Bloomberg Businessweek* published a report detailing how the company had made billions by going into states with "absolute capture" laws—such as Maine and Texas—which allow private landowners to pump as much water from the ground as they want, and sell it for however much they want. According to *Businessweek*, Nestlé has "come to dominate a controversial industry, spring by spring, often going into economically depressed municipalities with the promise of jobs and new infrastructure in exchange for tax breaks and access to a resource that's scarce for millions." In 1994 the company's former chief executive officer, Helmut Maucher, told the *New York Times* that springs are "like petroleum. You can always build a chocolate factory. But springs you have or you don't have."

Nestlé aims to own every spring it can. The company buys what should be a public resource and sells it back to the public, while paying minimal extraction fees. (In Michigan, *Businessweek* reported, Nestlé pays just $200 for the privilege of bottling and selling the state's clean water.) The company has also been known to buy water from small municipalities—Fryeburg, Maine, for example—and sell it under its private labels, meaning that the same water flowing through faucets in Fryeburg for free is distributed in convenience and grocery stores throughout the country for around $1.99 a liter. One of those private labels is Poland Spring. The employees at Poland Spring would, of course, prefer you forget about all that and focus on only the good stuff, like the jobs the company provides—some of the higher-paid positions in the region—and the spring's fabled history. Poland Spring community-relations manager Heather Printup, who has lived in Maine her entire life, relays the tale of Poland Spring's discovery in the 1840s in a tone that implies both the appropriate skepticism and company pride.

Long before Poland Spring fell into Nestlé's hands, in 1992, it was owned by a group of crusty old Maine pioneers. According to the legend, the Ricker family, who controlled the spring, had an unruly herd of cattle that kept sneaking off into the woods, day after day. After a time, a few curious farmhands began following the herd into the forest, where they discovered a bubbling source of water that the animals had been attracted to. The farmhands began to drink.

"Apparently, a magical power came over them, like they could do anything," says Printup. The farmhands informed their boss, Hiram Ricker. All his life, Hiram had been beset with abdominal troubles. Once he began to drink the water, the story goes, he felt great. He looked great, too. His doctor, thrilled by the change in his patient, began prescribing the water—which Hiram dubbed Poland Spring—to others. Word spread far and wide, and in 1859 Hiram began bottling and selling it on a commercial scale. By the early 1900s, a hotel built on the site had become a hot spot for socialites, celebrities, and even presidents. After the Ricker family lost control of the company in the 1930s, it passed through a series of different owners before it was snatched up by Perrier in the 1980s. In 1992 Nestlé acquired Perrier, and thus, Poland Spring officially became one of the big guys.

Though the label and the brand name have stayed the same over the years, Poland Spring no longer draws from one bubbling source. Rather, it utilizes the flow of water from springs across Maine. According to Poland Spring geologist and natural resource manager Mark Dubois, who manages and monitors the company's eight spring sites, Nestlé is looking for new sources.

It's hard to find a spring that meets the specifications of both

Nestlé and the Food and Drug Administration, but that hasn't
stopped the company from trying to (forcibly) expand. Unlike
Summit Spring water—which, Pullen says, only takes "what Mother
Nature is giving"—Poland Spring drills boreholes into the ground
near existing springs in order to harvest more water. According to
Dubois, this is a safer way to collect spring water, because it allows
the company to have complete control over the purity of its product. "A lot of springs have beaver activity and other animals that
drink from them," he explains.

The FDA allows Poland Spring to label its water "spring water"
because, according to government standards set in the 1990s, it
is spring water: sourced from the same aquifer as the water that
bubbles to the surface outside of Poland. The only difference is
that it doesn't come to the surface naturally. For people like Pullen, this is an important distinction: while Poland Spring water
could eventually make its way to the surface without assistance,
many people think that the intermediary action of drilling boreholes should disqualify this product from being defined (and marketed) as "spring" water. Spring water, they say, should emerge
from the ground naturally after moving its way through layers of
silt and sand and soil. This is, after all, what makes a spring: the
word comes from the Old English *springan,* which means to "leap,
burst forth, fly up." Spring water should move, not *be* moved.

Multiple lawsuits alleging mislabeling of water have been
brought against Poland Spring over the past 20 years. A 2017 class
action lawsuit argued that "not one drop of Poland Spring Water
emanates from a water source that complies with the FDA's definition of 'spring water.'" The 11 plaintiffs, who, according to the
New York Times, come from "various northeastern states," believe
they have been misled, and that Poland Spring has been selling
one billion gallons of well water to Americans each year.

Nestlé tried to get the lawsuit thrown out, issuing a statement
that same year that called the suit "meritless" and saying, "Poland
Spring Brand natural spring water is just what it says it is . . . 100
percent natural spring water." In March 2019 a federal judge in
Connecticut ruled that the complaint could proceed in eight
states, including Maine.

The lawsuit also claimed that the famous Poland Spring, the
one found by curious cows and patronized by American presidents, "ran dry nearly 50 years ago." But when I visited in March,

the original Poland Spring appears to still be running. Located in the middle of the company's groomed grounds—which include a Victorian mansion originally built for the 1893 Chicago World's Fair and a half-timbered Gothic stone chapel that can be rented for weddings—the spring itself is easy to miss, surrounded by marble tiles and columns, which visitors can glimpse only from the comfort of wicker chairs set up behind glass walls, like a museum display. A tour guide tells me that when rich guests would come to Poland Spring in the mid-1800s, they would be presented with a chalice of spring water and given a tour of the factory, where all the workers wore white linen and showered in Poland Spring water before every shift. It sounds, I can't help but think, a little too good to be true.

There is no marble observation area at Bond Mountain Spring—no fancy plaques, no decorative signs. This spring is located on the side of a mountain on the side of a road in a little Maine town near the White Mountains called Newfield. It took me 45 minutes to get there from my house, my white Subaru trailing Justin King's hunter-green Dodge pickup though backcountry roads lined with five-foot-tall snowbanks, around sharp turns that revealed long-dormant fields and lumberyards with felled trees piled higher than my head, ready to be milled. In the back of King's truck sat several three-gallon jugs and one eight-gallon jug, containers to hold enough water for King and his wife, Kasey—who live in Windham, a half-hour outside of Portland—to drink for the coming week.

Bond Mountain Spring is free and open to all. Drinking from spring sources is an old tradition in Maine: Poland Spring's Printup remembers when her parents used to visit a local aquifer before going camping, and there's a section on the Maine.gov website that explains how to properly patronize roadside springs, and warns about the dangers of contaminated water. ("Often people use roadside springs as dumping grounds for car waste," the site advises. "Drinking Water Program field staff have found diapers, garbage, and other waste in close proximity to some springs. One spring had earthworms living in it.") When it comes to private springs, it's up to owners to get their water tested; King assures me that Bond Mountain Spring's current landowners are "old school" and want to keep their spring free and open to the public.

I'd expected King, who works as a butcher in Portland, to be a fervent believer in the magic of spring water. I half-expected him to come at me with conspiracy theories and pseudoscience, particularly given the media coverage around the raw-water trend and how it intersects with doomsday-prepper culture. But he didn't. Unlike Pullen and Printup, King isn't trying to sell me anything or protect his employer's reputation, and is therefore able to discuss his water choices freely. King explains that he doesn't believe that Bond Mountain Spring is healing, or more hydrating than regular water—though he has met people who hold such beliefs. He just doesn't trust public water. "I do believe that municipal water is harmful. Especially chronically. The chlorine and fluoride that's used in a lot of supplies is terrible for you," he says. "Not to mention issues that arise, like in Flint."

In 2014, after years of being served by the Detroit water system —which gets its water from Lake Huron and the Detroit River— Flint, Michigan, switched its municipal water source to the Flint River. Local officials had been attempting to save money; as a result, the city's residents, most of whom are Black and many of whom are poor, found themselves with undrinkable tap water. As officials dismissed complaints about smelly, discolored water, Flint residents were exposed to elevated lead levels, *E. coli,* coliform bacteria, and other contaminants. To this day, the drinking water in Flint is still unsafe for some, and many children continue to suffer from medical complications related to lead poisoning. (Since May 2018, Nestlé has been making a weekly donation of 100,000 bottles of Ice Mountain brand water to community centers in Flint, a program the company says it will continue until August 2019.) It's unclear exactly how many Americans live without safe drinking water, but estimates based on EPA levels put the number between 9 and 45 million, according to researchers at the University of California, Irvine.

Justin and Kasey King started drinking self-harvested spring water four years ago. Then, while living in Maryland, they learned about spring hunters on an episode of the podcast *ReWild Yourself.* "Most people don't understand why we go through the effort," King says. He's leaning over the PVC pipe that flows down the mountain into a small gravel pit as Kasey looks on. She tells me that they gather spring water for the same reason that they gather bunches of sweet fern and baskets of fiddleheads: it makes them

feel good, like they're in control of their food and of their bodies. It's not just the water that they like, but the entire process of
driving together into the mountains, spending a few hours in the
truck, and filling up their heavy jugs. Though they can't collect
enough water for bathing or laundry, they'll be able to drink it
all week long. (They bring metal bottles of it to work so they can
avoid drinking Portland's municipal offering.) As they wait for the
containers to fill, they discuss what they're going to have for dinner. Venison, probably, with tomatoes they canned that summer,
and maybe some ramp oil for seasoning.

"So much of modern life feels fake," says King. "Everything is
canned. I go to the store and get a slab of red meat on Styrofoam and buy asparagus from Argentina and it just feels so empty."
Spring water, he explains, is "coming from the earth, and I have
to put in the labor to collect it." Work performed for its own sake,
by choice, with no money changing hands, feels spiritual to him.
Every time he visits, Justin likes to offer a silent prayer of sorts to
the land. "I like to thank the mountain for filtering the water, and
the snow for becoming the water," he says. "It all means something
to me."

My parents raised me to believe wholeheartedly in the following
things: Catholicism, public school, and tap water. I never saw a water filter growing up, and we never bought bottled water. We drank
from the tap or, if we were outside, my three siblings and I would
drink right from the garden hose. We were suburban, middle-class
kids in a relatively upscale part of Massachusetts (ironically, we
lived in the same county in which the 1982 Woburn water crisis
took place, a case that was inspiration for the 1998 John Travolta
film, *A Civil Action*) and my parents often reminded us that our
neighbors were richer than us, that we had to be practical. What
was good enough for most people was good enough for us.

I no longer believe in Catholicism, nor do I believe in the in-
nate goodness of public schools or the safety of tap water. All these
wells have been poisoned—by money, mostly. I know now that all
tap water isn't created equal, that all schoolchildren aren't given
the same books or access to skilled teachers. I wouldn't learn this
lesson until after college. I knew it logically before then—I had
read the right books and had been educated about environmental
racism at my private liberal arts college—but it wasn't something I

saw, or something I understood, until I started living in cities and talking to people who grew up beyond the suburban bubble, people who didn't take clean water for granted, who didn't get to feel safe and coddled at their public schools.

I don't believe a spring will heal me, nor do I think spring water is necessarily healthier than what comes out of my tap. I don't really know which bottled water is best—every company claims it provides a superior beverage, the cleanest water with the best balance of minerals to make consumers feel more hydrated or more whole. My well water could be toxic, I know. (We've had it tested, but it's unregulated, as both the representatives at Poland Spring and the owners at Summit Spring repeatedly told me.) I'm visibly pregnant, and Pullen is quick to point out on our tour that well water could be bad for my baby. "All pregnant women should be drinking our water," he tells me.

I can't imagine I will. I'll probably keep doing exactly what I have been doing and drinking from the tap, from the garden hose, from the shower head. But even though I won't be going to springs to gather water, it's still the Kings' belief system that aligns closest with my own. I believe in small rituals of daily labor that allow me to obtain some measure of control over the world—the spring shoots that come up with much coaxing, the successfully mended jeans, the little jars of homemade jam that line the walls of my refrigerator. I believe in feeling self-sufficient. And I do believe there's magic in the trees and the snow, in the quiet burbling of a brook, in the act of praying to a sky, to a stream, to a place.

Peter Luger Used to Sizzle.
Now It Sputters.

FROM *The New York Times*

I CAN COUNT on Peter Luger Steak House in Brooklyn to produce certain sensations at every meal.

There is the insistent smell of broiled dry-aged steak that hits
me the minute I open the door and sometimes sooner, while I'm
still outside on the South Williamsburg sidewalk, producing a
raised pulse, a quickening of the senses, and a restlessness familiar
to anyone who has seen a tiger that has just heard the approach of
the lunch bucket.

There is the hiss of butter and melted tallow as they slide down
the hot platter, past the sliced porterhouse or rib steak and their
charred bones, to make a pool at one end. The server will spoon
some of this sizzling fat over the meat he has just plated, generally
with some line like "Here are your vitamins."

There is the thunk of a bowl filled with schlag landing on a bare
wood table when dessert is served, and soon after, the softer tap-
tap-tap of waxy chocolate coins in gold foil dropped one at a time
on top of the check.

And after I've paid, there is the unshakable sense that I've been
scammed.

The last sensation was not part of the Peter Luger experience
when I started eating there, in the 1990s. I was acutely aware of
the cost back then because I would settle the tab by counting out
$20 bills; cash was the only way to pay unless you had a Peter Luger
credit card. At the end of the night my wallet would be empty.
Because a Peter Luger steak made me feel alive in a way that few

other things did, I considered this a fair trade, although I could afford it only once a year or so.

I don't remember when the doubts began, but they grew over time.

Diners who walk in the door eager to hand over literal piles of money aren't greeted; they're processed. A host with a clipboard looks for the name, or writes it down and quotes a waiting time. There is almost always a wait, with or without a reservation, and there is almost always a long line of supplicants against the wall. A kind word or reassuring smile from somebody on staff would help the time pass. The smile never comes. The Department of Motor Vehicles is a block party compared with the line at Peter Luger.

The management seems to go out of its way to make things inconvenient. Customers at the bar have to order drinks from the bartender and food from an overworked server on the other side of the bar, and then pay two separate checks and leave two separate tips. And they can't order lunch after 2:30 p.m., even though the bar and the kitchen remain open.

Since its last, two-star review in the *Times,* written by Frank Bruni in 2007, the restaurant has started taking online reservations. It accepts debit cards, too, which is nice. But the credit card you use to buy a cortado at the café or a bag of chips at the bodega will still not buy you a meal at Peter Luger.

The servers, who once were charmingly brusque, now give the strong impression that these endless demands for food and drink are all that's standing between them and a hard-earned nap. Signals that a customer has a question or request don't get picked up as quickly; the canned jokes about spinach and schlag don't flow as freely.

Some things are the same as ever. The shrimp cocktail has always tasted like cold latex dipped in ketchup and horseradish. The steak sauce has always tasted like the same ketchup and horseradish fortified by corn syrup.

Although the fries are reasonably crisp, their insides are mealy and bland in a way that fresh-cut potatoes almost certainly would not be. The sole—yes, I'm the person who ordered the sole at Peter Luger—was strangely similar: the bread crumbs on top were gold and crunchy, but the fish underneath was dry and almost powdery.

Was the Caesar salad always so drippy, the croutons always

straight out of a bag, the grated cheese always so white and rubbery? I know there was a time the German fried potatoes were brown and crunchy, because I eagerly ate them each time I went. Now they are mushy, dingy, gray, and sometimes cold. I look forward to them the way I look forward to finding a new, irregularly shaped mole.

Lunch one afternoon vividly demonstrated the kitchen's inconsistency: I ordered a burger, medium-rare, at the bar. So had the two people sitting to my right, it turned out. One of them got what we'd all asked for, a midnight-dark crust giving way to an evenly rosy interior so full of juices it looked like it was ready to cry. The other one got a patty that was almost completely brown inside. I got a weird hybrid, a burger whose interior shaded from nearly perfect on one side to gray and hard on the other.

The same issue afflicted a medium-rare porterhouse I was served one night: the fillet was ideal but the other side of the T-bone, the strip, ranged from medium-rare to medium-well. I could live with this; big cuts of meat don't always cook evenly. What gnaws at me every time I eat a Luger porterhouse is the realization that it's just another steak, and far from the best New York has to offer.

Other restaurants, and not just steakhouses, can put a formidable crust on both sides of the cut; Luger caramelizes the top side only, while the underside is barely past raw, as if it had done all its cooking on the hot platter.

Other restaurants, and not just steakhouses, buy beef that is tender, richly marbled, and deeply flavorful; at Luger, you get the first two but not the third.

Other restaurants, and not just steakhouses, age that beef to make flavor grow and intensify and double back on itself; dry-aging at Luger still results in a tender steak, but it rarely achieves a hypnotic or compelling or even very interesting one.

But those other restaurants are not Peter Luger, as Friedrich Nietzsche might have said.

"When in this essay I declare war upon Wagner," Nietzsche wrote in "The Case of Wagner," "the last thing I want to do is start a celebration for any *other* musicians. *Other* musicians don't count compared to Wagner."

I could say the same thing about other steakhouses—compared to Peter Luger, they don't count. Luger is not the city's oldest, but it's the one in which age, tradition, superb beef, blistering heat, an instinctive avoidance of anything fancy, and an immensely attractive self-assurance came together to produce something that felt less like a restaurant than an affirmation of life, or at least life as it is lived in New York City. This sounds ridiculously grand. Years ago I thought it was true, though, and so did other people.

The restaurant will always have its loyalists. They will laugh away the prices, the $16.95 sliced tomatoes that taste like 1979, the $229.80 porterhouse for four. They will say that nobody goes to Luger for the sole, nobody goes to Luger for the wine, nobody goes to Luger for the salad, nobody goes to Luger for the service. The list goes on, and gets harder to swallow, until you start to wonder who really needs to go to Peter Luger, and start to think the answer is nobody.

AMELIA NIERENBERG

Hard Times for a Hot Commodity, the Prized New Mexico Chile

FROM *The New York Times*

IN ALL HER eight decades of farming in southeastern New Mexico, June Rutherford has never seen a chile season this bad.

"The weather hasn't been a bit good for chile," said Ms. Rutherford, who was recently crowned Queen of the Great New Mexico Chile Taste-Off, in Socorro, New Mexico, about 110 miles north of Hatch.

At 95, Ms. Rutherford is the matriarch of the Franzoy family, one of the first to commercialize the Hatch chile, a mainstay of the farm-based economy here and a brand known around the world.

"It's been hot," the queen said, sitting at her dining room table, a crown atop her curls. "Hot and dry."

More than two decades of drought have drained the reservoirs, which are fed by the Rio Grande, a river that—even on a good year —flows shallow in the parched riverbed. But a shortage of water for irrigation is just one of many forces threatening the future of the state's signature food.

The peppers depend on hot days and cool nights, growing comfortably between 55 and 95 degrees, to develop the desired taste and heat. Since at least the 1970s, summer daytime temperatures have reached 100 degrees or higher. The excessive heat, a symptom of climate change felt across the Southwest, can blister the chiles' fragile skin and interrupt the growth cycle.

"You put all your effort into it, all of your money, but if there's no water, you won't get anything," said Edgar Grajeda, 25, an owner of Grajeda Farms in Hatch. "It's getting drier and drier."

Some farmers who have grown chiles for generations are cutting back acreage to save their limited water for more reliably profitable crops like onions or watermelons. After decades of driving the Hatch Valley brand and agricultural economy, the chile has become less dependable.

Water and labor costs are fixed, but growers cannot increase their prices by much; farms in Mexico, which sell their chiles in the United States, often pay workers less and can sell their product cheaper. Scientists are trying to find a way to automate the harvest, but for now, chiles have to be picked by hand because they bruise easily.

Some farmers are having a hard time finding pickers, as tightening immigration policies have slowed the flow of temporary workers from Mexico.

"This year, we were faced with more challenges from weather and labor than ever before," said Chris Franzoy, 50, Ms. Rutherford's great-nephew and an owner of Young Guns, Inc., and the Hatch Chile Factory. "We've got a much higher cost, but we're not able to pass that along to the consumer."

Few other foods embody a state's identity like the chile, one of New Mexico's two official state vegetables (alongside pinto beans). Chiles are pictured on license plates, sold flame-roasted by roadsides, and served on just about every food you can order. It's even the subject of the official state question: "Red or green?"

"It's who this state is," said Teako Nunn, 70, an owner of Sparky's, a popular restaurant in Hatch. "For the people that live here, it's like milk, or American cheese, or ketchup, or mustard. It's like that, except better."

Red chiles dry on the vine and are served in a smoky, spicy sauce. Green chiles are usually fire-roasted, chopped, and used as a relish over anything from omelets to pasta to burritos.

For the unaccustomed, the heat is a slow build; by the seventh bite of a Sparky's burger, customers are often red-cheeked and sweating. (The restaurant's chocolate ice cream shake is meant to soothe, but that's got chile in it, too.)

Other crops—like blueberries in Maine and peaches in Georgia and South Carolina—have also landed in the crosshairs of climate change. Many, like wine grapes, are being moved to more hospitable climates to the north or at higher elevations.

But New Mexican chiles can't be grown just anywhere: the state's high elevation provides the required temperature swings between hot days and cool nights. (Hatch, which is in a lower part of the state, is still over 4,000 feet above sea level.)

"It's hard to say that you could just move to a cooler environment," said Jonathan Overpeck, the dean of the School for Environment and Sustainability at the University of Michigan, who studied the Southwest when he held a similar post at the University of Arizona. "I just don't think there's an obvious place to move to grow our chile."

Farmers have started growing chiles in Colorado, which is directly north and has the highest mean elevation nationwide. (This kicked off an amusing spat on Twitter between the two governors.)

But the soils are different in Colorado. The water is, too. And much like wine connoisseurs, chile enthusiasts claim they can taste the difference. Something about the Hatch Valley, they say, crisps up the texture and balances the taste.

That belief comes at least in part from a decades-long marketing campaign, led by farmers and town officials, hailing the valley as the Chile Capital of the World. There is now an annual Hatch Chile Festival and a state chile association.

There's even a state law, enacted in 2013, that defines the parameters of a "New Mexico Certified Chile," to keep other states and countries from fraudulently labeling their peppers New Mexican.

"Hatch is considered the Napa Valley of chile," Mr. Franzoy said, standing in his fields as workers knelt around him, snapping the green peppers off plants with gloved hands. "There's a misconception. Hatch is not a variety. It's a place, an origin."

In 2017 sales of the state's chiles totaled $44.6 million, placing the crop seventh in New Mexico's $3.38 billion agriculture sector. They trailed pecans ($221 million), hay ($109 million), and onions ($107 million), according to the United States Department of Agriculture.

Different parts of New Mexico grow different chiles: a teaching garden run by the Chile Pepper Institute at New Mexico State University in Las Cruces, 40 miles southeast of Hatch, has more than 150 varieties.

But all varieties are facing an uncertain future. In the 1990s more than 35,000 acres of chiles were grown in New Mexico, compared with about 8,400 in recent years, according to Sonja Schroeder, the executive director of the New Mexico Chile Association.

"It's talked about, kind of on the same level as politics would be," said Nelle Bauer, a chef at Frenchish, a restaurant in Albuquerque, speaking of the drought and fears of a future chile scarcity. "It's at the forefront of most New Mexicans' minds."

In 2018 the Elephant Butte Reservoir, which supplies water to southern New Mexico, Mexico, and parts of Texas, was at only 3 percent capacity. The riverbed of the Rio Grande cracked in some places, and farmers watched their chiles wither in the fields.

Thanks to a snowy winter and a cooler spring, the reservoir was fuller this year, reaching about 26 percent capacity, according to David DuBois, the state climatologist and a professor at New Mexico State. It's been a good growing season as a result, and the fields around the valley are filled with pepper plants.

Still, the trend points down: New Mexico "is at the very top" of water-insecure states, with 80 to 100 percent of available water used every year, said Betsy Otto, who directs the global water program at the World Resources Institute.

"Our drought pretty much started in 1999," said Dr. DuBois, who added that "2011 and 2012 were really dry. I called those harbingers of the future. I'd ask farmers: 'Can you adapt? Because that's the direction we're heading.'"

Not every farmer sees the unpredictable weather as caused by human actions and industry, but nearly all agree: the past few years have been harder. The weather has been more erratic, with winds, unpredictable frost, and wetter growing seasons, which can bring pests.

Warmer winters drop less snow in the mountains, leading to less runoff to fill reservoirs. Windier spring weather shakes the fragile sprouts, kicking up dust that can cut down new growth.

Most farms, like Morrow Farms, have converted to irrigation that runs under the ground, at the root of the plants. (Some farms rely on aquifers, but pumping the water from underground can be expensive and it can be too salty.) That's a more efficient system, but it's far from a permanent solution.

"It'll keep you up at night to worry about the weather," said Tyler Holmes, 35, who intends to take over part of the farm from her father, Harvey Morrow.

In the 1980s Morrow Farms planted hundreds of acres of chiles, but Ms. Holmes's uncle John, another owner, stopped planting chiles on his section 10 to 15 years ago. He doubts he will plant any next year; watermelons are just better for business.

Ms. Holmes and her father still plant chiles, but only on about 80 acres of the 1,200 they irrigate. They mostly sell to people in town who like their product.

"We talked about not growing it, but that's not possible," she said. "It's who we are."

Other families, like the Franzoys and the Grajedas, are still holding strong, expanding their operations and breeding new varieties.

Ms. Rutherford, the chile queen, demands it: she watched her father, Joseph Franzoy, start with just two acres, and picked chile for 10 cents a bushel with her first husband, Jim Lytle, during World War II. In his honor, she bred the Big Jim variety, one of New Mexico's most popular.

But even as she sat at her dining room table wearing the plastic crown, she worried those days might be over.

"Do you think any of our kids are going to carry on the legacy?" she asked. "Why should they come and farm if they can't make a living?"

TAMAR HASPEL

Here's What the Government's Dietary Guidelines Should Really Say

FROM *The Washington Post*

I HAVE A confession. When the call went out to recruit members of the 2020 Dietary Guidelines Advisory Committee, I thought about throwing my hat in the ring. I've got a few things to say, and I figured maybe there was room on the committee for a journalist.

But then I took a cold, hard look at my lack of advanced degrees, as well as all those elementary school report cards that said I didn't play well with others, and I thought better of it. Besides, who needs all those tedious meetings when you can just use your column to tell everyone what you think they should eat?

So here goes. If I were writing the dietary guidelines, I would give them a radical overhaul. I'd go so far as to radically overhaul the way we evaluate diet. Here's why and how.

The reason we know so little about what to eat despite decades of research is that our tools are woefully inadequate. Lately, as scientists try, and fail, to reproduce results, all of science is taking a hard look at funding biases, statistical shenanigans, and group-think. All that criticism, and then some, applies to nutrition.

Prominent in the charge to change the way we do science is John Ioannidis, professor of health research and policy at Stanford University. In 2005 he published "Why Most Published Research Findings Are False" in the journal *PLOS Medicine*, and he's been making science headlines (although not always friends) ever since.

He came down hard on nutrition in a pull-no-punches 2013 *British Medical Journal* editorial entitled "Implausible Results in Human Nutrition Research," in which he noted, "Almost every single nutrient imaginable has peer reviewed publications associating it with almost any outcome."

Ioannidis told me that sussing out the connection between diet and health—nutritional epidemiology—is enormously challenging, and "the tools that we're throwing at the problem are not commensurate with the complexity and difficulty of the problem." The biggest of those tools is observational research, in which we collect data on what people eat, and track what happens to them.

The trouble begins with that "collect data" part. There are a few ways to do this, none of them particularly good. You can use a 24-hour recall, which gives respondents a fighting chance of remembering what they actually ate but doesn't give you a representative sample of overall diet. Food diaries over a long period do that better, but people tend to eat differently when they're tracking their diet for researchers. Most large population studies use food-frequency questionnaires (FFQs, in industry lingo), where they ask people to count up the servings they've eaten of a wide range of foods, often over the course of a year.

There's no better way to understand the shortcomings of an FFQ than to fill one out. Maybe you know how often you ate pie last year, but do you know how often you ate "foods with oils added or with oils used in cooking (do not include baked goods or salads)"? A host of studies of self-reported data have found that up to two-thirds of respondents report eating a diet so inconsistent with their caloric needs as to be implausible.

Give tens of thousands of people that FFQ, and you end up with a ginormous repository of possible correlations. You can zero in on a vitamin, macronutrient, or food, and go to town. But not only are you starting with flawed data, you've got a zillion possible confounding variables—dietary, demographic, socioeconomic. I've heard statisticians call it "noise mining," and Ioannidis is equally skeptical. "With this type of data, you can get any result you want," he said. "You can align it to your beliefs."

Ah, beliefs. Just about every week there's a new study of a food funded by the people who profit by it (New York University's Marion Nestle has been tracking this for years; her 2018 book *Un-*

savory Truth details her findings). But funding bias isn't the only kind. "Fanatical opinions abound in nutrition," Ioannidis wrote in 2013, and those have bias power too.

So what do we do about this? "Definitive Solutions Won't Come From Another Million Observational Papers or Small Randomized Trials," reads the subtitle of Ioannidis's BMJ paper. His is a burn-down-the-house ethos.

Frank Hu lives in the house and is understandably less enthusiastic about the incendiary approach. He chairs the department of nutrition at Harvard's T. H. Chan School of Public Health, arguably ground zero of nutritional epidemiology. While he acknowledges shortcomings of the research in his field, and is respectful of Ioannidis's criticism, he says nutrition researchers have brought much to our understanding of a healthful diet, and can address the problems.

He pointed out that data collection is improving, with new tools to better assess diet, and reality checks with measurable biomarkers (testing the urine of respondents in a salt study for sodium, for example). And he doesn't believe biases undermine the credibility of the field. Often, they cancel each other out, he says, and the most authoritative recommendations, such as the dietary guidelines (he was on the 2015 committee), are the consensus of large groups looking at the preponderance of evidence. Still, he acknowledges that there's work to be done. "If we don't have challenges, our life will be very boring."

When it comes to actual dietary recommendations, the disagreement is stark. "Ioannidis and others say we have no clue, the science is so bad that we don't know anything," Hu told me. "I think that's completely bogus. We know a lot about the basic elements of a healthy diet." He lists plant-based foods—fruit, veg, whole grains, legumes—but acknowledges that we don't understand enough to prescribe specific combinations or numbers of servings. The ongoing controversy, he says, has generated "a lot of heat but not much light," and he's afraid Ioannidis's dismissal of the entire field undermines nutritional advice.

But if nutritional advice is unsupported, a little undermining is in order. Ioannidis is in favor of fruits, vegetables, and whole grains, but "the evidence behind them is pretty soft," he wrote in an e-mail. Older observational studies showed big reductions in cancer risk, but newer studies show small benefits, if any. "When the benefit in published studies in the literature shrinks 10-fold or 100-fold over time," he continued, "you have every reason to worry about whether this type of research effort can give you any reliable answers." Heart disease risk reduction has remained sizable, Ioannidis noted, but it's still observational data, and confounding and data-reporting issues mean we can't definitively link diet to health, a point Hu makes in his own research.

Big differences in what people eat track with other differences. Heavy plant-eaters are different from, say, heavy meat-eaters in all kinds of ways (income, education, physical activity, BMI). Red meat consumption correlates with increased risk of dying in an accident as much as dying from heart disease. The amount of faith we put in observational studies is a judgment call.

In the two decades I've been writing about nutrition, my confidence in what we know about food and health has eroded, and I find myself in Ioannidis's camp. What have we learned, unequivocally enough to build a consensus in the nutrition community, about how diet affects health? Well, trans fats are bad. Anything else, and you get pushback from one camp or another.

And then there's eggs, poster food for we-don't-know-jack-about-diet. We used to think they were bad, because their cholesterol content contributed to heart disease. Then they were exonerated. Eggs are okay! And just last week, a new study came out saying not so fast, they might be bad after all. Let the eye-rolling begin.

Over and over, large population studies get sliced and diced, and it's all but impossible to figure out what's signal and what's noise. Researchers try to do that with controlled trials to test the connections, but those have issues too. They're expensive, so they're usually small and short-term. People have trouble sticking to the diet being studied. And scientists are generally looking for what they call "surrogate endpoints," like increased cholesterol rather than death from heart disease, since it's impractical to keep a trial going until people die. While I hold out hope that we'll get better at all this, it's going to take a while.

Meantime, what do we do? Hu and Ioannidis actually have similar suggestions. For starters, they both think we should be looking at dietary patterns rather than single foods or nutrients. They also both want to look across the datasets. Ioannidis emphasizes transparency. He wants to open data to the world, and analyze all the datasets in the same way to see if "any signals survive." Hu is more cautious (partly to safeguard confidentiality), but does believe wider access to data and checking results against multiple datasets will help identify genuine effects.

I don't think anyone would be against this—I'm certainly not —but remember those FFQs? You're still working with flawed data, and I am not optimistic that we'll get much actionable advice out of the effort. Neither is Ioannidis. When I asked him whether that approach would be more likely to solve the dietary-advice problem or tell us how little we know, he said "probably the latter."

The important question—what are we supposed to eat already?! —is still on the table, and I have a suggestion. Let's give up on evidence-based eating. It's given us nothing but trouble and strife. Our tools can't find any but the most obvious links between food and health, and we've found those already. Instead, let's acknowledge the uncertainty and eat to hedge against what we don't know. We've got two excellent hedges: variety and foods with nutrients intact (which describes such diets as the Mediterranean, touted by researchers). If you severely limit your foods (vegan, keto), you might miss out on something. Ditto if you eat foods with little nutritional value (sugar, refined grains). Oh, and pay attention to the two things we can say with certainty: keep your weight down and exercise.

When I first started writing about nutrition, I used to say I could tell you everything important about diet in 60 seconds. Over the years, my spiel got shorter and shorter as truisms fell by the wayside, and my confidence waned in a field where we know less, rather than more, over time. I'm down to 5 seconds now: eat a wide variety of foods with their nutrients intact, keep your weight down, and get some exercise.

Oh, and playing well with others is highly overrated.

PAIGE WILLIAMS

The Spice Trade

FROM *The New Yorker*

THREE DAYS AFTER Christmas, in a part of Northeast Nashville that many locals describe as "dicey," a Ford Explorer crashed
through the front of a discount-tobacco shop at one end of a strip
mall. Police later called the incident an attempted burglary. The
vehicle, which had been reported stolen, was propelled by a brick
weighting the accelerator. The store was empty—it was four-thirty
in the morning. The authorities arrived to find the Ford abandoned and the shop on fire.

Two doors down, just past Jennifer Nails, Tyreese Lawless had
come to work early, as usual, to clean the fryers at Prince's Hot
Chicken Shack. After hearing a boom, he got out of there, in
case the flames reached the restaurant. Lawless began calling colleagues—to them, and to generations of customers, Prince's is a
kind of second home. Firefighters went inside and started yanking
down ceiling tiles and singed insulation. Ducts and wiring lay exposed, and there was extensive damage from smoke and water. As
a precaution, the fire department shut off the strip mall's gas and
electricity. Yellow police tape outside Prince's front door stretched
toward the shattered glass of the targeted bodega.

When Nashville residents learned that Prince's would be closed
indefinitely, a minor panic ensued. In the past decade or so, the
restaurant's signature dish, hot chicken, has proliferated worldwide, and the original incarnation, fried chicken bathed in fiery spices, has been subjected to relentless permutation—tacos,
ramen, sushi, oysters, apple fritters, empanadas, pâté, poutine.
The invention, now known everywhere as Nashville hot chicken,

sounds like a viral novelty, like the Cronut, but it long predates Instagram: it became popular more than 80 years ago, in the city's Black community, and the recipe originated with one family, the Princes. After the fire, @ThuggBugg_ tweeted, "Literally any other hot chicken place coulda burned down but it had to be prince's." Addressing the driver of the Ford Explorer, @OcifferJJ declared, "All of Nashville hates you sir."

In November, *Eater* named Prince's one of the 38 essential places to dine in America. Six years ago, the James Beard Foundation gave the restaurant its America's Classics award, which honors "timeless" establishments serving "quality food that reflects the character of its community." Nashville hot chicken, the foundation said, was a "totemic" creation. The proprietors of Prince's, and its many imitators, regularly appear on TV food and travel shows. Anthony Bourdain, after sampling the hot chicken of a competitor, Bolton's, said, "I eat many strange and spicy things around the world, but never in my life have I experienced something like this." He added, "Is it food? Or an initiation ritual for Yankees?"

Such comments can make eating Nashville hot chicken sound like one of those "challenges" in which people choke down spoonfuls of cinnamon. But for many diners the dish is an obsession. In a short documentary for the Southern Foodways Alliance, a Prince's devotee describes hot chicken as "worse than dope" in its addictiveness. When Isaac Beard, who owned a massage-therapy clinic in Nashville, first ate Prince's hot chicken, he thought that it was just okay; then, about a month later, he woke up in the middle of the night with an enormous craving. "From that moment on, I was licked," he later told Timothy Charles Davis, the author of *The Hot Chicken Cookbook*, adding, "There's something legitimate there in hot chicken that's not there with, say, Buffalo wings." (Beard now owns a hot-chicken restaurant, Pepperfire, four miles south of Prince's.)

On Fridays and Saturdays, Prince's stays open until 4:00 a.m., and in those early hours graveyard-shift workers share vintage wooden booths with country music artists and fans emerging from the honky-tonks. A Prince's employee once said that Beyoncé and Jay-Z always "send somebody down" for takeout when they're in Nashville. Devotees from out of town are known to head to Prince's straight from the airport. In the Reddit thread FoodPorn, someone once reported that a friend "flew from Nashville with Prince's Hot Chicken in hand like she was carrying a donor organ."

Ira Kaplan, of the indie band Yo La Tengo, heard about Prince's from Richard Baluyut, of the band Versus. Kaplan has recalled, "We were told it came in 'mild,' 'medium,' 'hot,' and 'extra-hot,' but if we'd never been there before we would not be allowed to have extra-hot. We asked if we could at least taste 'extra-hot sauce.' What rubes we were—we were informed that there *is* no sauce." Kaplan found Prince's hot chicken "simultaneously delicious and practically inedible." He ate it four days in a row. The band wrote a song about it, "Flying Lesson (Hot Chicken #1)," and then another, "Don't Say a Word (Hot Chicken #2)," and then another, "Return to Hot Chicken."

The weekend of the Ford Explorer crash, Prince's had been expected to be even busier than usual: the Tennessee Titans were at home, playing the Indianapolis Colts, and the Predators, Nashville's popular hockey team, were also in town. One vehicle after another pulled into the empty parking lot and idled, the occupants confounded by the CLOSED sign.

The day after the crash, the woman who has been called the "queen mother" of Nashville hot chicken, André Prince Jeffries, drove to Prince's and parked in her usual spot, four feet from the front door. Jeffries, who is in her early 70s, has run the restaurant since 1980. She wears glamorous hairstyles, plum-colored lipstick, a smoky eye, and long lacquered nails. (That day's shade was lavender.) She also had on gray sweatpants, a matching shawl, Ugg-style boots, and a red-and-purple crocheted cap. Enormous earrings dangled halfway to her chin. When she knows she'll be interviewed on camera, she may dress in a Prince's T-shirt; otherwise, she does not advertise. She regularly declines offers to open franchises—she recently rejected a request from Dubai—and to star in reality-TV shows.

Clutching a cane, Jeffries made her way into Prince's, where a few employees had started cleaning up. Spotting a brick near the front door, she shrieked, "Is that the brick that was on the accelerator?" Her event planner, Katrina Ware, laughed and said, "Naw, that brick's in *evidence* now." Jeffries said, "Have mercy!" Her tinkly voice is laced with cackle and rasp.

People eat at Prince's because of the chicken but also because of the story behind it. Jeffries has spent the better part of her adulthood recounting the legend, for she inherited both the recipe (which is secret) and the family lore (which is unverifiable). In the 1930s her great-uncle Thornton Prince III was a handsome pig farmer and fond of women. One Saturday night, he dragged home late, angering his girlfriend. The next day, Prince asked her to make his favorite food, fried chicken. The girlfriend complied, but with a furious twist: she saturated the bird in cayenne pepper and other spices.

No doubt, Prince was expected to suffer, and did—but he also enjoyed the experience. He began replicating the spicy fried chicken and selling it on weekends, out of his home. He eventually opened a small restaurant, the BBQ Chicken Shack, which became beloved in the Black community. It became popular with white people, too, especially after the restaurant moved to a location near the Grand Ole Opry. Under Jim Crow, the Princes were not free to dine wherever and however they wanted, or to use the front door of white establishments, but they never told their own customers where to sit or what door to use. The matter handled itself: Black patrons sat up front; whites entered through the back door and sat in back.

Nashville, which was chartered in 1806, on the Cumberland River, is closer to Bowling Green, Kentucky—Union territory— than to Memphis. By the start of the Civil War, it was one of the country's 60 largest cities, with a population of 17,000. The Union army saw Nashville as a potential supply center, and captured the city in 1862. Escaped slaves flocked there, adding to an already sizable African American population. The Prince family had been enslaved at a plantation south of town. Thornton Prince III seems to have been born around 1893.

The civil rights leader Ralph Abernathy once said that, in the Black community of the 1930s, "chicken was the best of all meals to serve," especially on Sundays: "Gospel bird" was "better than ham, better than pork chops, better even than roast beef or steak." Timothy Charles Davis, in his cookbook, points out that poor people don't tend to document their lives the way well-off people do, and that American journalists of the early 20th century covered only "high-end, white-tablecloth places, not workingman joints peopled by African Americans." The name of the girlfriend whose attempt at revenge inspired a culinary phenomenon is unknown. The story is "so perfect, it almost—*almost*—seems created out of whole cloth," Davis noted, but he added, "Does the lobster roll have such a story? I think not." The chef and TV personality Carla Hall, a Nashville native who made hot chicken the main attraction at her former restaurant in Brooklyn, has said that, whatever the details about Thornton Prince III's love life, "the chicken ain't nothing but the truth."

After Prince died, around 1960, the restaurant got passed around to relatives, eventually landing with Jeffries, the granddaughter of one of his brothers. She made some tweaks. First, she changed the name to Prince's Hot Chicken Shack. "Hot chicken is *not barbecue!*" she told me. She replaced the restaurant's 19-inch cast-iron skillets with deep-frying vats. Then, after a mother asked her why Prince's didn't serve chicken that wouldn't terrify her children, Jeffries introduced varying levels of spiciness. The current maximum level, XXXHot, is irresistible to spice-hounds and fools. The menu board, hanging above the order window, features an image of flames.

YouTube is filled with footage of people trying hot chicken. Rendered speechless, they cough, tear up, towel off. The best way to eat fried chicken is with your hands, but Nashville hot chicken leaves the fingertips glistening with red residue. Jeffries still talks about the customer who made the mistake of wiping his eyes with his fingers—he knocked over furniture in his agonized rush to reach the bathroom faucet.

Jeffries enjoys pointing out that men tend to order the hottest varieties to see if they can stand them, whereas women order their chicken that way because they like the heat. Hot chicken's unofficial ambassador, the former mayor Bill Purcell, likes to say that, at Prince's, anything hotter than Hot "ain't chattin' food." When the English food writer Tom Parker Bowles, the son of Camilla, ate at Prince's, in 2004, he ignored a recommendation to start with Mild or Hot and instead ordered XHot, telling himself, "This will show these lily-tongued Southerners what true British grit is really about." He was soon silently berating himself as a "vainglorious twat."

In 2013 Sean Brock, then a celebrated chef in Charleston, showed up at Prince's with a pal. Jeffries took their order. "Am I crazy if I get the extra-hot?" Brock asked.

"That's suicidal chicken," Jeffries told him.

"I gotta do it," Brock said. "But I'm nervous."

The friend asked him, "What's the worst that could happen?"

Jeffries said, "Just don't let it happen *in here*."

Prince's is so secretive about its recipe that employees must agree in writing not to divulge details. Cameras aren't allowed in the kitchen, which is mostly walled off from customers' view. Devotees are left to guess at the ingredients: paprika, garlic, onion powder, vinegar, pickle juice, pork fat, bacon grease, sugar? Perhaps the chicken is marinated in spiced milk, dredged in spiced flour, fried in spiced cooking oil, and then coated in a spicy paste. (*"Milk?"* Jeffries told me. "No, no, no!") On Reddit, someone theorized that, during the preparation of hot chicken, "the oil combines with the chili to make some kind of undigestible lava." Semone Jeffries, André's daughter, who is in her early 50s and runs Prince's with her mom, can be seen in the background of one video, ladling out a rich, auburn liquid; but the secret isn't "just dousing some spicy stuff on top at the last minute." A customer once described Prince's hot chicken as spice "down to the bone."

A food's spiciness can be measured in Scoville Heat Units, a gauge developed, in the early 20th century, by Wilbur Scoville, a pharmaceuticals chemist from Connecticut. A jalapeño, at its hottest, measures 8,000 SHU. Cayenne, the only confirmed hot-chicken ingredient, is at least four times hotter than that. There is a growing market for peppers that have been cultivated expressly for pungency. At last check, the hottest chili pepper, as recorded in August 2017, by Guinness World Records, was the Carolina Reaper, which comes in at 1.64 million SHU. Prince's fundamental recipe predates newfangled peppers.

Cayenne stimulates the nervous system, awakens mucus, and can cause the heart to beat faster. The heat builds on itself. Jeffries likes to say that hot chicken will sober you up and clean you out. She calls it "a twenty-four-hour chicken." Activities that may not pair well with Nashville hot chicken include a road trip, a long flight, a first date, work, sleep, and your wedding. First-timers have been advised to prepare for hot chicken by putting a roll of toilet paper in the freezer at home.

As Brock, the chef, started to eat, he took off his eyeglasses. Jeffries told him, "Start out slow." She added, "Say your prayers."

Brock soon said, "This has ruined fried chicken for me."

"This is not a boring chicken," Jeffries agreed. "It's a *passionate* food."

His face flushed, his nose running, Brock said, "I think I'm hallucinating."

At one point during the global spread of Nashville hot chicken, someone bad-mouthed the dish as a "stunt food." Andrew Zimmern, the host of the Travel Channel show *Bizarre Foods,* disagreed. He first tasted hot chicken 40 years ago, at Prince's. "This is not gimmick fare," he said. "This is not a scorpion you get inside a lollipop at the museum gift shop. This is a way of eating."

Decades ago, a former cook at Prince's left and started his own place, Columbo's, in downtown Nashville. In the '90s Bill Purcell, who at that time worked as a lawyer, represented the restaurant in a tax matter. After trying its hot chicken, he ate at Columbo's at least once a week. When Columbo's closed, amid downtown redevelopment, Purcell shifted his allegiance to Prince's, even though it was a 20-minute drive to Northeast Nashville.

In that part of town, 42 percent of the children live below the poverty line. Prince's zip code, 37207, has one of the country's highest incarceration rates. Recent neighborhood crimes have included assault, robbery, and break-ins. Jeffries often refers to "my little thugs"; she is talking about the reputed drug dealers who "watch over" her and protect her business from harm.

Purcell noticed that Prince's attracted an unusually broad cross-section of residents. The mixture of race, income, and ethnicity struck him as representative of the city he wanted Nashville to be. He told me, "This particular food is one that, literally from the start, has brought people together who otherwise would not be in the same place." Hot chicken, he realized, might be Nashville's "only indigenous food." In 1986 Purcell, a Democrat, was elected to the state legislature, and he eventually became the majority leader of the Tennessee House of Representatives. In 1996, in his last official act as a lawmaker, he declared Prince's to be the best restaurant in Tennessee, and presented Jeffries with a printed proclamation. She hung it on the wall at Prince's. After it grew yellow and grease-stained, she framed it.

In 1999 Purcell was elected mayor. He served two terms, until 2007. He ate at Prince's so often that people joked the restaurant had become his second office. During his final year as mayor, Nashville had its bicentennial, and Purcell commemorated it by creating the Music City Hot Chicken Festival. The event, held each Fourth of July, begins with a parade of fire trucks.

Other local restaurateurs began attempting to replicate Prince's hot chicken, often adding their own twists. Dozens of places in the Nashville area now specialize in hot chicken—Slow Burn, 400 Degrees, Party Fowl, TNT BBQ—and indicate the level of spiciness with such terms as Poultrygeist, Executioner, and Shut the Cluck Up. Fans plan entire weekends around which hot-chicken restaurants they'll visit. Zimmern, the Travel Channel host, told me that the mystery surrounding Prince's recipe has led to a range of innovation: "All Nashville hot chicken is not created equal. The seasoning dredges are getting more complex, the oil baths are becoming more bespoke. Safflower oil, heated to three hundred degrees and then cooled before adding the ground hot chilies, is one famous joint's secret."

Nashville hot chicken can now be found everywhere from Los Angeles (Howlin' Ray's) to Melbourne (Belles Hot Chicken) to Singapore (Chix Hot Chick'n). In Chicago, the chef Jared Van Camp started Leghorn Chicken after developing a "hot tooth." A dreadful form of hot chicken is now on the menu at KFC, and Pringle's recently introduced a flavored potato chip that the *Washington Post* called "an insult to the fine citizens of Nashville."

Although certain upstarts have earned admirers, Prince's remains the gold standard. Bolton's, which grew out of Columbo's and developed "hot fish," is also a favorite, and, like Prince's, it remains embedded in the Black community. A lot of the new places were started by white people, including, in 2001, the country music star Lorrie Morgan. (Her restaurant has since closed.) In 2012 Hattie B's Hot Chicken opened and became popular, especially with tourists; the company, which is family-owned, now has several Nashville locations and has opened outposts in Birmingham, Memphis, Atlanta, and Las Vegas, with plans to expand throughout the Southeast.

A few years ago, at a conference in New York, Devita Davison, the executive director of FoodLab Detroit, used Hattie B's and Prince's as examples in a lecture about restaurants and race, titled

"Black Food Matters: Race and Equity in the Good Food Movement." Recounting the story of Prince's, she said, "Hot chicken, particularly in the African American community, was more than just about eating chicken." She cued up an image of an article, in the magazine *Food Republic,* bearing the headline "Meet the Man Who Launched the Nashville Hot-Chicken Craze." The man in question wasn't Thornton Prince III; it was John Lasater, the chef at Hattie B's. Lasater, who is white, trained at the French Culinary Institute in New York. His brother-in-law, Nick Bishop Jr., who is also white, cofounded Hattie B's; Bishop's grandfather was a CEO of the Morrison's Cafeteria chain.

As Davison observed, when "African American entrepreneurs don't grow rich" from an invention like hot chicken, it's not necessarily because rivals make superior food; it's because Black entrepreneurs still struggle for such resources as bank loans and industry networks. The food world had been talking about "who gets credit for what cuisine." Davison said, "I don't think that white voices should be centered around a dish" invented and popularized "by Black businesses eighty years ago." She concluded, "We cannot afford to have a movement that is based" in "white privilege."

Jeffries often jokes that Prince's success allows her to "pay one more bill," but her modesty is considered part of her shrewd business sense. She lives in a one-bedroom place but owns several properties in the Nashville area. Whenever Jeffries is asked what the Prince family thinks of copycats, she demurs; Thornton Prince, after all, was the first of the opportunists. The *Nashville Tennessean* recently tweeted, "What does the owner of Prince's think about all these hot-chicken imitators?" One Prince's fan replied, "Ms. Andre has always been so gracious about the Nashville Hot Chicken trend popularizing other restaurants. But Prince's is the OG. And that's that on that."

On the Friday before the fire, Bill Purcell met me for an early lunch at Prince's. The restaurant opened at 11:30, and by 11:15 the line outside was a dozen deep. Jeffries wasn't expected until the late afternoon, because she always works the shift that ends at 4:00 a.m.

After serving as mayor, Purcell had returned to practicing law; he arrived at Prince's in an overcoat, a blue blazer, and a striped scarf. Inside, he was pointed toward a table by the window, where an overturned Styrofoam plate, on which someone had Sharpie'd the word RESERVED, sat atop a Christmas-themed tablecloth. Purcell, who is in his 60s, with silver hair and an amused demeanor, said, "If I haven't had hot chicken in a week, I feel a little puny."

Customers place their orders at a cutout in a plywood wall that separates the kitchen from the dining room. After paying, they listen for their number to be called. Each dish is made to order —veterans know they'll wait 45 minutes or more.

"What you need to decide is really very simple—leg or breast, and what temperature," Purcell told me. The leg quarter, which costs six dollars, consists of a drumstick and a thigh; the breast quarter, seven dollars, comes with a wing. Purcell only gets the leg quarter, Hot. "This is a hot-chicken shack," he said. "If you wanted medium, you'd go to a medium-chicken shack." We both got the leg quarter, Hot.

Bad fried chicken isn't worth the loss of the bird; on this I am a reliable judge. Born and raised in Mississippi, I am the granddaughter of a fried-chicken savant who always managed to keep the meat tender and the skin crispy. The chicken that I saw on the plates at Prince's looked like my grandmother's, only much darker —an almost umber shade. "It's such a *personal* chicken," Jeffries told me later. "Our hands touched every piece. It's not like in a machine."

Our server was Tyreese Lawless—the man who was later cleaning the fryers when the Ford Explorer rammed into the tobacco shop. Purcell introduced Lawless, a former semipro football player, as a rising "superstar" of hot chicken. Lawless told me that when Semone hired him she had warned, in her soft-spoken way, that if he discussed the marinade with anyone he'd "never work in the hot-chicken world again." When he brought us our lunch, he described the secret ingredient as "love."

Prince's hot chicken is served on two slices of white bread. A short stack of dill-pickle chips sits atop the chicken, speared with a toothpick. The bread and pickles may appear to be garnish, but they are, as the Beard Foundation put it, "the closest things to life rafts your taste buds will find." The bread, having absorbed the spices and oil, appears to be soaked in blood.

The two chief attributes of hot chicken—fried chicken and

spice—aren't an inevitable pairing. Southern food tends not to be spicy, except for tangy barbecue. A lot of Deep Southerners like jalapeño jelly (with cream cheese, on crackers); and we may add jalapeños to corn bread, or to pintos or collards, and speckle our turnip greens with pepper sauce. But, beyond Cajun territory, spice isn't a staple, making hot chicken an outlier in southern cuisine. Fans have noted the convergence of several pleasures at Prince's: the quality of the fry; the "complexity" of the seasoning; the degree of the burn. You either get it or you don't. I got it. The spices were deep and smoky, and as we ate, Purcell said what I was thinking: "I wouldn't want the chicken to be hotter, and I wouldn't want it to be *less* hot."

Nearby, a customer named Ashenae Goins and her daughter, Madison Steptoe, were waiting for their order. We invited them to sit with us until their number was called. Goins, who is 35, works for Verizon, and Madison is in the ninth grade. Both were wearing hijabs. When Purcell and I mentioned that we'd been talking about where Prince's customers come from, Goins said, "We're from here. We're natives."

Goins had eaten at Prince's all her life. An uncle who worked the third shift used to bring it home, in an oily brown bag. "Prince's would be our Saturday-night thing," she recalled. Madison had just been saying that one of her earliest memories was standing in line at Prince's with her mother. When the other hot-chicken joints started opening, Goins tried them, but declared everything but Prince's "fake." At work, her colleagues call her "the hot-chicken connoisseur."

Goins was visibly pregnant. Jeffries generally advises prospective mothers to choose Plain or Mild (unless the baby is due—some believe that spicy food induces labor). Goins told me, "Since I've been pregnant, it's not always hot *enough* for me. I *dream* about it. The other day, I called my husband and said, 'Can you stop and get me some Prince's?' He was, like, 'Right now?' I said, 'Right now.'" Goins said that her doctor had told her, "I don't know if you should be eating that," and that she had responded, "If I don't, I'll die."

As she waited for her lunch, she thought about it and said, "I *could* go to Medium."

Madison said, "You can't go Plain, though. I know that."

*

The next day, I went to Hattie B's with old friends who live in the Nashville area. Hattie B's is their favorite. They especially like the sides—the black-eyed-pea salad, the pimento mac and cheese. The restaurant was spacious and loud, with piped-in pop music. The crowd was predominantly white. The line moved swiftly, past a self-serve soda station. I ordered my chicken Hot. The food showed up within minutes.

At that point, I had eaten Nashville hot chicken only once in my life, and yet I felt a snobbish disdain for the spices that ostentatiously coated the crust; the granules resembled crimson sand. I also tasted too much sugar. That night, I was back at the strip mall, where dozens of cars stretched from the Prince's parking lot all the way to a nearby highway.

For years, fans of Prince's clamored for a second location. Jeffries didn't want to do it. "If you franchise something like this, you miss all of that intimacy," she once said. In 2016 she gave in, and Prince's Hot Chicken Shack South opened, in a former sports bar, on the other side of town.

Employees jokingly call the Northeast Nashville location "the shack" and South "the palace." The shack seats two dozen people; the palace seats more than a hundred. It's got big-screen TVs, and beer on tap, and it closes well before four in the morning. On the walls, instead of the grease-stained proclamation and posters, there are enormous photographic portraits of Jeffries and Thornton Prince III. Aesthetically, it's not all that different from a Ruby Tuesday (or a Hattie B's). On Reddit, someone wrote, "Bougie Prince's is much nicer in every conceivable way than OG Prince's. And somehow for that, it's just less magical."

The night after the fire, every seat was taken at the palace, with a line to get in. Whenever someone entered, an employee hollered, "It's a forty-five-minute wait for all orders!" I ordered a leg quarter, Hot, to go, and sat at a table near the entrance to wait. Julie Tracy and Eric Hinton were sitting there, too. Tracy, an out-of-work hotel clerk in her late 50s, was lamenting the damage at the other Prince's and decrying its rivals as diabolical impostors. She has lived in Nashville for 31 years and had brought Hinton to Prince's for his first visit. He had moved to the city only recently, from Illinois, and kept a pen in his pocket in case he felt the urge to write a song. He'd decided to "ease into" hot chicken, with Medium, while Tracy adheres to the maxim "*Mild,* baby!" She told me, "The Medium about melted my face off—and I *like* spicy." She and Hinton had also placed an XXHot order for Tracy's ex-boyfriend, whose diabetes had cost him a leg and an eye. Tracy told me that when she worked in hotels she steered tourists to Prince's. "It's important for people to hear how places like Prince's came about," she said. "In the new Nashville, I see too many things gone."

A few hours earlier, I'd been with Jeffries at the damaged location, as she supervised the cleanup with Semone and several employees. "I'm having the hardest time, trying to adjust," she told me. "I'm usually here until four in the morning. After all these years, I can't believe I was off on a Friday."

Looking around, she noticed that the vintage booths were missing. "Wait a minute," she called out. "Where are my benches?"

"They went into storage," Semone explained. She had also stashed away the kitchen equipment, the menu board, and the best-restaurant proclamation. The shack had become such a landmark that, she worried, thieves might try to steal artifacts.

Jeffries looked alarmed. "We ain't gonna be closed that long!"

Semone explained that there were insurance matters to deal with, and the entire strip mall would need to be repaired and inspected before Prince's could reopen. She told her mother, gently, "You're gonna be closed for a few minutes."

Jeffries absorbed the news. "Life is full of transitions," she said. "Like my mama always told me, 'No matter what happens, keep moving.'"

We All Scream

FROM *Eater*

ICE CREAM IS not the American Dream, not exactly. It's more like the American Way. It has countless stories to tell, and anyone can tell them. Walk up to the freezers at Whole Foods and stare at the rows and rows of primo pints. Which will you choose? Will it be a Van Leeuwen, wrapped in clean, modern, Easter egg monochrome? A whimsically hand-doodled Ample Hills? Or a McConnell's, the epitome of old-fashioned?

They're all selling the same thing: a trip to Bountiful—an Instagram-filtered memory of one's own past, and a greater, collective American promise. Whether their designs evoke the Yankee-Doodle optimism of Norman Rockwell or the hazy, impasto California Dreaming of Wayne Thiebaud, they're all tapping a kind of bygone patriotic ideal. With this modern repackaging of Americana comes an additional tenet of our mythical history: the virtue of artisanry. No, they're not churning ice cream in wooden buckets, but they want you to know that there is care and craft in each and every pint. That they're making the brownies in your scoop of chocolate fudge brownie from scratch, in-house. That they're using responsibly sourced produce from small, local farms. This handmade's tale may be the most important story they tell—and sell.

Capitalism is the American Way, too. You can always get someone to pay more for something—in fact, it's encouraged. Still, $8, $10, $12 dollars is an awful lot for a pint of ice cream, which was one of the few staples that, no matter where or how we lived, it seemed we could all rely on enjoying. As our egalitarian treat becomes another common good that's been "elevated" into a luxury item, we might want to ask a few questions of the national pas-time-as-dessert—like, how did we get here? How good is $10-good? And if it's really that good, how much better might $15-good be?

Eve Babitz, who, like most of us, has been known to succumb to a craving for a scoop, may have been more inclined to lose it over boys than anything else, but her relative objectivity about the rest makes her observations reliably perceptive. In *Eve's Hollywood*, the same book in which she recounts wearing her "leopardskin bath-ing suit and eating a [Wil] Wright's chocolate burnt-almond ice-cream cone" as a gorgeous young man in a Jaguar chucks a U-ey to check her out at 13, only to drive off just as abruptly, leaving her with a broken heart, she writes:

> My mother once told me that in high school she won the state champi-onship for catsup making. The girl with whom she'd shared a kitchen only won 4th place though they'd made the catsup in the same pot and there was no difference. My mother puts hers in a glass jar with flowers painted on it that she painted herself. Packaging is all heaven is.
>
> It's the frames which made some things important and some things forgotten. It's all only frames from which the content arises.

If you asked kids what they imagine people eat in heaven, ice cream would probably be one of the most popular answers. As they get older, they might stop believing in heaven, but not in ice cream—although these prices could make a person question their faith. What if it is all just packaging?

Hard-packed pints, even the $10 ones, are made from the same fundamental ingredients—milk, sugar, air—with the same basic technology as the $5 pints, and even the $5 not-quite-half gallons. The people responsible for these pricey pints will tell you that the cost is justified. They incorporate more butterfat; their milk is or-ganic and comes from grass-fed, deliriously happy cows; and they use the best ingredients possible, whether direct-trade coffee or gently smoked cherries. These details—signifiers that speak to a contemporary antibourgeois bourgeois culture that selects for "au-thenticity," "mindfulness," and "transparency"—go into their ice cream, and the story that their ice cream tells, one as conscien-tiously fashioned as the other.

You can put organic bilberries or biodynamic sapodillas foraged by an elite cult of yodeling eunuchs into your product and slap a

$20 price tag on it, for all the United States government cares, but what's inside had better be ice cream, if that's what you're calling it. Not gelato, not sorbet, not ice milk, not frozen yogurt, and definitely not the ever-enigmatic "frozen dessert."

The FDA has a specific legal definition of "ice cream" that stipulates both the process by which it's made—"freezing, while stirring"—and the minimum amount of dairy fat it must contain (10 percent). There are other rules, ones about pasteurization or the use of "hydrolyzed milk proteins" and "optional caseinates," but the important thing to know is that anything labeled "ice cream" contains a legally mandated amount of dairy and dairy-derived fat, or butterfat, determined by weight: a gallon of ice cream must contain 1.6 pounds of dairy solids and weigh at least 4.5 pounds. So there's a limit to how far even Halo Top, the world's preeminent seller of fantastically branded pints of exquisitely flavored air, can stretch the definition.

Butterfat gives ice cream its richness, density, and luscious mouthfeel. It is the most essential—and, traditionally, most expensive—raw material in ice cream making. The more butterfat that's in there, the richer it feels, and the more it costs to make. In her cookbook *Hello, My Name Is Ice Cream*, Dana Cree, the former executive pastry chef for several One Off Hospitality restaurants and current owner of Pretty Cool Ice Cream in Chicago, explains that it's "key to ice cream's flavor, not only by contributing its own deliciousness but also by absorbing flavor from other ingredients like mint leaves or coffee beans."

But there's a "physical limit" to how much butterfat an ice cream base can take, Cree writes. More than 20 percent and "the ice cream feels flabby on the palate—more and more fat compounds on your cold tongue before your mouth has a chance to warm it and swallow it. Within a few bites, you'd notice your entire mouth has a slick of fat coating it." This is something you may have experienced, especially with the deluxe stuff. That greasy, creamed-soup texture is not a measure of fanciness; it's an indication that the ice cream may be full of first-rate ingredients, but the quality of those items isn't matched by the technique applied to them.

In a given batch of ice cream, the amount of butterfat is more or less inversely proportional to that of its overrun, or how much air it contains. More air means more fluff, and less room for other

ingredients, according to Jill Moorhead, who wrote the Grocery
Insider column for the Kitchn, and, at one point, was the wholesale marketing director for Jeni's Splendid Ice Creams. And it
turns out that a good way to spend less money on ingredients that
you have to pay for is to add more of the one that you don't.

Within the industry, ice cream is classified into "quality segments," which are based on price, the caliber of ingredients, overrun, and butterfat content, among other factors. The lowest quality segment is "economy," a label applied to a product that has
the maximum overrun (100 percent, or equal parts air to dairy
base)—and the minimum butterfat (10 percent)—permitted by
the FDA; it is the least ice cream that ice cream can be and still
legally be called "ice cream."

One step above that is "regular," which covers the standard supermarket half-gallon that usually has between 10 and 12 percent
butterfat. This is probably the fluffy ice cream of your youth—the
Breyers, the Dreyer's, the Edy's, and the Blue Bells; even as you
read this, future memories are being spooned into the mouths
of America's children. Then there's "premium," which runs the
gamut from the Whole Foods' in-house brand to the scoops you
might get at your local ice cream shop, with between 12 to 14 percent butterfat and less overrun than the generic.

For a long time, that was it. Things didn't get any more deluxe than premium until 1960, when Reuben Mattus came along
with the idea that there were people out there, unabashedly bour-
geois types, who might be interested in a more rarefied option. He
upped the butterfat to at least 15 percent, shunned preservatives
and stabilizers (we'll get to those, don't worry), and cut the overrun to 20 percent. He may have been just another macher from
the Bronx, but his ice cream conjured European sophistication:
his wife and cofounder, Rose, called it Häagen-Dazs. They rolled
their pints out in just three flavors—vanilla, chocolate, and coffee
—and sold them for what, at that time, was a higher price than any
other ice cream on the market, 75 cents each, or roughly $6.40
today. The "superpremium" quality segment was born.

The Mattuses had impeccable timing: over the next two decades, Americans became turned on to all things "imported." If it
came from Europe (or seemed to), it was perceived as finer, fan-
cier, and more desirable, and marketed accordingly. Häagen-Dazs

did more than fit right in; it spawned a number of knockoffs (this is why everyone ate all the Frusen Glädjé). By 1982, high-priced pints from Häagen-Dazs and its clones comprised 20 percent of total ice cream sales.

This was the scene that a pair of Long Island–born hippies named Ben Cohen and Jerry Greenfield burst onto when they took over a former gas station to sell "Vermont's Finest All Natural Ice Cream" in zany flavors like mint Oreo, mocha walnut, honey coffee, or wild blueberry. Their scoops—and pints—offered the same superior quality as the Fauxropeans' in terms of butterfat and overrun, but with a folksy, decidedly All-American ethos. They had little black-and-white spotted cows drawn onto their packaging, colorfully illustrated like a children's picture book, and where their continental competitors prided themselves on the elegance and purity of their products, the hippies packed their pints with Heath bars, or a "dastardly" mix of pecans, raisins, and chocolate chips. The duo's success posed enough of a threat to Häagen-Dazs that in 1984, its owner, Pillsbury—which had purchased the brand a year earlier—tried to block distributors from carrying Ben & Jerry's.

For all the folksiness, Ben & Jerry's pints were still among the most expensive ice cream sold in supermarkets at the time—$1.69 to $1.79, or more than $5 in today's dollars—though they came with a money-back guarantee. The twosome managed to leverage populism to charge more for one of the most populist things around, projecting good, clean, homegrown fun in direct opposition to pretentious European airs—all while asking customers to pay the same price. It was marketing genius, and it has served as the template for a new generation of ice cream makers.

You might have imagined that ice cream couldn't get any better than "premium"; the word indicates the ultimate in quality, the top slot. But this is America, a place where brands regularly transcend the limits placed upon them by science or decency, where terms like "fast casual" or "wellness" can become synonymous with "lifestyle," and where no one has ever minded the redundancy of a superlative like "superpremium."

More recently, an insurgent category, informally called "ultrapremium," has emerged. These ice creams have pornographic amounts of butterfat—17 to 20 percent—while their branding reflects the new artisanal-American vernacular of "hand-packed," "locally made," and "small batch." Ingredients aren't just "the best," they're seasonal, organic, heirloom, "crafted in-house," and sometimes, savory (fennel), unexpected (pickled mango), or disarmingly paired (milk chocolate and tarragon). Ultrapremium ice cream is also exceedingly expensive, with pints generally running between $8 and $12.

We can thank—or blame—Jeni Britton Bauer for the existence of ultrapremium ice cream. In November 2002 she opened the door to the first Jeni's Splendid shop in Columbus, Ohio. At the time, Häagen-Dazs's four-year-old dulce de leche was still all the rage, Ben & Jerry's had just retired Wavy Gravy, and brownie batter was about as exciting as it got. Britton Bauer exposed the midwestern city to the craft-beer equivalent of ice cream: flavors like sweet curry, basil honey pine nut, El Rey single-origin chocolate, and, the brand juggernaut—and a now-ubiquitous dessert conceit—salty caramel. "Ylang-ylang fennel ice cream sounds weird," she admits. But, she adds, there's a "method to that madness." The essential flavor derived from the flower is "similar to vanilla" and, she emphasizes, creates a nostalgic effect, which is what everything hinges on for Britton Bauer.

She priced it accordingly, and claims Jeni's Splendid was the first ice cream to cross the $10-a-pint mark—a milestone she takes pride in. "When we think about what's happening in flavor right now and ice cream, if you can't make ice cream better than Häagen-Dazs, you really can't charge that much," she says. She still loves Ben & Jerry's too, for its character and its mission—it's no coincidence that Jeni's Splendid is a certified B Corp—but says that "we don't have a twenty-first-century version of those companies. We don't have that next great American ice cream." Becoming that is her raison d'être.

"Most ice cream recipes are still based on those from the 1950s," Britton Bauer says. If that sounds surprising, think about the FDA standards: ice cream is required to contain a certain amount of fat, in specified proportions, and the source of that fat has to be dairy—the processing of which is governed by yet another set of rules—meaning the boundaries of an ice cream base, the liquid that eventually becomes the lickable heap perched on a cone, are relatively fixed. This means that the best way to maximize your flexibility or autonomy in recipe development is by having total control of your dairy source.

The only proven avenue for total control is owning every step of the process, a fact Michael Palmer can probably retire on. In 2011 Palmer, a winemaker, and his wife, chef Eva Ein, bought McConnell's Fine Ice Creams. Based in Santa Barbara, California, McConnell's was established as a dairy in 1934, 15 years before it launched its ice cream business. Palmer thinks that he is sitting on a pot of churnable gold, and is doubling down on his investment by constructing what will be California's first built-from-the-ground-up dairy in close to 60 years. When it's finished, it will have 8 to 10 times the capacity of his original dairy.

A licensed dairy doesn't just have access to the raw material straight out of the cow, it has the equipment and legal permission to pasteurize the cream and milk. Becoming licensed to pasteurize is onerous, to say the least, so ice cream makers are often beholden to a dairy like Palmer's to blend and sterilize their ice cream base. Many simply work with a standard, widely available commercial dairy base. Not only do most of their flavors probably start with the same ratio of milk, cream, sugar, and maybe eggs, they potentially share that base with competitors who depend on the same dairy source.

Some ice cream makers are able to develop an original recipe for their base with a dairy partner, which allows them to retain more autonomy over their product. But they're still dealing with a fixed entity, and ice cream, at its best, isn't a one-size-fits-all proposition: What works for peanut butter might not be optimal for mocha almond fudge. Some flavors, like strawberry, do better with less butterfat; or, like lemon, without eggs; if some of your mix-ins are particularly sweet (or salty) they require a more (or less) saccharine background. But if you're relying on one or two premixed bases, you're stuck. Either make do, or scrap your dreams of creating a new ice cream flavor.

For some ultrapremium producers, securing a dairy license for on-premises pasteurizing is a priority from the start. The license allows them to take raw milk and cream from their dairy source, then mix it themselves, so they can make as many different bases as they want, as long as they have the manpower, time, and equipment to handle it. Although Britton Bauer became certified in 2006 and previously pasteurized her bases in the back of her first Jeni's store in Columbus, she's found that doing everything at the dairy she collaborates with most closely yields better results. She uses the dairy's facility to do everything herself, including the churning. "Their ice cream machines are better than any we've ever had," she says.

It may be disappointing to learn that the machines are more important to how we physically experience ice cream than any perfectly calibrated ratio of butterfat to overrun, or the psychic well-being of the cows whose udders produced the milk and cream. A recipe is really just a measure of potential—of how good each bite-size gob could feel in your mouth, how its flavor might open up to you. If the recipe determines how much ice your finished product will have, the equipment used to process the ice cream determines the size of those crystals; the smaller the crystals, the better the ice cream.

The technology behind ice cream machinery dates back to 1843, when a woman named Nancy Johnson secured a patent for her hand-cranked "artificial freezer" that improved upon the jerry-rigged contraptions of the Ma and Pa Ingalls crowd. No more vigorously shaking a bucket full of salted ice one moment, then whipping and scraping the sweetened, flavored cream the next. This new device was the prototype for the familiar, ever-churning canister system widely used today. Explained by Laura B. Weiss in *Ice Cream: A Global History*, with Johnson's invention, "all that was required of a cook was to give the crank several good turns. That action would turn the dasher, ferrying the ingredients from the edge of the freezer to the center and back again." The mechanism, as detailed in US patent No. 3254, functioned by "constantly allowing fresh portions of the cream or other substances to be frozen to come in contact with the refrigerating surface."

In 2019 commercial-grade equipment is, obviously, electric, and can accommodate larger quantities of ice cream. You can program it for churn rate and length, and for the amount of aeration. But these systems operate exactly the same way and rely on the same architecture as Johnson's: a canister filled with an ice cream base spins inside a larger vessel. Industrial-grade machines fall into two categories, batch freezers and continuous freezers. The first is smaller and demands more human attention on the inputting and receiving ends—to load your base into the canister, feed in the flavorings, and then to collect the ice cream as it snakes out of the spigot like cold, bloated toothpaste being squeezed out of a tube.

Today's heroes of the artisanal startup brigade were batch-freezer babies, and Tyler Malek, the chef behind Salt & Straw, which he runs with his cousin Kim, remains faithful to the batch machine. He wants to figure out how to use its limited capacity and functionality to make the best ice cream, period. He claims he prefers it to the continuous freezer, equating the difference to hand-rolling pastry dough as opposed to sending it through a sheeting machine. "There's something you can taste in ice cream when it's handmade," Malek says.

An asshole might ask, "What is handmade ice cream, really?" They would have a point. Anyone using an electric churner, whether a batch machine or continuous freezer, is not, technically, making the stuff by hand. What can be done by hand, as the ultrapremium parties tend to do, is make the mix-ins from scratch, and that Malek does, more meticulously—perhaps maniacally— than anyone. "The pint we've brought to market that had the most hands, was nine," he says, before Kim explains: "He marks an ice cream by how many hands it takes to make it." When he wants to put gummy candies in his ice cream, he doesn't stop until he's figured out how to build the chewy, waxy bears of his dreams.

Like Miley Cyrus, Malek seems to enjoy the climb. He loves hand-packing pints—"scooping the ice cream in, ladling in the caramel, adding nine pieces of ganache to each"—and he and his cousin refuse to adjust their local point of view even as they expand the eight-year-old Salt & Straw beyond Portland, Oregon, to Los Angeles, Seattle, and San Francisco. Danny Meyer's Union Square Hospitality Group has invested in the company, allowing them to grow their business at their own leisurely pace. If the only way to move forward is to think inside the box, chefs like Malek are taking that to its furthest conclusion; you could call it thinking inside the coffin. Who's to say it can't lead to better results?

McConnell's Palmer, for one. "The term 'small-batch,' people think it refers to those tiny batch machines," he says with exasperation in his voice. "I will tell you it's an awful way to make a very good, consistent product." This is why, he adds, "so many people co-pack."

Co-packing—using a third-party contract manufacturer—is the

workaround for anyone without the capital or space who wants to scale up their production and access a continuous freezer. Jake Godby and Sean Vahey of San Francisco–based Humphry Slocombe continue to use a batch freezer at their first, freestanding location, but they have turned to co-packing to expand their business into supermarket aisles. "Since we don't have enough equipment capacity for grocery, we have partnered with a co-packer in the East Bay to help make our pints," Vahey said. "Our production team prepares all of the ingredients, and the co-packer runs it through their machines for us." He insists that they work "very closely" with the co-packer to ensure the "quality and taste" in their pints is up to par with what they scoop out of their storefront.

It's even possible that the quality and taste of those grocery pints surpass that of their shop scoops. Because, hold on to your hats, "ice cream should get better if you scale up," says Ben Van Leeuwen, cofounder of the eponymous brand. After getting his start selling ice cream out of a pastel-yellow truck in Brooklyn in 2008, he and his partners now operate a bicoastal empire. The enormity of Van Leeuwen's continuous freezer strikes you immediately when you walk through the company's Brooklyn facility, which Ben and his business partners Pete (his brother) and Laura O'Neill (his ex-wife) leased in 2015 and upgraded in 2016. At 5,000 square feet, the factory is more than six times the size of their previous space. A continuous freezer is self-loading, self-depositing, and yields consistently better results: bigger machines are able to freeze ice cream more quickly, and the faster it freezes, the smaller the ice crystals—and the smaller the crystals, the smoother the ice cream. "We joke it's kind of like Walter White's lab," O'Neill said, standing among the large, stainless steel cylinders connected by overhead pipes. As you look at them, you begin to understand this isn't as simple as buying just one (huge) piece of equipment —it requires an entire family of machines, such as special clean-in-place food-grade piping to transfer bases from pasteurizer to freezer, with numerous procedural stations along the way.

Due to its capacity, size, and cost, installing and operating a continuous freezer is only an option for brands that aim to produce vast quantities of ice cream. In the not-so-distant past, among superpremium brands, that mostly meant Ben & Jerry's and Häagen-Dazs, outfits that have the demand and distribution to justify (and afford) continuous freezers. Van Leeuwen's growth in New

York, LA, and Whole Foods global allowed the business to invest in the new factory and equipment, which currently produces around 2,000 gallons per day.

There's a point where that kind of setup begins to pay for itself. Before that, though, there's a tentative phase where batch equipment doesn't cover the desired output, but demand isn't quite high enough to fully support the cost of the tricked-out gear. Brian Smith of Ample Hills was in that kind of growing-pains stage when he moved his Gowanus-based operation into a larger space in Red Hook, with a brand-new continuous freezer. Before that, he was at capacity with his batch freezer, doing 450 to 500 gallons a day, or 12 to 15 gallons every 15 minutes. His latest facility will allow him to increase that tenfold and beyond.

Each batch freezer costs $36,000, Smith says. A continuous freezer is a lot more—he wouldn't say how much his new one cost, all told—but it's a behemoth. It will, he says, "allow us to regulate it and make it more consistent. The machine itself makes a creamier product. It will include a homogenizer, which we don't have now." The homogenizer is the second step—and piece of equipment —in the ice-cream-making process; it comes after the pasteurizer. Think of it like a rock tumbler for fat molecules; it blasts them into small, evenly sized particles, which will more readily emulsify (or divert) the water. After it's been blitzed in the homogenizer, the base is transferred to an aging vat, where it cools to a churnable temperature and its flavors have more time to develop.

An added perk of the continuous freezer is its fruit feeder, which allows mix-ins to be mechanically incorporated. Now, no one needs to stand by to collect the finished product, so Smith can cut down on manpower and rest assured that the contents of each pint are uniformly distributed. "I went from being terrified that we wouldn't be able to make a better product," he said. "Now I'm excited we can make a better ice cream at scale . . . and be able to lower prices."

Everyone seems to have scale on the brain—not just how to do it, but the optics of the endeavor. "Should we define super-super-premium by the size of its batches?" Palmer asks. The real "art in artisan," he asserts, "is how you scale your product." This flies in the face of everything we've been taught as consumers of specialty goods. "There's this automatic—you would defer to the smaller brand's quality, thinking, Oh, if they're smaller, they must be bet-ter," Ben Van Leeuwen complains.

You can see how this looks: A generation of ice cream makers develops their products, builds their brands, and cultivates their followings in thrall to a zeitgeist whose most hallowed values up-held the handmade over the mass-produced, the local over the (multi)national, and the notion that smaller isn't just better, it's the best. Now that they stand on the brink of potentially becoming the next Häagen-Dazs or Ben & Jerry's, they're declaring that ac-tually, maybe, that's all wrong. For ice cream, unlike cult breads or heritage meats or hand-jarred jam, they're saying, perhaps bigger really is better.

Anyone who makes ice cream, whether they have the most ram-shackle of rigs or the newest gadgetry on the market, is fighting the same battle: against time. Ice cream is best the instant it leaves the machine; every second after that, it's a little worse than it was before. No one, not even Michael Laiskonis, the James Beard Award–winning pastry chef who, as creative director of the Insti-tute of Culinary Education in New York, spends his days contem-plating the molecular structure of ice cream, can escape this iron-clad law of dessert thermodynamics.

Every time Laiskonis pumps a soft inflated, nougat-thick rib-bon out of his commercial-grade batch freezer for testing, he is reminded of his friend, a fellow pastry chef, who once confessed how profoundly sad it left him, knowing that the people he made ice cream for would never taste it at its peak.

This is just as true for the most incredible ice cream as it is for the worst; you could eat whatever just came out of a Halo Top or Turkey Hill spout and it would probably still be terrific. That's be-cause ice crystals are at their smallest at the moment the ice cream meets the world, just as it crowns and leaves the machine, where it turned over and over so that its water content was unable to clump together and seize up into crunchy ice. The second the water be-gins to freeze, Laiskonis says, "you've lost the battle."

Things only get worse from there. The machine—any and all of them—is designed to create a certain, fixed number of ice crys-tals, explains Salt & Straw's Malek. "Regardless of how cold your freezer will be going in, your crystal count drops immediately," he says. "So if we start with one thousand ice crystals, as soon as you pull it from the machine, you drop and start losing the smallest ones and say you drop down to nine hundred. Then you put it in a holding freezer and it drops to eight hundred and then it travels to another really cold freezer and it drops again to seven fifty . . . The biggest crystals that are left grab up that water, suck it up, hold it in and you get really large crystals." Every time you open the door to a freezer, in your kitchen or at your local supermarket, you injure your pints, loading them down with ever larger, smoothness-shattering crystals. There's only one proven, if partial, remedy: stabilizers.

Stabilizers were introduced to ice cream around the time we started pumping it full of air. After World War II, Americans lost interest in soda fountains and ice cream parlors, and grocery stores became the primary point of purchase as people brought their cartons home rather than socializing over ice cream. By the mid-1980s, as the *New York Times* reported, more than 80 percent of all ice cream sales were transacted at convenience stores or supermarkets. The rise in mass production brought the ubiquity of the carton, which needed to hold up for a lot longer than the scooped-to-order ice cream on a cone.

It should be obvious but may require saying: the primary job of stabilizers is to keep whatever solution they're added to stable. And yet people seem to dislike stabilizers, or the idea of them. They get lumped in with the phrase "artificial additives or preservatives," the lists of ingredients that no one can pronounce or spell, which must surely describe something unnatural and evil.

Yet ice cream makers who proudly—and often self-righteously—trumpet their avoidance of stabilizers and insist that their said absence improves the product and makes it more "natural," aren't being entirely straight with us. By and large, these additives are derived from natural ingredients and as long as they're used in the correct, small doses, they can produce ice cream better suited to withstanding the journey from the factory to your freezer without becoming too haggard.

A few hours with Laiskonis might disabuse the stabilizer truthers of their contempt. "Most of cooking is trying to manipulate water," he says. He could, he suggests, write a single-subject cookbook about that element. Ice cream, which is 60 percent water, would definitely get its own chapter. To make it, you're forced to complete an impossible task: Freeze a solution that, despite being called ice cream, is more than half full of water, all while avoiding the formation of ice. Ice is, well, icy—it's watery and crunchy, two attributes that make for a shitty pint. As your base churns in its chilled container, it begins to freeze, and thickens as it does so, in part because that water is forming crystals. If you can keep the crystals to a minimum number and size, you will produce decent ice cream.

Along with acting as thickening agents, stabilizers bind water that would otherwise turn to ice. Their binding properties allow them to do more than impair water's ability to freeze; they keep it tied up so that the fluctuations in temperature that would cause your ice cream to begin to melt, then subsequently refreeze and form new icicles, have less impact. And today's stabilizers derive from plant-based ingredients. Those most commonly deployed for ice cream are locust bean and guar gum, and they tend to be used in tandem. Their names sound scary, and the inclination is to assume they're artificial chemicals. But the layperson's term for locust bean is carob bean. Guar's a plant, too. Another common stabilizer, carrageenan, is seaweed-based. Options that sound even more science-y, like xanthan gum and pectin, come from natural sources.

The better ice cream stabilizers are blends—those from Italy developed for gelato are thought to be the best. They generally incorporate emulsifiers (elements that fuse otherwise incompatible compounds like water and fat), so they're all the more efficient. Used correctly, they "increase viscosity" and give you a "creamier mouthfeel," Laiskonis says. "Too much gets you something gummy, and increases overrun, too." That's what gives stabilizers a bad rap: several mass-market brands cut costs by using less-expensive stabilizers in place of milk fat, milk solids, or eggs.

Laiskonis has determined that perfection is achieved when stabilizers comprise less than half a percent of the base ("typically zero-point-two to zero-point-four percent if we're getting technical"). At such a low concentration, your taste buds won't detect any of it. Your mouth will pick up on a more substantial, appealing texture in the ice cream—that slight "chew" that gives the impression of extralusciousness. If you want to know what stabilizers taste like when there are enough of them present, just ask Britton Bauer. She calls it "a mouth-watering metallic flavor" that "has a slight bitterness." If you haven't experienced that flavor, eat a Twinkie, she advises. Laiskonis insists you'd need to add a hell of a lot of them for your taste buds to register what Britton Bauer described. She concedes that "the natural ones are fine," but where many would argue that, when used wisely, they improve the texture, and possibly flavor, she thinks the former suffers for them and the latter is muted.

She has sympathizers, Ben Van Leeuwen and Palmer among them. Van Leeuwen, for his part, likes to remind everyone that Häagen-Dazs doesn't use stabilizers either; Palmer admits that leaving them out of his pints gives him less control over their fate once they leave the McConnell's facility. Still, it might leave you wondering why you'd spend so much money on something that will never be as good as it once might have been.

That is the question, after all: Is the $10 pint worth it? And how different are these ultrapremium products from each other—or the rest, really? You'd think a blind taste test would help answer those questions. It did not.

Some of New York City's finest ice cream minds—and palates —generously volunteered their services and were put through a rather rigorous two hours of eating and assessing ice cream. Max Falkowitz, editor, journalist, and ice cream expert? Fany Gerson of La Newyorkina? Meredith Kurtzman of gelato? Natasha Pickowicz of Café Altro Paradiso and Flora Bar? Alex Stupak of Empellón? Nancy Druckman (ice cream fanatic and definitely a relation of the author—i.e., her mother)? Laiskonis? All present. There were numerous flights, and the judges were asked to consider each item they tried on the basis of the intensity and quality of its flavor, its texture, and its finish. Samples of Häagen-Dazs and Ben & Jerry's were slipped into each round to determine how the ultrapremium products compared to those in the price bracket beneath theirs.

The results of this test were hilariously ambiguous and mostly inconclusive. The tasters barely agreed on anything, except that none of them was particularly excited about a single item he or she tasted. Opinions varied, not just from one brand to the next, but from one flavor to the next of a single brand. Common complaints were of samples having "no character" or being "too sweet."

A tester who will remain nameless (okay, it was the mom) said it was the first time she had ice cream that "tasted terrible." Possibly the most telling information to emerge was that, out of nine vanillas, Häagen-Dazs came out on top, and it wasn't very close. (One of the test coordinators decided they liked the Van Leeuwen vanilla best because it tasted like marshmallow, which makes you wonder if anyone knows what vanilla tastes like, and why that company doesn't name that flavor "marshmallow.") In related news: Ben & Jerry's chocolate chip cookie dough scored solidly, too.

Whatever the answer to the question of "worth it" may be, Britton Bauer doesn't "see ice cream going back to five dollars from here." And why should she? She's been making and selling a lot of it, and her success shows no signs of slowing. But she wants to change her pricing model: Why not, she asks, charge by the flavor? Special flavors that are limited by access to products or require extra manpower should fetch a higher price than some of the less complicated, perennial offerings. You could "find a pint at nine ninety-nine at Whole Foods, or one that's close to fifteen dollars at a specialty market for a more labor-intensive pint," she suggests, quick to mention that distributors determine prices. "I think nine ninety-nine is pretty great," she says. For now, when you order through the Jeni's Splendid website, $12 is the damage per unit.

Ample Hills is distinguishing itself by going low when everyone is going high. Smith decreased the price of his pints in groceries in early 2018 from $9.99 to $8.99, and his latest packaging uses hand-drawn cartoon animals that have been part of the company's in-store and online imagery since he and his wife, Jackie Cuscuna, opened their first location in Prospect Heights in 2011. The look suits the brand's ongoing Disney affiliation; in addition to special-edition Star Wars pints, Ample Hills opened a storefront at Walt Disney World Resort nearly three years ago. "We're making ice cream that's more geared [to] a Ben & Jerry's version two-point-oh," Smith says.

Smith sees Ample Hills as less "intellectual" than the brands with which he shares retail real estate, and believes this curtails his ability to charge as much as they do. At the same time, he sees a gap in the high-end market where outstanding quality and kitsch overlap. He doesn't use the word "stoner," but it's easy to infer that Smith is speaking to the more laid-back foodie who doesn't take himself too seriously and digs artisanal junk food. "Our goal is not to be the most expensive pint in the freezer. As long as we've got Jeni's to the right of us at eleven ninety-nine, we feel at least we're not out there on a limb."

Cracking the mass market will require a slightly different algebraic set. "If we're in Target, it's going to be the most expensive pint by far. The goal then will be seven ninety-nine. But that's a ways off. You can't go up in price." Van Leeuwen, which took on investment last year to fuel national expansion, is now regularly $7.99 at Whole Foods, but it's using a trick pioneered by its forebears—one of its "pints" contains just 14 ounces of ice cream, not 16. It's a clever way to raise prices, or keep them the same while becoming more accessible; people rarely notice when a pint isn't a pint, as long as it looks like a pint.

Some might say no matter how delicious the ice cream or how big the pint, $10 is an absurd amount. Britton Bauer confesses, "I think fifteen dollars is too much for a pint." Others might be offended by the very idea that any American could be priced out of enjoying this once-accessible treat. We have a right to happiness; ergo, we have a right to ice cream.

Maybe the truth is that all ice cream, even the worst, is good enough. Ice cream tastes like something forgotten. It's a perfect example of synesthesia—faded memory in the edible form of perfectly smooth, barely frozen butterfat. Its flavors, no matter how long you infused those tea leaves or spices in its base, are fuzzy around the edges. When we indulge in it, we're not looking to experience the purest, most concentrated version of a bunch of fresh mint leaves, or for the deepest expression of caramel with salt. We do so to access a feeling. That is why, as Smith says, "even the cheapest, crappiest commodity stuff is good on a summer day, because it's still ice cream." And if you grew up on that cheapest, crappiest commodity stuff, you might even prefer it, because its familiarity makes that nostalgic connection stronger. Or, to put it more cruelly, a line from Sam Lipsyte's novel *The Ask:* "It was horseshit, of course, nostalgia for a nonexistent past, but it warmed the cheap parts of me."

Ice cream reduces grown people to the children they once were. It's why the entrepreneurs who have committed to improving or "elevating" ice cream stubbornly, maybe irrationally, believe in their fool's errand. It's why those who are willing—and able

—pull out their wallets for $10 pints, convinced that what's inside is worth it. Our faith in heaven may be long gone, but we haven't given up on ice cream, even if packaging is all it is. Here, the frames are often the content, the source of a holy commercial aura that comforts and drives us. It's the American Way.

DAN NOSOWITZ

What the Heck Is Crab Rangoon Anyway?

FROM *Atlas Obscura*

OF ALL THE wonders of the modern American Chinese menu, crab rangoon is one of the strangest. It consists of cream cheese, sometimes sweetened, plus, usually, very small bits of imitation crab, stuffed into a wonton wrapper and deep-fried, served with a syrupy, neon sweet-and-sour dipping sauce. It is, essentially, deep-fried cheesecake with fake crab in it—as sweet as any dessert, but served as an appetizer. It has a Burmese name, is served in a theoretically Chinese restaurant, and its main component was created in its modern form in New York in the late 19th century.

I conducted a survey through Twitter, in which more than 650 people responded with their experience of crab rangoon. The vast majority adore this dish, as I do. I asked respondents to state where they live, whether they order crab rangoon, and to describe the version they get. Responses came from New York, Chicago, Los Angeles, and other major American cities, in addition to Chattanooga, Tennessee; Tampa, Florida; Madison, Wisconsin; Boulder, Colorado; and many smaller towns. I also got replies from Dublin, Ireland; Vancouver, British Columbia; and other places outside the United States.

In all of these places, people love and order crab rangoon from their local takeout American Chinese (or Canadian Chinese or Irish Chinese) restaurant. In all of these places, crab rangoon is essentially the same dish. With a few exceptions (P. F. Chang's, Panda Express), none of these restaurants are formally associated with one another in any way, yet the dish is consistent, and consistently beloved.

What the heck is crab rangoon, and how did it happen?

One thing to get out of the way is that crab rangoon is not inauthentic, and you should not be embarrassed to order it. American Chinese food is its own cuisine, with its own staples and a reasonably long and fascinating history. There's a fundamental problem with the concept of authenticity in food, because cuisine is constantly mutating and adapting to new ingredients, new people, new techniques, and new ideas. Mexican food would be completely different without the influence of the Spanish and Arab immigrants and colonists; the tomato is not native to Italy; the chili pepper is not native to Thailand. There are old dishes and there are newer dishes, and that can be an interesting distinction. And there is tasty food and lousy food, but using some concept of authenticity alone as a criteria is a flawed approach.

American Chinese food did not arise with the first major influx of Chinese migrants to the United States, during the Gold Rush in the American West. These people cooked Chinese food for other Chinese people, who happened to be in the United States. By the end of the 19th century, other Americans had begun to discover Chinese food, which was to be found in the various Chinatowns that had sprouted up in cities large and small. But American Chinese food, as a distinct cuisine, was born thanks to a loophole in the racist laws aimed to keep Chinese immigrants out of, or at least marginalized in, the United States.

Those exclusionary laws allowed certain kinds of "merchant visas" to let Chinese Americans find workers who wanted to emigrate from China. In 1915 a court decided that restaurant owners qualified for those merchant visas, and the number of Chinese restaurants immediately ballooned. One economist estimated that the number of them quadrupled between 1910 and 1920.

A restaurant was one of the few ways for a Chinese American to own a business, and they began to blossom outside of Chinese enclaves. Chinese food was the first Asian cuisine to take hold in the United States; it was unlike the more Eurocentric restaurant scene at the time, and that made it exciting to some Americans.

This is the period when American Chinese food begins to

evolve. Chinese restaurateurs began to change menus to suit the tastes (and/or perceived tastes) of their new clientele. Jennifer 8. Lee, author of *The Fortune Cookie Chronicles,* in which she examines American Chinese food through the lens of the fortune cookie, says that the availability of ingredients was a major influence. Many ingredients that were expensive in China were cheap in America, and vice versa. Oil, for deep-frying, was cheap, as was white sugar and many cuts of meat, such as chicken breasts, which weren't prized in China. Szechuan peppercorns, on the other hand, were for a long time expensive and largely inaccessible in the United States.

Thus began a period of experimentation, when American Chinese restaurants—many of which were fancy, date-night places— began trying a whole bunch of stuff to see what stuck. Sometimes they modified older Chinese dishes. Szechuan kung pao chicken, for example, got sweeter, added Western ingredients such as bell pepper, and lost the expensive, distinctive peppercorns. Sometimes dishes were created out of whole cloth, like chop suey or General Tso's chicken. The latter, as revealed in the documentary *The Search for General Tso,* shares a name with a dish on the menu of a Hunanese restaurant in Taiwan, but is neither Hunanese nor Taiwanese. It is a perfect icon of American Chinese food: deep-fried, sticky-sweet and sour, barely spicy.

Through the 1950s and 1960s, much of the modern American Chinese oeuvre developed and was codified, especially the proven hits, the stuff you had to have if you wanted a packed dining room. A few companies further standardized things. Kari-Out, for example, today sells most of the little soy sauce packets nationwide. Menu printing was and remains dominated by a few printers in New York City and the Bay Area—menus used by tens of thousands of independent restaurants.

The dishes on these largely standardized menus came from a hive-mind of restaurateurs. "Something pops up and people copy it," says Lee. That's why it's nearly impossible to credit an original inventor for many of the classic dishes. Lee likens the process to open-source software, where anyone is free to make modifications to, or outright copy, the work of anyone else. Eventually, there emerged a pattern: if you wanted to have an American Chinese restaurant, certain menu items were expected.

But the inspiration had to come from somewhere. American Chinese chefs are still experimenting with dishes to suit their own hyperlocal customer bases. Yakamein, in New Orleans, combines Cajun seasoning with a beef noodle soup. Cashew chicken, from Springfield, Missouri, pairs southern-style fried chicken with cashews.

Crab rangoon has its roots in another quintessentially American cuisine. Starting in the 1940s, thanks to returning World War II veterans, the country began a decades-long obsession with the aquamarine hues and tropical vibes of Polynesia, or at least a vague idea of what Polynesia might be. It manifested as what we know as tiki culture.

Tiki bars and restaurants have even less in common with their ostensible international roots than American Chinese restaurants do. They were based instead on an American obsession with leisure, danger, and exoticism—along with what now reads as a racist stew of imagery: palm-thatched roofs, canned pineapple, ceramic Easter Island head mugs, white sand beaches.

The history of crab rangoon leads back to tiki culture. The dish was probably invented by Victor Bergeron, best known as the namesake founder of the Trader Vic's chain of tiki bars. (Trader Vic's, in turn, inspired the Trader Joe's grocery chain—you can still see some of that weird colonialist imagination in its design motifs.) In 1934 Bergeron opened a saloon called Hinky Dink's in Oakland, California. Capitalizing on the new craze for the South Pacific, Bergeron began integrating island signifiers into his decor and bar lineup. In 1937 Hinky Dink's became Trader Vic's, and began selling many of the cocktails now associated with tiki culture. (He is one of two disputed creators of the mai tai.)

Also in 1937, Bergeron started selling food at the new Trader Vic's. Eve Bergeron, head of marketing and public relations (and also Victor's granddaughter), sent me that original 1937 menu. Eve says that Joe Young, a Chinese American barback at Trader Vic's, was a major influence on the early menus. That first one has a couple of nods toward tiki culture: pineapple spareribs, imported New Zealand clams. But it is, largely, early American Chinese food.

Bergeron, though, was a joyful experimenter with both cocktails and food. Sometime in the 1940s, says Eve, he started messing around with wonton wrappers. "Knowing my grandfather, he probably just started to play with it," she says. "Just put stuff in here, fry it up, and see what we get."

The predecessors of cream cheese—a high-fat cheese made

with cream rather than milk and usually not aged at all—date back a few hundred years, but it was first mass-produced in New York in the late 19th century. Modern cream cheese, with its distinctive flavor and texture (imparted, to be honest, by a selection of stabilizers), is an American creation. In the United States, cream cheese became a staple of 1940s and 1950s American cuisine. This is a bit of a generalization of hindsight, but midcentury cookbooks seem to offer no end of creamy, cheesy sauces. With celery, with Spam, formed into balls and rolled in nuts, baked into cheesecake, the ultimate decadent dessert: it was the age of cream cheese.

Several people in my survey expressed embarrassment, or at least puzzlement, that crab rangoon violates the taboo against eating seafood with cheese. Though pervasive, this is a mild and inconsistent prohibition originating in Italy. But cream cheese has always somehow been exempt. Bagels with cream cheese and lox is a relevant, beloved example, and many famous dishes from the 1940s and 1950s use the combination as well. There's clam and cream cheese dip or those cucumber rounds with cream cheese–based salmon mousse on top.

Trader Vic's crab rangoon recipe, which remains largely unchanged over the decades it's been on the menu (at 20-odd locations today, including a notable cluster in the Middle East), has several major differences from American Chinese crab rangoon. Trader Vic's version uses real crab meat, for one thing: Canadian blue. It also includes A1 Steak Sauce and Lingham's Chilli Sauce, a bottled sweet-and-sour hot sauce created in Malaysia to suit the tastes of British colonists, in addition to cream cheese. Eve seemed offended when I suggested the cream cheese in a crab rangoon might be sweetened, as it is in many American Chinese restaurants. Trader Vic's is not (though the sauces mixed in are).

The name, too, is emblematic of tiki culture. Rangoon, now Yangon, is the largest city in Myanmar, formerly Burma. Myanmar has a substantial Chinese cultural and gastronomic influence, as the two countries share a border. But neither uses cream cheese in its food. There's plenty of crab in Burmese cuisine, but it's pretty clear that Trader Vic didn't name his dish after the city because there was any connection there. It is simply a place in a general Southeast Asia–Polynesia–South Pacific zone, suitably exotic-sounding but still easy for native English speakers to pronounce.

Tiki culture's widespread popularity occurred in the 1940s and

1950s, just when American Chinese cuisine was also gaining huge mainstream acceptance. The food served in tiki restaurants shared a lot with American Chinese food: vaguely Asian, very sweet, deep-fried. So it shouldn't come as a surprise that the cuisines cross-pollinated. Some tiki food gained a spot on those centralized menus. The pupu platter, for example, derives, sort of, from the Hawaiian pū pū, essentially Hawaiian meze: a selection of appetizers.

There was a strange, circular movement between tiki food and American Chinese food. Trader Vic's created tiki food by making American Chinese food seem more tropical; American Chinese restaurants took his dishes right back and made them more American Chinese. The American Chinese version tends toward cheaper imitation crab, which is made, usually, of pollock blended with starch and other binders, crab flavoring, and red food coloring. Imitation crab simply wasn't available to Trader Vic—it started being produced in 1975—and it's also neither Polynesian nor Chinese, but Japanese. American Chinese crab rangoon is a 1940s crab-and-cream-cheese dip stuffed into a wonton and deep-fried —a pure distillation of tiki fusion weirdness.

Crab rangoon is, after all, a preposterous dish. Many of the responses I got in my survey were sheepish, or seemed overly proud, as if to mask the problem of loving a dish that is utterly uncool, wildly outdated, and not even in the same ballpark as authenticity.

But that notion is even more preposterous than the dish. Making this crazy thing took years of work, ingredients from around the world, and who knows how many restaurateurs. Those little packets are strangely, psychotically perfect, designed to appeal to our base instincts: creamy and fatty and crispy and sweet and sour and savory, all at once. No modern food conglomerate would ever come up with something as deranged as crab rangoon, and if it was new today, nobody would buy it. And yet somehow it survived, watching food trends be born and die, outliving them all.

SARA KAY

Yelp Reviewers' Authenticity Fetish Is White Supremacy in Action

FROM *Eater NY*

OVER GRILLED CHEESE sandwiches at a pub on the Upper East Side of Manhattan, a friend and I discussed our favorite topic—eating. Up for debate this lunchtime was Foursquare; she explained that the review-driven app allowed users to rate restaurants on a multitude of factors. We reviewed our current restaurant to explore how it worked: "Good for Kids?" Sure. "Vegetarian Friendly?" Not really. "Authentic?" Skip. Woah, woah, woah—I asked her to slow down. What does "authentic" mean in this context? And how do I judge the authenticity of my grilled cheese sandwich?

The term "authenticity" is everywhere. Pundits claim that millennials crave it, restaurants boast authentic dining experiences, and Foursquare asks us to make judgments about it. These claims, often used as markers of quality, are employed by diners and restaurateurs alike—often used by owners to evoke a homespun or faraway romanticism. Nowhere does that come into play more than on user-based review sites like Yelp.

I would know: I have read and studied 20,000 Yelp reviews—part of my thesis as a master's student at New York University in the food studies program. I can tell you a lot about what I concluded about the depths of the internet, but I'll start with this one: the word "authentic" in food reviews supports white supremacism, and Yelp reviews prove it.

There are 17 million restaurant reviews on Yelp from over 30 different countries. Of course, not all of these reviews support white supremacy, or even mention authenticity. I narrowed my data collection to reviews from New York, and focused my field even further by picking from Zagat's top 10 most popular cuisines in New York City: Mexican, Thai, Japanese, Chinese, French, Italian, Korean, and Indian, adding Mediterranean and soul food based on recent dining trends. Over the course of six months, from September 2016 to March 2017, I read 100 reviews (written at any point prior to March 2017) for each of the top 20 Mexican restaurants on Yelp, recording how often commenters used the term "authenticity" or its synonyms, like "legitimate," or the phrases like "this made me feel like I was in Mexico." Then I kept going, ultimately reading 2,000 reviews for each of the 9 other popular cuisines.

Seven percent of the 20,000 reviews I read—or 1,400 reviews —contained some sort of authenticity language. While I don't know anything about the specific demographics of the reviewers I studied, trends in the reviews I read reflect some of the more troubling themes seen on the internet these days. In particular, the large sample size of reviews reflects the dominant culture: one that is continuously and historically rooted in favoring the white, Eurocentric experience.

When reviewers picture authenticity in ethnic food, they mentally reference all the experiences they've had before with that cuisine and the people who make it—and most of the time, reviewers view those experiences, whether from personal interaction or from interacting with media, as not positive. Reviews tend to reflect the racism already existing in the world; people's biases come into play.

According to my data, the average Yelp reviewer connotes "authentic" with characteristics such as dirt floors, plastic stools, and other patrons who are nonwhite, when reviewing non-European restaurants. This happens approximately 85 percent of the time. But when talking about cuisines from Europe, the word "authentic" instead gets associated with more positive characteristics. This quote from a reviewer commenting on popular Korean barbecue restaurant Jongro illustrates the bias: "We went for this authentic spot with its kitschy hut decor much like those found in Korea" (Celine N., 2016). Even though it's possible Celine N. liked the decor at the restaurant, "kitschy" is not a descriptor generally used in reviews serving modern Western cuisine. For example, a review from French restaurant La Grenouille reads: "Old elegance at its best! Yes, the ambiance is lovely with all the fresh flowers" (Alexandra C., 2013).

The distinction in tone extends to restaurant staff, too. Tamar G. writes about French restaurant Pardon My French in 2016: "The waiters are so good looking and so cute with their French accents!" In stark contrast, Kenny C. writes about his experience at Chinese restaurant 88 Lan Zhou Handmade Noodles: "One of the [servers] asked a lady (quite rudely in Chinese . . . as if there's any other way) to move." Not only do Yelp reviewers talk about non-Western workers differently, but the difference is racist, rude, and frightfully mimicking of other supremacist trends on the internet and in American life.

However, the distinction in how people talk about restaurants and authenticity doesn't just fall between Western and non-Western restaurants—there's nuance within the non-Western cuisines. The restaurants most impacted by this difference serve Mexican and Chinese food, according to my research.

The reasoning for this can be determined by looking at how American culture has viewed immigrant-population foods in the past. Historically in the United States, immigration rates dictate not only population wealth, but also cultural cuisine acceptance. For example, as Italians migrated to the United States in record numbers during the late 1800s, becoming the dominant poor and working class, popular sources such as magazines and papers counseled against aspects of Italian cuisine for fear of health risk. As Italian Americans have gained social status in the United States, we don't see magazine advertisements advising against eating garlic.

But we do still see signs waging war on MSG. This can partly be attributed to the fact that people from Mexico and China immigrate to the United States with the least amount of money. Reviewers tended to use authenticity language far more to talk about those cuisines, and in doing so, had expectations of authenticity aligned with characteristics that they associate with foreign-born poor. Cuisines from countries with wealthier immigrants, such as Japanese and French, are less beholden to these stereotypes.

While it might seem good to label restaurants as authentic, the usage of the term builds an authenticity trap where reviews reinforce harmful stereotypes that then become nearly impossible for restaurateurs to shake off. Negative traits like "gaudy signs" and decor, as well as price, end up becoming necessary to maintain positive reviews for being "authentic." But those same traits impact overall Yelp review rating; there's a negative correlation (–0.17) between star rating and the amount reviewers use the word "authenticity" in Chinese and Mexican food. As people talk about authenticity more online, star ratings decrease, independent of food quality.

It's a reality that restaurateurs and chefs have spoken about publicly. Amelie Ning Kang, an *Eater* Young Gun and owner of MáLà Project, was cognizant of these expectations when she opened her restaurant in late 2015, refusing to include dragon decor or more Americanized flavors on her menus. Similarly, Momofuku kingpin David Chang has widely discussed his dislike of expectations for low-priced ethnic food: "It pisses me off that Asian food has to be cheaper. Why? Not one person has given me a reason why," he said in 2016. Other studies similarly show the dichotomy in the way cuisines are viewed. Yelp reviewers tend to attribute food poisoning to Asian or Latin American restaurants, blaming it on low health grades, but statistically, lower health ratings aren't tied to food poisoning outbreaks.

This puts restaurateurs—particularly non-European immigrant owners—in a bind that makes it hard for chefs and owners to break out of stereotypes. Bringing in newer decor, sourcing local produce, charging higher prices, or taking creative liberty with a menu might allow non-Western restaurants and cuisines to compete in the larger dining landscape. But then, the restaurant might not meet the expectations of diners who expect authenticity in the "correct" way. Many restaurants end up losing either way: stay "gaudy" and authentic, and receive lower ratings; or update and be "not authentic," and receive lower ratings.

Of course, there are restaurants that have managed to fight negative stereotypes, including MáLà Project. But my data shows that the search for authenticity is still alive. And when reviewers use "authentic," they put unfair expectations on restaurateurs to maintain a low set of standards for their establishment—much lower than any restaurant serving Western cuisines. The language directly supports a hierarchy where white, Western cuisine is allowed more creative latitude to expand, explore, and generate profits than its non-Western counterparts.

The use of "authenticity" in the dining landscape is counterintuitive. It's usage to promote white supremacist norms furthers an atmosphere that's antithetical to the spirit of authenticity. The language of authenticity holds up the supremely inauthentic—a single ideology that supports possibly the most powerful social group: white people.

Contributors' Notes
Other Notable Food Writing
of 2019

Contributors' Notes

Burkhard Bilger has been a staff writer at *The New Yorker* since 2001, where his work has focused on food, science, and American subcultures. His pieces have included portraits of ginseng poachers, deep-cave explorers, child bull-riders, and a cheese-making nun, and have been anthologized ten times in The Best American and Best Food Writing series. Bilger's first book, *Noodling for Flatheads* (2000), was a finalist for the PEN/Martha Albrand Award, and he is at work on a book about his grandfather's experiences in World War II. Bilger is a Branford Fellow at Yale University.

Charlotte Druckman is a journalist and food writer. She conceived and edited the collection *Women on Food* and is the author of *Skirt Steak: Women Chefs on Standing the Heat and Staying in the Kitchen*. In addition, she has written two cookbooks—*Stir, Sizzle, Bake: Recipes for Your Cast-Iron Skillet* and *Kitchen Remix: 75 Recipes for Making the Most of Your Ingredients,* and cowrote chef Anita Lo's *Cooking Without Borders*. She's a proud New Yorker, born and raised.

Joe Fassler is deputy editor of *The Counter.* His first novel, *The Sky Was Ours,* is forthcoming.

Hannah Goldfield is the food critic for *The New Yorker,* where she writes the weekly Tables for Two restaurant column as well as food-related essays and reported stories.

Dr. Cynthia R. Greenlee is a writer, editor, and African-Americanist historian based in Durham, North Carolina. She is a southerner by birth, residence, choice, and culture, but does not eat/consume fried chicken, collard greens, or iced tea. She's also co-editor of *The Echoing Ida Collection* (forthcoming), an anthology of Black women and nonbinary people writing about reproductive justice. Her work has appeared in publications such as *Elle, Gravy,* the *Guardian,* the *Nation, Smithsonian, Vice, Vox,* and the *Washington Post.* You can see more of her work at cynthiagreenlee.com.

Tamar Haspel is a James Beard Award–winning *Washington Post* columnist. She writes about food and science, and has contributed to *Discover, National Geographic, Fortune,* and *Vox,* among other outlets. When she's tired of the heavy lifting of journalism, she helps her husband on their oyster farm, Barnstable Oyster, where they grow about 300,000 oysters a year in the beautiful waters off Cape Cod.

Laura Hayes is the food editor and Young & Hungry columnist at *Washington City Paper,* a position she's held since July 2016. She covers issues impacting the restaurant industry, including mental health, labor, immigration, race, and accessibility, as well as topics related to food access, food policy, and urban agriculture. Before joining *City Paper* in 2016, she wrote for the *Washington Post, Washingtonian, Arlington Magazine, Bethesda Magazine, Food Network Magazine,* and *Thrillist.* The Philadelphia native studied broadcast journalism at Syracuse University before pursuing a career in television news writing and production. She also spent two years teaching English in Japan and worked as the senior communications manager for the US-Japan Council for three years.

Sara Kay is a writer and educator based in Oakland, California. Her work has appeared in *Eater,* as well as cookbooks including *The Nimble Cook* and *The Bastard Cookbook.* She has an MA in food studies from New York University. Learn more at saraflkay.com.

Katy Kelleher is a writer and editor who lives in the woods of Maine with her dogs, husband, and daughter.

Kat Kinsman is senior editor at *Food & Wine,* author of *Hi, Anxiety: Life with a Bad Case of Nerves,* host of *Food & Wine's Communal Table* podcast, and founder of Chefs with Issues. Previously, she was the senior food and drinks editor at Extra Crispy, editor in chief and editor at large at Tasting Table, and the founding editor of the CNN blog *Eatocracy.* She is a frequent public speaker on the topics of food and mental health.

Brett Martin is a correspondent for *GQ* magazine and the author of *Difficult Men: Behind the Scenes of a Creative Revolution.* He has won two James Beard Awards for journalism.

Meghan McCarron is a special correspondent for *Eater.* She lives in Los Angeles.

Tim Murphy is a senior reporter at *Mother Jones* magazine, where he's reported on everything from presidential politics to freight-hopping. His writing has appeared in *Slate, Foreign Policy,* and *Stranger's Guide.* He lives in New York.

Amelia Nierenberg is a writer from New York. She spent a year as a fellow with the *New York Times,* covering food and climate. She was an Overseas Press Club fellow posted in the West Africa bureau of the Associated Press and has worked for the *Boston Globe* and the *Pittsburgh Post-Gazette.* A graduate of Yale University, she has reported in from 17 states and four countries.

Dan Nosowitz is a writer and editor currently living in Los Angeles. His articles have appeared in the *New York Times, New York Magazine, GQ, Esquire, Vox, Bloomberg Businessweek,* and elsewhere.

Kwame Onwuachi is the James Beard Award–winning executive chef at Kith/Kin and author of *Notes from a Young Black Chef.* He was born on Long Island and raised in New York City, Nigeria, and Louisiana. Onwuachi was first exposed to cooking by his mother, in the family's modest Bronx apartment, and he took that spark of passion and turned it into a career. From toiling in the bowels of oil-cleanup ships to working at some of the best restaurants in the world, he has seen and lived his fair share of diversity. Onwuachi trained at the Culinary Institute of America and opened five restaurants before turning 30. A former *Top Chef* contestant, he has been named one of *Food & Wine's* Best New Chefs, *Esquire* magazine's Chef of the Year, and a 30 Under 30 honoree by both *Zagat* and *Forbes.*

José R. Ralat is *Texas Monthly's* taco editor and the author of *American Tacos: A History and Guide* (2020). He has written for national and local print and online media outlets, including *Dallas Observer, Texas Highways, D Magazine, Vice's* food vertical *Munchies, Eater,* and others. He lives in Dallas with his wife, their son, and two dogs.

Kim Severson is a national food correspondent for the *New York Times* covering food trends and news across the United States. She was previously the *New York Times* Atlanta bureau chief and, before that, a staff writer for the Dining section of the *Times*. Her first full-time food-writing job was with the *San Francisco Chronicle*. She also spent seven years as an editor and reporter at the *Anchorage Daily News* in Alaska. Before writing about food, she covered crime, education, social services, and government for daily newspapers on the West Coast. Severson won the 2018 Pulitzer Prize for Public Service for her contributions to the team that investigated sexual harassment and abuse against women. She has also won four James Beard Awards and the Casey Medal for Meritorious Journalism, for her work on childhood obesity. She has written four books, *The Trans Fat Solution; The New Alaska Cookbook;* a memoir, *Spoon Fed: How Eight Cooks Saved My Life;* and, in 2012, *Cook Fight!,* a collaborative cookbook with fellow *New York Times* food writer Julia Moskin.

Sho Spaeth is a staff editor and writer for *Serious Eats*.

Joshua David Stein is an author and journalist. Formerly a food critic for the *Village Voice* and the *New York Observer,* Stein is the coauthor of *The Nom Wah Cookbook, Il Buco: Stories and Recipes,* and *Notes from a Young Black Chef,* and author of the children's books *Can I Eat That?, What's Cooking?, The Invisible Alphabet,* and others, and the essay collection *To Me, He Was Just Dad.* His work has appeared in publications including *New York Magazine,* the *Guardian,* the *New York Times, Esquire, Taste,* and *Food & Wine.* He is currently the host of *Story Casual,* a fiction podcast for children, and makes a food zine, *Reduced Circumstance.* He lives in Brooklyn with his two sons.

Kaitlyn Tiffany is a staff writer at *The Atlantic,* living in Brooklyn. Her first book is about One Direction fans, forthcoming.

Pete Wells has served as restaurant critic for the *New York Times* since 2012. He has become the first *Times* critic to give starred reviews to restaurants in all five boroughs and to genres of restaurant that were widely seen to be outside the scope of a *Times* critic, such as a pizza-by-the-slice joint and a taco truck. Mr. Wells joined the *Times* as dining editor in 2006. From 2009 until January 2011 he wrote a column for the *New York Times Magazine* called Cooking with Dexter, about the kitchen life of a working father. Prior to joining the *Times,* he was articles editor at *Details* for five years. He also wrote a column, Always Hungry, for *Food & Wine,* where he worked as an editor from 1999 until 2001. Mr. Wells has received five James Beard Awards for his writing about eating and drinking. He lives in Brooklyn.

Paige Willams is a staff writer at *The New Yorker* and the Laventhol/Newsday Visiting Professor at Columbia University's Graduate School of Journalism. Her book *The Dinosaur Artist* was a *New York Times* Notable Book of 2018 and was chosen as one of the year's best books by *Publishers Weekly,* the *Paris Review, Library Journal, Smithsonian,* and NPR's *Science Friday,* and was a finalist for the 2019 Mississippi Institute of Arts and Letters prize in nonfiction. Her journalism has appeared in anthologies including *The Best American Magazine Writing* and *The Best American Crime Writing.* Williams, a winner of the National Magazine Award in feature writing, has been a fellow of the MacDowell Colony and was a Nieman Fellow, at Harvard.

Korsha Wilson is a food writer and graduate of the Culinary Institute of America. She is the host of *A Hungry Society* on Heritage Radio Network, a podcast that takes a more inclusive and diverse look at the food world. She has written for the *New York Times, Eater, Bon Appétit,* and *Food & Wine.* She is a 2019 Southern Foodways Alliance Smith Fellow and was part of Jack Jones Literary Arts' inaugural #CultureToo fellowship. She's obsessed with negronis, authentic Maryland crab cakes, and french fries.

Alex Van Buren is a freelance writer, editor, and content strategist living in the greater New York City area. She has written for the *New York Times,* the *Washington Post,* Gourmet.com, and many other national publications.

Other Notable Food Writing of 2019

CATHY ERWAY
Why Are We Still Drinking the Paul Newman Lemonade? *Taste,* May 20, 2019

DAVID FARLEY
Everyone Who Invented the Everything Bagel. *Taste,* November 12, 2019

BOBBY FINGER
My Obsession with the *Bon Appétit* Cinematic Universe. *Jezebel,* November 4, 2019

MADHUSHREE GHOSH
At the Maacher Bazaar, Fish For Life. *Longreads,* April 2019

AARON GOLDFARB
The Art of the Cooking Demo Disaster. *Taste,* November 26, 2019

J. J. GOODE
Things Chefs Do That You Should Not Do. *Taste,* September 30, 2019

JEFF GORDINIER
René Redzepi Gathered the Best Chefs in the World—and Me—for a Wild Cooking Competition. *Esquire,* July 9, 2019

DAVID GAUVEY HERBERT
On the Trail of New York's Nutcracker Kings. *Grub Street,* June 13, 2019

LISA LEE HERRICK
We Learned to Fear Tiger and to Love Squirrel. *Emergence Magazine,* October 23, 2019

ERIKA HOWSARE
Shovel, Knife, Story, Ax. *Longreads,* May 2019

BROOKE JARVIS
The Launch. *The California Sunday Magazine,* July 18, 2019

CAREY JONES
The Obscure French Bitter That Took Over Nevada. *Saveur,* September 6, 2019

JENNIFER JUSTUS
Country Cooking: Minnie's Corn Pudding and Tammy's Better Than Sex Cake. *The Bitter Southerner,* January 2019

MIRANDA KAPLAN
Knights, Horses, and . . . Hummus? An Evening at Medieval Times. *Serious Eats,* February 6, 2019

ALICIA KENNEDY
One Mai Tai, Hold the Colonialism Please. *Eater,* October 7, 2019

GIAAE KWON
Finding Home and Comfort in the Food of Korean-American Chef Eunjo Park. *Catapult Magazine,* December 3, 2019

THE BEST AMERICAN SERIES®

FIRST, BEST, AND BEST-SELLING

The Best American Essays

The Best American Food Writing

The Best American Mystery Stories

The Best American Science and Nature Writing

The Best American Science Fiction and Fantasy

The Best American Short Stories

The Best American Sports Writing

The Best American Travel Writing

Available in print and e-book wherever books are sold.

Visit our website: hmhbooks.com/series/best-american